THE POLITICAL
ECONOMY OF
WEST GERMANY

THE POLITICAL ECONOMY OF WEST GERMANY

Modell Deutschland

edited by

Andrei S. Markovits

foreword by

George K. Romoser

PRAEGER SPECIAL STUDIES • PRAEGER SCIENTIFIC

Library of Congress Cataloging in Publication Data

Main entry under title:

The Political economy of West Germany.

Bibliography: p.
Includes index.
1. Germany (West)—Economic conditions—Addresses,
essays, lectures. 2. Germany (West)—Politics and
government—Addresses, essays, lectures.
I. Markovits, Andrei S.
HC286.5.P624   330.943′0878   81-20996
ISBN 0-03-060617-9   AACR2

Published in 1982 by Praeger Publishers
CBS Educational and Professional Publishing
a Division of CBS, Inc.
521 Fifth Avenue, New York, New York 10175 U.S.A.

© 1982 by Praeger Publishers

23456789   145   987654321

Printed in the United States of America

FOREWORD

George K. Romoser

As these lines are written in the autumn of 1981, increasing concerns are being expressed in some quarters about the deterioration in relationships between the United States and the countries of Western Europe. Protest demonstrations in the latter against nuclear arms contrast with the Reagan administration's "neoconservative" emphasis on a policy of military strength. The specter of fragmentation in the Western alliance even, or perhaps especially, at a time of great tensions in Eastern Europe reminds us how intricate is the maintenance of some degree of stability in international affairs.

In this international scenario, the Federal Republic of Germany inevitably has a highly important role. The strength of its economy remains impressive, despite West Germany's dependence on exports, some structural problems, and considerable disarray in the international economy. The significance of the central geographical position of the two German states, moreover, can hardly be overemphasized. Finally, relations between the United States and West Germany have been particularly close in the postwar world; any hint of disorder in that relationship deserves careful attention.

The intricacies of international affairs, however, frequently have their roots in the intricacies of internal politics. The priorities of a given government may arise from real or imagined internal conditions and involve a more or less muddled desire to create a new direction or "get our own affairs in order." Such is certainly the case with the Reagan administration in the United States, for example. Under such circumstances, foreign policy tends to become an extension of the psychology and priorities of the domestic situation. Thus, regarding West Germany, policy makers no less than professors, students, and the general public need adequate information about the intricacies of that country's internal politics.

This volume is intended as a contribution to that end, and it succeeds very well in that endeavor. It is a particularly timely book, and while not everyone will agree with all of the points of emphasis, it is an important addition to the literature on West Germany. I am grateful to Professor Markovits and the other authors for undertaking this volume and pleased that it resulted from the 1981 New England Workshop on German Affairs.

The importance of the book's contribution is underlined by at least two considerations. The political economy approach, which tends to be central to this volume (that is, exploration of linkages between the economic system of a country and its politics), is one that is finding an increasing emphasis among younger scholars. Several of the studies in this book show how fruitful this approach can be and how the field of comparative studies can be enriched by attention to what Professor Katzenstein refers to in his chapter as parapublic institutions. Indeed, though this approach can provide, in my opinion, only part of a comprehensive framework for the study of politics, it represents a crucial addition to the kind of material used in the study of various regimes. The focus on Modell Deutschland as a political-economic whole connects analysis of the structure of economic life with the political question, Who rules?

Another striking fact about this volume is precisely that a number of the contributions are by members of the younger generation of scholars interested in West Germany. Concerns have also recently been expressed about signs of a decline of interest in West German affairs in this country, no less than about growing indifference among young West Germans toward the United States. Fears about the growth of "anti-Americanism" in Europe and about revived suspiciousness of West Germany in the United States also trouble experienced scholars and public officials. While such concerns are sometimes overdrawn, they are not without a basis in reality. Thus, it is important to recognize that efforts at enriching our understanding of West Germany continue in this country, as illustrated by the organizational efforts that led to this volume and by its content. The New England Workshops on German Affairs, inaugurated in June 1980 with the support of the Goethe Institute in Boston and Munich, are intended to solidify a network of contact among scholars interested in various aspects of West German affairs and to contribute to the future of scholarly and public affairs communication across the North Atlantic. I am happy to say that, although much more could be done with a broader resource and staff base, they have been successful beyond my expectations.

The dramatic traumas of the Third Reich were such that, in my judgment, it will be many generations before numerous persons can think of Germany or the Germans without at least some lingering suspicion, if not outright hostility. This fact, and the continuing attention West Germany's recent past inevitably receives in so many facets of literature, art, the media, and reflections on the violence of the twentieth century, must be recognized by all who deal with German affairs. These traumas should not be forgotten or suppressed, but as Professor Markovits indicates in his conclusion to this book, there is also considerable need to understand West Germany as it is today and West Germans as they are today. Very much has changed, and those of us who were drawn to a certain emphasis on "things German" in our studies and subsequent professional work by being students of the emigré generation of central European professors, or by our fascination with the question of how the Third Reich could happen, should welcome every effort to deepen our understanding of today's realities. The authors in this volume have not ignored the past but have sought to show, along with the changes, such elements of continuity in the West German economic and political systems as may actually still be relevant.

The approach in this volume has a broad relevance that involves more than the study of West German politics. Issues of continuity and change in the U.S. political economy deserve continuing attention, for example, especially given the question, How do changes in a domestic scenario impact on foreign policies and attitudes toward other countries? However, the insights in many of these studies can help one assess the likelihood of basic crises or transformations in the West German regime. Thus, the present volume will be essential reading for a broad range of scholars and policy makers.

Durham, New Hampshire
November 1981

PREFACE

The origins of this book date back to the fall of 1980, when the editorial collective of the Berlin-based quarterly Prokla invited my colleague Thomas Ertman and myself to contribute an article to the journal's tenth anniversary, which featured the topic: Modell Deutschland. Our essay, entitled "Das 'Model Deutschland': Eine Herausforderung für die U.S.A." (" 'Model Germany': A Challenge to the United States"), focused on the disparate forms of conflict management in the Federal Republic of Germany and the United States since the reconstruction period following the end of World War II. Very much connected to my detailed research project on trade unions in the Federal Republic of Germany (FRG), I continued to pursue this new, albeit related, interest throughout the winter and spring of 1981. At this point, a number of us in the greater Boston area, sharing an academic interest in the FRG, assembled under the leadership of George K. Romoser to plan various panels for the Second Conference on German Affairs to be held in Boston on May 15 and 16, 1981. I was put in charge of organizing a panel on Modell Deutschland. This effort proved the decisive stage in the creation of the present volume. Being very fortunate, I secured the participation of three first-rate scholars—David Abraham, Peter Katzenstein, and Willi Semmler— who, with my addition, formed the panel discussing "Politics and Economics in Germany: The Historical and Contemporary Perspective of 'Modell Deutschland'." During the presentations and ensuing discussions, my initial hopes changed to a firm conviction: the quality of the panel left no doubt in my mind that we had the makings of an important and controversial volume. Indeed, our four contributions to this book all originated in one form or another from our talks on the morning of May 16, 1981. Charles Maier's stimulating keynote address to the conference focused on issues related to the topic of our panel. His chapter in this volume also had its source at the Boston conference. Finally, the chapters by Guido Goldman, Carl Lankowski, and Jeremiah Riemer represent valuable additions by scholars who have worked on this topic over the last few years.

I owe a great deal of gratitude to two groups of people whose continued assistance and support proved indispensable in producing this volume. The first, smaller in number, helped me directly in one way or another with the immediate creation of this book. Here, I would like to express my appreciation to George K. Romoser, who has been the indefatigable dynamo behind various cross-disciplinary West German studies in New England for the last few years. He not only had the excellent idea of holding two conferences on West German affairs in the late springs of 1980 and 1981, for which the latter proved the cradle of this book, but unlike many others, he also knew how to implement his ideas. This, of course, would have remained impossible had it not been for the generous financial support of the Goethe Institute in Boston. I would like to take this opportunity to thank the institute's director, Gerhard Kirchhoff, whose active interest in the proceedings extended well beyond financial help and manifested itself in genuine enthusiasm and intellectual engagement. A word of thanks is also in order to my colleagues in the volume, who completely reversed usual academic manners by handing in their contributions on time and in excellent shape. I would also like to thank Princeton University Press for giving us permission to reprint several pages from Peter Katzenstein's review essay "Problem or Model? West Germany in the 1980s" and two tables from David Abraham's book The Collapse of the Weimar Republic: Political Economy and Crisis. Moreover, thanks are also due to Olle and Wolter publishers in West Berlin for granting us permission to reprint several tables and figures from a book by Elmar Altvater, Jürgen Hoffmann, and Willi Semmler, Vom Wirtschaftswunder zur Wirtschaftskrise: Ökonomie und Politik in der Bundesrepublik. Finally, I am greatly indebted to two young scholars who have helped me at every stage of this book's production. Gary Herrigel proved an excellent editor and a superb critic; I continue to cherish his opinions. Hardly a paragraph in this volume remained untouched by our lengthy discussions, which compensated very pleasantly and beneficially the chores accompanying the task of editing such a book. Thomas Ertman, more than anyone else, deserves credit for my intellectual development over the last few years. Our association has not only produced the already-mentioned article on Modell Deutschland, but it is also in the process of finishing a major work on trade unions in the Federal Republic of Germany. In addition to Tom's invaluable intellectual input into much of my writing since 1980, he has also proved to be a trusted friend, which I see as being even more important than his assistance as a colleague.

The second group, somewhat larger, exercised an equally important, albeit indirect, influence on the creation of this volume. It consists of all my West German friends and colleagues whose true interest and unselfish support for my various projects over the years proved absolutely indispensable for my work. Their expertise helped my research and taught me much I would otherwise never have had the chance to learn. To me, they all represent the most positive side of Modell Deutschland. They are Hermann Adam, Elmar Altvater, Gerhard Armanski, Volker Bahl, Angelika Bahl-Benker, Iris Bergmiller, Hans-Joachim Bieber, Reimar Birkwald, Ulrich Borsdorf, Rüdiger Bouillon, Ulrich Briefs, Wolf-Gunter Brügmann, Knuth Dohse, Rainer Erd, Tilman Ernst, Günter Friedrichs, Ina Frieser, Hajo Funke, Gerhard Gerlach, Helmut Görlich, Angelika Griess, Alice Hänsel, Karl Hauenschild, Achim de Heer, Hans-Otto Hemmer, Detlef Hensche, Eckart Hildebrandt, Jürgen Hoffmann, Willi Hoss, Otto Jacobi, Hans Janssen, Karl-Heinz Janzen, Jürgen Jöns, Reinhard Jordan, Rudolf Judith, Ulrich Jürgens, Wilhelm Kaltenborn, Erwin Kastleiner, Franz Kersjes, Jutta Kneissel, Heribert Kohl, Manfred Krüper, Hartmut Küchle, Rudolf Kuda, Friedrich Knilli, Klaus Lang, Wolfgang Lecher, Gerhard Lehmbruch, Stefan Leibfried, Manfred Leiss, Gerhard Leminsky, Konstanza Löwenstein, Uwe Magnus, Heinz Markmann, Helmut Martens, Margit Mayer, Hans-Peter Michaelis, Norbert Möller-Lücking, Bernd Mülhaupt, Gernot Müller, Walther Müller-Jentsch, Wolf-Dieter Narr, Frieder Naschold, Oskar Negt, Hans Nutzinger, Peter von Oertzen, Claus Offe, Martin Osterland, Annemarie Ott, Detlef Perner, Ernst Piehl, Hans-Adam Pfromm, Manfred Piecha, Christian Rabe, Hermann Rappe, Brigitte and Martin Riesebrodt, Gunter Rose, Harald Russig, Ina and Tilo Schabert, Claus Schäfer, Willi Scherer, Walter Schneider, Annemarie Schrey, Hartmut Seifert, Rolf Seitenzahl, Willi Semmler, Werner Sengenberger, Dieter Senghaas, Werner Sewing, Alfons Söllner, Franz Steinkühler, Wolfgang Streeck, Karl-Heinz Tiedtke, Hartmut Tofaute, Kurt Tudyka, Karl Ullrich, Werner Vitt, Hajo Vitzthum, Karsten Voigt, and Ulrich Zachert.

CONTENTS

LIST OF TABLES

LIST OF FIGURES

1
INTRODUCTION: MODEL
GERMANY—A CURSORY OVERVIEW
OF A COMPLEX CONSTRUCT

ANDREI S. MARKOVITS

One could see it everywhere in Germany during the summer
and early fall of 1976. It simply read Modell Deutschland ("Model
Germany"), but its overall implications stirred a more passionate debate on the national and international level than perhaps any other
slogan in the Federal Republic of Germany's young history. On the
most immediate level, these two words were nothing more than the
Social Democratic Party's (SPD) campaign motto for the Bundestag
elections in October 1976. They were to convey to the German
voter that the SPD's stewardship in Bonn forged a model out of the
Federal Republic of Germany (FRG). Thus, a renewed Social Democratic victory at the polls would ensure a continuation of West Germany's model existence. So much for the specific origins and
short-term dimensions of this slogan.
    Clearly, however, it was the slogan's deeper connotations
that triggered such a lively interest in both the FRG and elsewhere.
It implied West Germany's successful coming of age, a triumphant
achievement to many, yet also a frightening fact to some. Having
gone from the world's pariah in the late 1940s and early 1950s to
the famous "economic-giant-political-dwarf" combination of the 1960s,
the FRG achieved a comprehensive model-like stature under Social
Democratic leadership by the mid-1970s. Few other countries in
the world provided its citizens with a better life than the FRG. On
almost any meaningful indicator measuring economic well-being,
West Germany ranked among the very top in the world. West Germans seemed to travel more, consume more, enjoy more extensive
social services, benefit from longer vacations, and suffer from less
inflation and unemployment than just about anybody else in the advanced industrial countries, with the possible exception of Austria
and Switzerland. Complementing this economic bliss was a domestic

stability that seemed to permeate all aspects of politics in an era
when other countries suffered from social upheavals. Having weathered the oil crisis of the mid-1970s better than any of its major competitors, West Germany's overall success seemed truly uncanny to
some, including many of its domestic critics. The FRG conveyed
this image of an island of stability, strength, prosperity, and confidence surrounded by a sea of nations plagued by insurmountable ad-
versities. Looking at West Germany from abroad, one had the feeling that if West Germans still had problems, they would not be
around for long, since they excelled in the art of problem solving.
That is exactly what Model Germany was all about. While the SPD's
slogan was meant to convey a sense of accomplishment and pride to
the West German voter, it left the rest of the world wondering in
awe and with envy. The title of the cover story in Newsweek's
European edition of September 27, 1976, best summarized the world's
mixed sentiments regarding West Germany's success: "Germany:
The Model Nation?"

As the 1970s continued, the salience of Model Germany assumed even greater proportions both in the FRG and abroad. In both
areas one could roughly discern two major dimensions in the scholarly and journalistic assessments of Modell Deutschland. The first,
perhaps appropriately labeled a "value dimension," separated those
that approved and praised the model from an equally vocal group
that criticized its existence and pointed to its faults. The second,
an "analytic dimension," debated the model's structural and temporal origins. Was it a creation of the SPD or social democracy more
generally? Could it be dated to West Germany's Bismarckian past,
or did the model's roots merely extend to the early years of the FRG?

While there were no predictable overlaps among advocates of
these various dimensions, it is interesting to note that the more positive, uncritical, indeed glowing, judgments about Model Germany
emanated more from abroad than from within the model itself. In
many ways, the various international reactions to Modell Deutschland had much more to do with the domestic situation of the respective country than with the ingredients of the West German success
story proper. Model Germany often served as a convenient vehicle
to indict the reasons for failure at home. It fulfilled the role of a
somewhat mythical structure whose imitation would yield instant
improvements in the troubles of the domestic economy and the turmoil of politics.

Perhaps nowhere did this rather one-dimensional image emerge
with such clarity as in the United States during the late 1970s.
Whereas the European accolades were somewhat more measured by
the mere fact that most of them analyzed this phenomenon in the larger context of their "coming to terms with the German question"

(a sort of "Bewältigung der Deutschenfrage"), no such ambivalence seemed to accompany the admiration of Modell Deutschland in the United States. While French, Italian, Dutch, and British discussions of the model frequently included mention of civil-rights violations in the FRG as perhaps an example of the seamier side of the West German success story, few such instances of the "ugly Germans" marred the model's image in the United States. If anything, the U.S. public received a personalized rendition of West Germany's superlatives in articles extolling Helmut Schmidt as the "superchancellor" who somehow seemed to embody all the virtues responsible for West Germany's economic success. Cool-headed, brilliant, far-sighted, determined, and competent were the attributes associated with Helmut Schmidt in U.S. public opinion of the late 1970s. He seemed almost invincible at the time, as did Model Germany, which mirrored all of Schmidt's qualities on a macro level according to the U.S. media.[1]

It was not by chance that 1979 and 1980 witnessed a proliferation of public preoccupation in the United States with what seemed to be the two most successful models of advanced capitalism: Japan and the Federal Republic of Germany. While the first achieved a cryptocult status confirmed by that rare, but enviable, occurrence wherein academic books become national bestsellers, "Number Two" (as one author of this volume calls it) did not do so badly either. Be it in the form of television documentaries or seminars on employment policy, the United States suddenly "discovered" West Germany in its quest to find solutions to its own economic problems. Some of the nation's most prestigious publications, such as Business Week, the Wall Street Journal, the New York Times, Fortune, the New Republic, Time, and Newsweek, carried substantial articles about West Germany's success.[2]

Seminars at leading universities attended by some of the United States' most important legislators, businessmen, and academics asked the question, "What can we learn from the German experience?" In short, the preoccupation with Model Germany in the United States seemed an accurate reflection of the pessimistic Zeitgeist that dominated much of the atmosphere in the U.S. business community and among leading opinion makers. Just as Schmidt's characteristics were always portrayed as an implicit, sometimes even explicit, criticism of President Jimmy Carter (soft, vacillating, incompetent, without a clear policy), so too was the success of the West German economy juxtaposed to the failures of the U.S. economy. The almost daily reports of near-catastrophic debacles in the mainstays of U.S. industry, such as automobiles, steel, and rubber, began to shatter the last, hitherto untouched, hegemonic myth from the days of Pax Americana: the superiority of U.S. business. The days when leading European politicians and intellectuals, such as Jean-Jacques Servant-Schreiber, exhorted their compatriots to emulate U.S. management techniques lest they succumb to the U.S. juggernaut were long gone.

The West Germans and the Japanese had not only successfully challenged the United States in the world market, they were about to extend this onslaught to the United States' hitherto sacrosanct domestic realm. Japan's "Number One" position in the process of U.S. soul-searching stemmed in good part from the visibility of that country's products in the daily lives of Americans. Transistor radios, portable televisions, cameras, hair dryers, and cars are much more noticeable to the general public than textile machines, pharmaceutical products, and various chemical goods. Yet, it was mainly in the latter area (that is, industrial goods) that the West Germans not only outdistanced the United States by wide margins in nearly every corner of the world market but also were in the process of making serious inroads on the U.S. home turf. What was the secret of their success?

It was this question that led to a rather glorified, but nevertheless useful, analysis of Modell Deutschland. Some qualities recurred in every account dealing with the subject. Thus, nearly every assessment dwelt on some key components of West German political culture. Discipline, punctuality, obedience, conscientiousness, thoroughness, and excellence were all seen as crucial ingredients of the model. Furthermore, these admirable qualities seemed not only to permeate West German society as a whole, but especially the country's workers. Hardly any account failed to mention the fact that West German workers compete with their Austrian and Swiss colleagues for the least number of strikes among Western industrialized countries. Labor peace was judged to be one of the lynchpins of the model. In this context, special attention was given to the moderate and reasonable nature of West German union demands. Unions, it was argued, behave in such a compliant manner because they derive important benefits for their members via the model's success. Moreover, they are included in the key decisions affecting the model by way of Mitbestimmung, or "codetermination," perhaps the most frequently mentioned mechanism in terms of the West German industrial relations system's contribution to the country's economic success.

Yet, another ingredient that attracted much attention was the rather well-developed societal consensus in the FRG concerning the detrimental consequences of inflation. An "inflation trauma," which has haunted the Germans since the 1920s, it was argued, was mainly responsible for a very careful and sensitive fiscal and monetary policy on the part of the West German state and the country's independent national bank, the Bundesbank. This "anti-inflation consensus" enhanced the legitimacy of certain austerity measures, which would otherwise have been much harder to implement. Yet, on the whole, it was often mentioned that part and parcel of the model was an elaborate web of social nets, which certainly cushioned the fall for the victims of austerity, if indeed it could not stop it altogether. Furthermore, the country's export orientation and dependence were also viewed as being salient to the model's existence. With one of every four jobs dependent on exports, the FRG had to develop a great sensitivity to the ebbs and flows of the international economic system. This meant that in addition to a basic understanding between the two social partners—labor and capital—as to the overall validity and beneficial nature of this export orientation, the West German state had to contribute quite actively to the maintenance of this arrangement. Indeed, the state's science policy, its active support for research benefiting export-oriented industries, and other forms of assistance, as well as coordination, were mentioned in this context. Finally, special attention was given to the country's political climate. Extremists of both the Right and the Left seemed completely discredited in the eyes of the vast majority of West Germans. All three parties represented in the Bundestag were deeply committed to the maintenance of the FRG's liberal democratic Rechtstaat. Although certainly existent, the political cleavages among them—as in West German society as a whole--were far from nonnegotiable à la the Weimar Republic. An astute, enlightened, and highly competent leadership complemented and furthered this atmosphere of moderation, restraint, and perspicacity. All in all, a healthy pluralism seemed alive and well for the first time in German history.

There is no doubt that, on the whole, these reports captured some of the most crucial elements of Modell Deutschland. Often presented in clichés, these accounts nevertheless gave a cursory but helpful overview as to why the West German system seemed to work so well. The key concepts were expertise, competence, moderation, and predictability. The more detailed analyses and criticisms of the model and its larger implications remained confined to a highly stimulating discussion among West German scholars. Emanating mainly from the left of the West German political spectrum, most of these contributions concentrated their attention on the costs of the model, which they argued, were unevenly distributed. These costs, the critics believed, manifested themselves in essentially two ways: a curtailment of civil liberties and the freedom of political expression as a consequence of West Germany's excessive security consciousness (one writer associated Modell Deutschland with a Sicherheitsstaat, a security state); and an appeasement/straitjacketing/repression of the working class since the reconstruction period of the late 1940s and early 1950s.

Both of these indictments of the model had, of course, one common denominator. They basically claimed that West Germany had traded democracy for efficiency. In other words, Model Germany could only be maintained by a conscious exclusion, perhaps even victimization, of certain nonconformist elements, critical intellectuals, the weak, and the poor. Precisely because stability was the paramount ingredient of the model, West Germany could under no circumstances jeopardize this valuable asset. To that end, it had to pursue a rigorous "carrot-and-stick" policy, which either co-opted the "losers" via social welfare programs or repressed them outright. The critics also pointed to the inherent dangers lurking in the main motor of the model, namely its excessive export orientation. In addition to splitting West German industry, the union movement, and the working class into export-dependent "winners" and increasingly domestic-market-oriented "losers," this economic strategy became ever more risky in a world of sluggish demand replete with uncertainties. A serious setback for West Germany's exports would mean a severe curtailment of the surplus necessary to maintain the high quantity and quality of "carrots" presently comprising the all-important welfare ingredient of the model. By following these criticisms to their logical conclusion, West Germany's vulnerability in the world market could not only shatter the model altogether, but in the very process make its inherent repression the only remaining component dominating West German life.

While none of the contributions in this volume address any of these apocalyptic visions of Modell Deutschland's future, most of them provide important insights into its main structures, their antecedents, and current operation. In Chapter 2, Guido Goldman delineates the model's major characteristics by contrasting some of its key features with the situation in the United States. Delivered as an address to the Conference on U.S. Competitiveness held at Harvard University in late April 1980, Goldman's optimistic analysis represents an excellent example as to the way most knowledgeable observers in this country assessed West Germany's success at the time. Yet, Goldman also wisely points to the potential trouble spots in the model's functioning, some of which have indeed gained in salience during the intervening 18 months. Nevertheless, the major structural components discussed in Goldman's contribution still very much pertain and determine the continuation of Modell Deutschland.

The United States continues to be a crucial reference point in the discussion about Model Germany in Chapter 3. By providing detailed comparative data pertaining to the post-World War II economic developments of the United States and the Federal Republic of Germany, Willi Semmler focuses his analysis on the profoundly different paths these two countries took over the last three decades. Semmler emphatically anchors the model's existence in the so-called reconstruction period of West German capitalism in the 1950s. Concentrating his empirical, as well as theoretical, argument on the uniqueness of this historical constellation, the author repeatedly points to some rather compelling evidence that this model remains not only inimitable and nontransferable, but that in fact it may be facing some insurmountable obstacles in the FRG itself. Semmler delineates three very exceptional conditions that helped in the creation of the model: social-technical advantages, early export orientation, and specific state activities. Among these, the author pays particular attention to the unique labor-market conditions in the first decade of the FRG's existence caused by the huge influx of refugees and expellees from East Germany and areas in todays Soviet Union, Poland, and Czechoslovakia. He also stresses the highly skilled nature of the West German work force accompanied by a political complacency resulting from the country's National Socialist past. Moreover, Semmler dispels an important myth about this period: he argues that contrary to common knowledge, the ruling Christian Democratic Union's (CDU's) economic policy was far from being liberal in the classical laissez-faire sense. Rather, Semmler emphasizes, one could discern a clear supply-side orientation, which stressed the state's active support for capital formation from the very beginning. This policy, according to the author, gave the model a crucial head start. Semmler concludes his contribution by pointing to West Germany's growing vulnerability owing to its export dependence in an increasingly uncertain world and by once again stressing the model's uniqueness in terms of its temporal and geographic existence.

The key factors characterizing the model's concrete implementation focus on overall stability, concern for moderation, and the reaching of compromise. In few areas vital to the model's successful perpetuation have these concepts guided the policy-making process to the degree they have in the realm of economic steering. This, briefly put, represents Jeremiah Riemer's major finding presented in Chapter 4. Riemer shows that the overriding concern of stability has continued to dominate the politics of economic policy in the FRG to the degree that all preconceived notions of particular economic schools (for example, Keynesianism, monetarism) are simply useless concepts for the purposes of understanding the formulation and implementation of economic policy in West Germany. The author shows that the formation of economic policy is a fundamentally political process surprisingly devoid of a particular ruler's ideological content. Rather, Riemer submits, economic policy in the FRG developed a certain continuity by being a major component in the very specific but highly political interaction among key institutionalized groups in West German society. In this context, Riemer pays special attention to the role of the Bundesbank and the Council of Economic Experts (the so-called Five Wise Men). The author concludes his analysis of the model by arguing that its main task has always consisted of providing expert management of stability under conservative auspices. Riemer describes the nature of the model's structure as a "congeries of peak associations allied on behalf of stability."

If Semmler is mainly concerned with the model's initial stages in the 1950s and thus—at least implicitly—links it to the CDU-state, and Riemer's contribution concentrates on the partyless presence of this stability-conscious system of conflict management, then Carl Lankowski's argument in Chapter 5 clearly demonstrates a closensss between Modell Deutschland and the Social Democratic party (SPD). Perhaps more than any other author in this volume, Lankowski uses the specific literature on Modell Deutschland from the FRG as his theoretical starting point. Concentrating on some crucial events in the early 1970s, Lankowski highlights the model's foreign relations, notably vis-à-vis the European Community (EC) and the Third World. The author points to evidence that would indicate that the model has been inextricably linked to the regional extension of West German hegemony, especially in Europe. By deploying perhaps its most potent weapon in the form of the Bundesbank's tight monetary policy, the model, according to Lankowski, has by and large succeeded in imposing its own strict parameters onto its important trading partners in Western Europe. West Germany's hegemonic relationship in Europe has thus not only benefited the model, it in fact has become one of its most prominent and indispensable prerequisites. Lankowski concludes his challenging paper by pointing to some of the potential domestic and international costs that this expansive hegemonic dimension of Modell Deutschland may exact in the near future.

All observers of West German politics credit labor with playing a particularly crucial role in the creation and maintenance of Model Germany. This topic forms the focus of the next two chapters in the volume. In Chapter 6, David Abraham anchors labor's contribution to the model in its often ambivalent and sometimes self-defeating policies during the Weimar Republic. In discussing labor's growth strategy, the author highlights how the unions and the SPD inevitably had to get entangled in corporatist structures, which necessarily had a weakening and coopting effect on the labor movement's political articulation. At the same time, Abraham argues, forces in the labor movement developed a competing model of economic democracy, which in fact opposed everything that the growth strategy implied. It stood for nothing less than the full and collective democratization of working life. Indeed, it was envisioned as a definite road to socialism. The ultimate failure to implement this alternative not only led to the destruction of all working-class organizations, but also to the failure of the Weimar Republic as a whole. By arguing that economic democracy and growth strategy remain mutually exclusive models for working-class politics, Abraham implies that by choosing the latter, the decision makers in the key working-class institutions were at least partly to blame for the eventual debacle of their politics. Although drawing constant parallels to labor's predicament in the FRG, Abraham certainly does not mean to imply that a fate similar to the one in 1933 will eventually befall the West German working class. His valuable parallels concerning crucial institutional arrangements between labor and capital in Weimar and Bonn not only highlight some important structural continuities between these seemingly disparate entities, but also point to the fact that labor's power, and thus democracy's full existence, will always remain curtailed as long as its vision of a growth strategy continues unchallenged by that of economic democracy.

Although also providing a brief historical overview, Markovits concentrates his analysis of labor's contribution to Model Germany primarily on the post-World War II situation. In Chapter 7 he shows what factors in the West German union movement's "liberal" and "collectivist" past accounted for the creation of certain new institutional arrangements in the FRG, all of which have thus far made labor a participant in the model. Markovits focuses his discussion on the unions' relationship vis-à-vis the state, political parties, and management. He also shows how the West German unions' particular handicap (that is, their weak presence on the shop floor of the country's plants) elicited response mechanisms on the part of the unions, which actually yielded further institutional support for the model. Following a detailed presentation as to how important structures such as the unitary and industrial trade union movement, codetermination, the collective bargaining system, and the juridification of German industrial relations contribute to organized labor's participation in the model, Markovits concludes the chapter by highlighting some of the problems the unions have had to confront since the onset of the economic crisis of the mid-1970s. The politics of compromise will become much harder, but it nevertheless will continue.

The essence of Model Germany consists in a particular form of institutionalized interaction among organized groups in society. This represents the main analytical axis of Charles Maier's thought-provoking argument in Chapter 8. Countering most stereotypical views of the FRG and of modern German history, Maier submits that Germany has consistently suffered from a lack, rather than an excess, of state power. Indeed, the common denominator between Weimar and Bonn rests precisely in the relative weakness of their respective states and the strength of group interactions within civil society. The difference between the two republics consists in the fact that in Weimar this interaction led to unmitigated conflict, whereas in Bonn it produced enviable compromise. The concept of the state, Maier argues, is of less help than is generally believed in understanding German politics. Restricted sovereignity and limited statehood may yield a centrifugal, self-destructive polity à la Weimar; they, however, may also attain a functioning liberal democracy à la Bonn. Both versions, according to Maier, fit squarely into the German tradition. The key as to which way things will develop lies mainly in civil society and not the state.

The primacy of institutional arrangements among key interest groups and their highly regularized form of interaction also represents the main theme of Peter Katzenstein's chapter. In Chapter 9, Katzenstein once again touches on all issues central to the previous essays in this volume. He focuses especially on the concrete institutional mechanisms designed to foster consensus and compromise among crucial elites. Katzenstein sees the source of stability, perhaps the model's main contribution and prerequisite, in these particular social compacts buttressed by strict rules and regulations. In discussing the major components of Model Germany, the author constantly reminds us of the uncanny proximity of a problem that he sees as inherent to all models. By anchoring the German Model and problem in the country's past, Katzenstein explains their symbiotic and also contradictory relationship in the contemporary Bundesrepublik. Moreover, the author ventures a few predictions for the 1980s, which are devoid of the euphoria often accompanying accounts of the FRG in this country, just as they also carefully refrain from predicting disaster, yet another increasingly trendy mode of analyzing the FRG's political future. Model Germany, Katzenstein concludes, is a particular West German way of reconciling stability and democracy in an industrialized environment. While far from perfect, it seems to have worked better than many other endeavors with similar aims, certainly as far as Germany's political history is concerned.

This volume should not be construed as a textbook on West German contemporary politics. It cannot even claim to offer an exhaustive treatment of the complexity related to the narrower concept of Modell Deutschland. Rather, this book presents some studies analyzing the FRG's formation of public policy, macroeconomic development, and an industrial relations system within a distinct historical context. The precursors of the model receive almost as much attention as its present manifestations. The chapters differ quite substantially in terms of their focuses, theoretical approaches, and conclusions. Still, there is a common theme to all of them. It consists in an earnest attempt to convey that ephemeral "something special" about West German political arrangements. This something special embodies a whole that clearly is more than the sum of its parts. By necessity, this book only represents a partial discussion of the latter. Yet, if a careful study of these papers will help the reader recognize the complexities of a particular system of conflict management referred to as Model Germany, this volume will have fulfilled its purpose beyond the original hopes of its editor.

NOTES

1. This symbiotic admiration of West Germany's overall success and Chancellor Schmidt's unusual qualities as a statesman and economic strategist found its prototypical expression in John Vinocur's much-noticed cover story for the New York Times Magazine of September 21, 1980, appropriately entitled "Helmut Schmidt: Asserting Germany's New Leadership."

2. Among the scholarly publications, two deserve special mention in this context. The first, edited by Wilfrid L. Kohl and Giorgio Basevi, is entitled West Germany: A European and Global Power and appeared in 1980. Comprising essays written mainly by West German scholars, the volume's focus revolves largely around West Germany's economic relationships vis-à-vis the world at large and the European Community. The second, published one year later, represented a similar effort mainly on the part of British scholars. The British journal West European Politics, vol. 4, no. 2 (May 1981), devoted all its space, including its extensive book review section, to a discussion of the contemporary FRG under the telling title "The West German Model: Perspectives on a Stable State."

2
THE GERMAN
ECONOMIC CHALLENGE

GUIDO G. GOLDMAN

In many respects the recent experience of West Germany re-
sembles that of Japan. Both lost the war, endured an allied occupation, and had to begin to rebuild their economies from a relatively
low level. West German conditions at the postwar outset may have
been even more adverse. The country had been extensively bombed,
it was divided, and it was at once confronted by a massive population
transfer as refugees poured into the western zone from various areas
of the East, which are now part of East Germany, the Soviet Union,
Poland, and Czechoslovakia.

In January 1980, in its economic report to Parliament, the
federal government forecast its predictions for West German economic performance for that year. The gross national product (GNP)
was projected to exceed 1.2 trillion marks with an increase of 2.5
percent for the year. Unemployment was expected to remain between
3 percent and 3.5 percent. And consumer prices would rise by just
4.5 percent. What an enviable performance one might conclude.
How did the Federal Republic of Germany (FRG) achieve the ability
or capacity to do so well where the United States appears to have done
so poorly? What is the origin and the explanation for West German
competitiveness?

The historical experience of the German people in this century
is an important factor explaining postwar developments. The recur-
rent instability of the recent past has placed a special value on political order and stability. The memory of just how badly democracy

---

This chapter was originally an address delivered to the Conference on U.S. Competitiveness held at Harvard University on
April 25, 1980.

fared in the Weimar Republic (and what that led to) has created a greater willingness to accept compromise this time around. Consensus, rather than confrontation, has typified the internal political (and economic) life of the FRG.

The political spectrum is narrower than elsewhere in Europe (or even Japan). Antisystem radical parties and movements have remained relatively weak, although active in promoting terrorism. Any substantial communist appeal would have to contend with the antipathy directed toward Soviet actions and presence in East Germany and the repugnant conditions of life there.

These political factors have important implications for economic life in the FRG. The quest for stability and consensus is reinforced by several significant recent experiences. One is the profoundly corrosive effects the inflation of 1922-23 had on middle-class savings and values in the Weimar Republic. That the value of the currency at the time, the reichsmark, could be reduced virtually to zero has left such a deep scar on the collective memory of the West German people as to create a much greater awareness of the dangers of inflation. A second experience was the totality of the defeat and destruction wrought by World War II. Not only did this create an enormous domestic demand for goods and services, but it also meant that the satisfaction of material needs ranked first when compared with other pursuits. The primacy of economic ends, especially in a country in which politics had been so tarnished by the Hitler experience, gained a broad legitimacy that goes far in explaining the "economic miracle" of West German postwar recovery.

Several specific features of the West German situation in the immediate postwar period contributed substantially to its economic success. West Germany (like Japan) was left with no overseas commitments and no painful and costly colonial entanglements from which to disengage. Its initial defense burden was virtually nonexistent. The propensity to accept a major role for government in the economy seemed natural given the needs of postwar reconstruction (and the sundering of the private sector). But decontrol and deregulation found wide acceptance as well because the FRG emerged from four years of stringent allied occupation with far too many restrictions for which there was little domestic demand since they had been imposed from outside.

In addition, two phenomena of the postwar years were of key economic significance. One was the steady flow of a very special labor supply in the form of 14 million German refugees who streamed to West Germany until the building of the Berlin Wall in 1961. This potential burden proved to be an extraordinary asset. For here were willing workers, masses of them, who, in their flight to freedom, placed relatively low demands on their initial conditions of work.

Furthermore, many of them brought not only high motivation but special skills and training.

Second, the establishment of a trading bloc in Western Europe —beginning with the Coal and Steel Commission—that was to become the Common Market created an enormous secondary demand for West German goods and made foreign trade as a whole, but exports in particular, an absolutely central feature of West German economic life from a very early stage in the postwar recovery. This meant that as economic activity resumed it had a fundamental trading orientation right from the start. Without the Common Market it would be difficult to explain the pace of West German economic recovery.

A great deal of what has been described so far is, or was, unique to the West German situation. While it may help to explain West Germany's performance, it is not relevant to choices or options available to the United States. There are several features in the West German experience that may contain some useful lessons because they are not so exclusively the product of West German history or of the postwar context. Instead they are the result of a number of deliberate and well-designed initiatives or practices, which have served well to enhance West German economic purposes. The three I would like to focus on are the role of government, the role of labor, and the behavior of the private sector.

The role of government in West Germany has been effectively conceived and implemented for the furtherance of economic goals. The institutions of government, especially the way in which federalism works in the FRG, make possible both firm leadership from above and effective responsiveness to pressures and demands from below. It encourages consensus within political parties and among them. All three present-day parliamentary parties have, for example, at one time or another been in partnership with each other. State coalitions do not always mirror those at the federal level. When a party is in opposition in Bonn, it will be entangled in government policies because of the way in which the bicameral parliamentary system operates. There are dozens of bodies—commissions and agencies of all sorts—that bring together representatives of state governments to address specific national needs with a common, supraparty, single voice.

State and federal governments in West Germany are active economic participants. The federal government alone owns and operates some $25 billion worth of assets, ranging from the railroads to the largest oil company (Veba), the largest automobile producer (Volkswagen), and many other firms. Approximately one out of every ten workers is employed by public enterprise. And this is not limited to the federal government. State governments, too, may invest in commercial ventures. For example, Hamburg, Bremen, and Bavaria share ownership with private sources in the two major aerospace companies in the FRG. Basically, West Germany has achieved a kind of mixed economy with extensive state involvement in what remains essentially a free enterprise system.

Government is highly responsive to the needs of the private sector. All kinds of subsidies abound in the FRG. Some are designed to promote industrial innovation. Here the role of the Federal Ministry of Research and Technology (a post that does not exist in the U.S. cabinet) has become increasingly important. That ministry, with a swelling budget, has recently supported important projects centered around microelectronics and silicon chips. It has funded programs on the gasification of coal and has provided major support for the modernization of steel-producing equipment.

Other subsidies have helped prevent the collapse of key companies or lagging sectors. Large subsidies have been directed to the coal, iron, and shipbuilding industries. Perhaps best known was the rescue of Krupp through government assistance some years ago. Such aid in West Germany (in contrast to U.S. practices) tends to involve more stringent government efforts to impose conditions and seek the rationalization of the subsidized industry. Here, too, the interplay between the private and public sectors is much more extensive than in the United States.

Cooperation between these two sectors is also enhanced by a variety of consultative arrangements. One is the so-called concerted action, which at one time brought together union leaders, managers, government officials, and representatives of other economic groups on a regular basis. Even where there is substantial opposition among these interests, there is also continuing contact among them. This is facilitated by the fact that interest-group representatives play an important role in West German political parties and are represented in the federal and state parliaments. The interaction between senior government officials and business and union leaders is extensive as well. In West Germany there is simply a much tighter grid encompassing private and public economic activity than in the United States, and the exceptional quality of the civil service plays a particularly strategic and constructive role in facilitating a high level of economic performance.

The federal government pays careful attention to the accuracy of its economic forecasts. Law requires that intermediate range, five-year projections be articulated (and revised) annually. The Ministry of Economics (which is separate from the Finance Ministry) sees its role in part as the creation of a more stable framework for long-term, stable planning by West German companies. The staunchly independent and highly competent federal reserve bank (Bundesbank) maintains a separate forecasting mechanism, which is carefully insulated from partisan considerations.

The result of this kind of government role has been salutary for economic performance. Thrift, often characterized as a particularly German virtue, has been encouraged. The rate of savings is more than three times that in the United States. This habit has helped to curb inflation, which in turn, tends to reward savings because the deferred purchasing power of those savings does not rapidly erode. While the United States experienced a continuing increase of consumer debt throughout 1979, West German savings expanded creating the base for a further 10 percent rise in capital spending. Here there are some real lessons for the United States to learn.

The FRG has benefited from the fact that the deutsche mark (DM) has not, until recently, served as a reserve currency. This has permitted the Bundesbank to keep a far tighter control on capital markets and money supply, although the sharp and sustained rise in U.S. interest rates has complicated this task.

Perhaps nowhere has the effectiveness of West German economic policy been more pronounced than in grappling with the problems of its energy supplies during the past few difficult years. West Germany imports all of its oil, which in turn, represents slightly more than half of its primary energy consumption. Government strategy after the 1974 price increases was to slow the rate of growth of the domestic economy, maintain a strong balance of payments, and encourage a strengthening of the mark, which meant that an export-led current account surplus would create sufficient demand for West German products to prevent a serious recession. A strong mark would reduce import costs to restrain inflation. But this required an intensification of the effort to sell West German products abroad. The federal government organized selling campaigns, especially to the Arab members of the Organization of Petroleum Exporting Countries (OPEC). In the mid-1970s it was not unusual to find the Minister of Economics (now head of the Dresdner Bank) selecting a dozen industrial leaders to join him on a marketing mission to Saudi Arabia or Iran. Apparently it succeeded. Despite the dramatic increase in the price of oil, the FRG for a time actually achieved a favorable balance of trade with the Arab members of OPEC.

Meanwhile, the West German government has vigorously promoted the search for alternative sources of supply. Here its options are more restricted than our own because of the weak domestic energy resources that are available. West Germany developed one of the most modern and sophisticated nuclear reactor programs (now installed because of environmental opposition). Its reactors are seen to be so good that they sell abroad at prices substantially higher than competing U.S. products. Gasification of coal has been strongly subsidized in the two major government-owned energy companies, Veba and Ruhrkohle. Efforts to develop natural gas imports from the USSR and to secure liquefied natural gas imports from Algeria have been the result of vigorous government initiatives. Oil has been stockpiled in sufficient quantities to sustain 110 days of consumption.

These are expensive measures. Their full effect was discounted in the recent past by the enormous upward valuation of the mark. This phenomenon has now, most likely, run its course. The mounting burden of oil and gas imports will take a greater toll in the years to come. The cost of oil imports spurted from DM30 billion in 1978 to DM45 billion in 1979 and may rise a further 50 percent this year. Oil imports would then absorb 4.5 percent of the GNP compared with 2.5 percent just two years ago. This cost will require a further intensification of the export drive in the years ahead.

The experience of the past decade has been remarkable. West German exports have increased since 1970 at an annual rate of 11 percent, soaring from DM125 billion in 1970 to DM315 billion in 1979. In part, this was the result of astute government policies and initiatives. The government has been instrumental in providing or ensuring credits for foreign purchases of West German goods. It has opened the door for major sales to eastern Europe, the USSR, and now the People's Republic of China. When Iran collapsed, the federal government was quick to establish a foothold in Iraq. Without the strong and effective support of government resources, it is unlikely that West German exports would so successfully have withstood the price effects of the strengthening mark.

But trade for West Germany is emphatically a two-way street. Imports, too, have been growing rapidly. The West German economy is basically an added-value manufacturing system. To prosper it must import vast quantities of raw materials. Despite the strength of the mark and the fact that oil prices are dollar denominated, raw material and energy costs increased by 31 percent in 1979. For a major chemical company such as Hoechst, that represented an additional cost of a half billion marks in just one year. It has been projected that raw material and production costs in the U.S. chemical industry may now be as much as 30 percent below those of West Germany.

Any serious erosion of West German capacity to export competitively could have serious consequences for its domestic economic equilibrium given its soaring energy import bill. In 1979, for the first time since the recession of 1966, West German balance of payments on current accounts did slip into the red by about DM9 billion. That deficit is now projected to exceed DM20 billion for 1980. Given its vast accumulated reserves, a year or two of deficit can be easily absorbed. Were this a harbinger of things to come, West German government initiatives would have to be further intensified to restore a positive balance, and it is a governmental system that is both sensitive to, and well designed for, playing that sort of role.

The second significant factor accounting for West German competitiveness has been labor. First, during the 1950s there was a
large, motivated reservoir of surplus labor, which helps explain both
the prodigious growth of those years and the relatively harmonious
labor relations that characterized them. Organized labor approached
the tasks of postwar recovery with a profound sense of partnership
and participation, rather than confrontation. This is partially the result of its historical experience. During the 1920s the labor unions
fought for a recognition and legitimacy that was never broadly accepted. Under Hitler they suffered the dictates of a totalitarian war
machine.

All is different in the FRG. Here the role of the unions is affirmed in the constitution. Trade unions are basically unified and
have gained overwhelming recognition. Three members of Helmut
Schmidt's cabinet, including the finance minister, Hans Matthöfer,
were union officials prior to taking government posts.

Labor bargaining is quite different in West Germany from the
experience elsewhere. Unions bargain for basic wages and fringe
benefits across the board for entire industrial sectors, often on a
national, or at least a state, level. Where strikes are threatened, the
role of government agencies, especially in arbitrating disputes, has
been significant. The part played by government in labor affairs has
to be substantial in West Germany because government is the single
largest employer.

The propensity to strike has not been great. This has several
explanations. First, and most important, wages have increased
enormously. Of course, the point of departure in the late 1940s was
rather low. Nonetheless, there has been a fourfold increase in purchasing power per capita in the FRG since then, and that kind of improvement diminishes dissatisfactions. From 1950 to the recession
of 1966 real wages grew by 140 percent while the work week decreased
by 10 percent; the record since the mid-1960s is about the same.

Much of the growth in wages is due to increases in labor productivity, which has been growing by more than 3 percent annually in
the last few years. This, in turn, is the result of the far higher per
capita investments in research and development (R&D) and new plant
equipment than occur here in the United States. But there may be
imminent limits to the West German experience. In the chemical
industry, wage costs in the FRG now exceed those in the United States
by 30 percent. In the highly competitive motor vehicle industry, West
German manufacturers in 1978 paid DM24.4 per manhour compared
with an equivalent of DM21.5 in the United States and only DM16.3
in Japan. It could be that West German labor costs may price West
German goods out of foreign markets in years to come, and that situation could feed back into the domestic arena with a much more contentious outcome for labor negotiations.

However, those negotiations do not rest with wages alone. West German unions have placed great emphasis on the way in which labor is organized in the plant and in the firm. The role of works councils in factories and codetermination (or Mitbestimmung) in the boardroom are seen as important gains for the labor movement, which helps explain the relative harmony of labor relations in the FRG.

Much as the state is a partner of private enterprise in West German business, so too are the trade unions. One of the giant banks (the Bank für Gemeinwirtschaft) is union owned. So is the largest building firm (Neue Heimat) in West Germany. This kind of partnership helps explain the unions' increased willingness to accept new technologies and to acknowledge the need for industrial innovation. West German labor seems to comprehend far better than our own the need to rationalize, because it has grown strong with an ongoing awareness of the need to remain competitive.

If West German labor has been cooperative, it has also reaped impressive gains. The average monthly industrial wage in West Germany today stands at about DM2,400. Unemployment has remained well below the 5 percent threshold and that under conditions in which millions of foreign workers have joined the labor force. These guest workers, who tend to be a kind of labor underclass, have been more easily expendable because they are not full-fledged members of the national labor constituency. Thus, when jobs become eliminated, some of these foreigners can be sent back home. To date these workers have been relatively docile in placing demands upon the system. That is beginning to change and may pose problems (and costs) for West Germany.

In many respects West Germany has become a social welfare society. Today about one-third of its GNP is directed toward social costs, which now total over DM400 billion annually and are presently rising by 6.3 percent per annum. If the guest workers are to increase their demands for full participation as beneficiaries of the social welfare system, the costs could escalate at a precarious pace. This indicates problems down the road, especially in view of the negative birthrate, which will place disproportionately heavy burdens on a reduced supply of wage earners in the not-so-distant future.

If labor has been the second important component in West German economic prosperity, the contributions of the private sector have been the third. The management and organization of West German finance and industry have played an absolutely essential role in fostering economic growth. Here there are several distinctive factors. First is the close fusion between banking and industry. In the FRG there is no separation of deposit and investment banking functions. Nor are banks limited—as they are in the United States—in their geographic spread. While some are regionally concentrated, all the large banks are national, countrywide institutions. Given West German thrift and prosperity, the major banks have had substantial capital at their disposal. They have used this capital both to finance industry and to acquire very significant industrial holdings. The Deutsche Bank, for example, owns more than 25 percent of Daimler Benz. Its directors sit on the boards of countless industrial firms.

This close relationship has important implications. West German industrial companies are not dependent upon equity markets for the raising of capital. The provision of massive funds by private banks permit more long-term, stable planning for firms, which are not as adversely affected by the collapse of stock prices as are their U.S. counterparts. Moreover, the closeness of industry to the major banking institutions makes unfriendly takeovers less likely and less rewarding. West Germany has been spared the creation of wide-ranging, internally inefficient conglomerates. Instead, banks and companies work together to rationalize where desirable and to salvage where necessary. A bankruptcy, such as Rolls Royce, would not occur in the FRG. When the giant AEG-Telefunken Company teetered on the brink of illiquidity, the banks, which were already important shareholders, stepped in to supply a billion marks of credit along with some stringent demands for reorganization.

Concentration is another central feature of the West German system. The chemical, electro-technical, and automotive industries are dominated today by monolithic giants who have become important multinational players. Here the interplay between size and commanding export roles has been of strategic value. All three sectors export more than 40 percent of their production. Their size has permitted extensive foreign market penetration and permitted effective competition with U.S. firms. The Volkswagen experience may be the best known. Not only are its exports formidable, but it has established assembly plants in Argentina, Brazil, Mexico, Egypt, and the United States and may even place one in South Korea (right under Japanese noses!). Indeed, Volkswagen today has displaced American Motors as the fourth largest U.S. domestic car producer. In chemicals, Bayer now has garnered 1 percent of the U.S. domestic market. In 1978 its U.S. subsidiaries had a combined turnover in excess of DM4 billion, which approached its total sales in West Germany.

The link between size and foreign sales is innovation. West German thrift, concentrated banking deposits, retained earnings, and government subsidies have permitted the allocation of substantial resources of R&D. West German companies have increased their R&D outlays from 0.5 percent of domestic output in 1964 to 1.5 percent in 1977. Today, that figure probably exceeds 2 percent, whereas in the United States it is less than 1 percent. Well supplied with capital, West German firms are less concerned with rate of return than

with the quality of the product. Since 1975 Siemens has raised sales
from products that are less than five years old from 39 percent to
48 percent. The Mercedes-Benz has replaced the Cadillac or the
Rolls Royce as the symbol of quality, workmanship, and status. West
Germany has produced goods that work and that are wanted and has
done so with sufficient prowess to sell them effectively, even when
they are no longer price competitive.

It has also invested heavily in new plants. Here spending increased by 14 percent in 1979. This is not just the result of innovative will and capital reserves; it also reflects labor's acceptance of
the necessity of modernization, even where it may spell job redun-
dancy. This enlightened outlook on the part of labor reflects the fact
that its leaders are often placed in relationships with business leaders from which the longer-term needs of the economy can be better
assayed. Organized interest groups play a very important role in
West Germany. There is a great deal of behind-the-scenes bargaining and accommodation. The state, labor, and business leaderships
coalesce in ways that have fed effective economic collaboration. Interelite relations have helped cement this process. The results can
be measured in performance figures, be they in growth, stability,
curbing of inflation, or export sales.

What can the United States learn from all this? There are lessons in the West German case. They are to be found in a much
stronger sense of the need to become and remain competitive, given
the less favorable circumstances of the country as a whole. That
sense and the rational effort to rebuild a society that had wrought such
destruction on itself have created a balanced mix of private and public
initiatives and institutions that have permitted a fundamentally weaker
economy to become a prodigious world leader. If the West German
experience exemplifies anything, it is that will and proper organization can attain remarkable achievements. Perhaps it is time that we
begin to do the same ourselves.

3

ECONOMIC ASPECTS OF MODEL GERMANY: A COMPARISON WITH THE UNITED STATES

WILLI SEMMLER

In comparison with other Western countries, the West German economy performed extraordinarily well in the postwar period. During the 1960s and 1970s, the wide productivity gap that existed in the 1950s between West German and U.S. industries became smaller and smaller and finally disappeared in many industries at the end of the 1970s.[1] By 1980 the per capita gross national product (GNP) for West Germany was higher than the U.S. per capita GNP. The declining growth rates for productivity of the U.S. industries caused a decrease in the international competitiveness of U.S. firms in comparison with European and Japanese rivals.

A common statement is that "while the United States experienced the highest growth rate among the industrial nations during the period from 1870 to 1950, its relative performance was below average for the period from 1950 to 1965, and it had the lowest rate during the period from 1965 to 1971."[2] The decline in growth rates continued during the 1970s: the growth rate of productivity dropped to -.05 percent for the period from 1973 to 1976.[3] After this period, productivity increased only slightly. In contrast, the West German economy has consistently shown a much higher growth rate of per capita GNP. After World War II West Germany's per capita GNP was only 50 percent that of the United States. In 1977 West Germany had a level of per capita GNP that was 95 percent of the U.S. level.[4] By the beginning of the 1980s it had surpassed the United States.

In this period West Germany's manufacturing sector grew rapidly. From 1950 to 1975 that sector increased from 31 percent of the GNP to 43.2 percent, whereas in the United States the manufacturing sector declined during the same period from 28.2 percent to 26 percent of the GNP. Today the West German economy has the strongest manufacturing sector among the developed countries (see Table 3.1).

TABLE 3.1

Manufacturing Output as a Proportion of GDP at 1963 Prices, in
Advanced Industrial Countries, 1950-75

	1950	1955	1960	1965	1970	1973	1974	1975
United Kingdom	29.3	30.6	31.0	31.1	31.7	31.5	30.6	29.1
Canada	25.1	24.7	24.2	27.1	26.4	27.1	26.8	25.5
Japan	n.a.	22.2	31.7	34.7	41.9	41.8	40.9	35.5
France	32.6	33.3	35.0	36.2	38.0	39.6	39.4	36.0
West Germany	31.0	37.2	39.9	42.6	44.5	44.6	44.5	43.2
Italy	17.9	22.6	25.5	27.6	31.2	32.0	n.a.	n.a.
Belgium	n.a.	n.a.	26.0	27.3	30.3	31.7	31.5	30.0
Netherlands	32.7	33.8	36.6	38.4	41.7	42.3	42.1	41.0
Sweden	25.2	25.6	27.7	29.8	31.9	32.5	32.6	33.8
United States	28.2	28.9	27.4	29.3	27.9	29.2	28.1	26.0

n.a. = not available

Sources: Organization for Economic Cooperation and Development, National Accounts of OECD Countries, 1952-79 (Paris: OECD, 1980); idem, Industrial Production, 1950-71 (Paris: OECD, 1972); ibid., 1971-73 (1974); and ibid., 1973-75 (1976).

Export-oriented industries within the manufacturing sector have been the leaders of this tremendous growth. The West German economy not only caught up with the level of productivity in the U.S. economy, but on the basis of its strong export-oriented manufacturing sector, it also replaced the U.S. economy in its leading role in world trade. The U.S. share in world trade declined from 15.9 percent in 1960 to 10.7 percent in 1977, whereas the West German share in total world trade increased from 3.5 percent in 1950 to 10.5 percent in 1977. These changes in the shares of world exports by West Germany and the United States are even more dramatic if we look at the export shares of manufactured goods. West Germany increased its share in world exports of manufactured goods from 19.3 percent in 1964 to 20.8 percent in 1977, whereas the U.S. export share dropped in the same period from 21.5 percent to 15.9 percent. West Germany is now the leading country in exports of manufactured goods, especially of investment goods.

These three indicators—the level of productivity, the share of the manufacturing sector in GNP, and the share in world trade—show that the West German economy became increasingly competitive in the postwar period and the U.S. economy lost the competitive advantage it had at the end of World War II. Numerous studies have already been conducted to explain the extraordinary success of the West German economy, as well as the impact of this economic miracle on the labor movement, the trade unions, the party system, and the stability of the political system.[5] This chapter deals with only three questions: (1) What are the specific causes of the rapid economic development and the long prosperity in West Germany? (2) Why do the growth rates of output and productivity differ from those of the U.S. economy? and (3) To what extent could the West German economy escape the long downswing and the increasing international instabilities beginning in the 1970s?

PRECONDITIONS OF THE ECONOMIC MIRACLE

The huge amount of economic literature on West Germany can be broken down into three basic positions that attempt to explain the rapid rise of the postwar economy. First, we find the neoliberal view. In its analysis, the West German success has to be explained by the initial political decision after World War II to turn the German war economy back into a socially oriented free market system. This was accomplished through the following:

1. The postwar reform of the monetary system and abolition of the price freeze,
2. Encouraging private initiatives,
3. A tough monetary policy that limited the growth of the money supply,
4. A tough antitrust law that led to an increase in economic competition and increasing efficiency of West German firms,
5. A reduction of state intervention, and
6. Putting industries back into private hands.

Representatives of this neoliberal interpretation of the West German Wirtschaftswunder ("economic miracle") dominated economic theory in West Germany until the middle of the 1960s. Writers such as Eucken, Erhard, Müller-Armack, Rüstow, and Ropke were not only the leading neoliberal theorists of the West German market system, but were very influential in the formation of economic policy.

A second position claims that the success of the German economy was due to the increasing public management of the private economy. Here the position is taken that the implementation of Keynesian economic policies, such as improvement of the national income account, macroeconomic demand management by the state, and an expanding state sector, were decisive in developing the West German, as well as other European, economies in the postwar period. Yet, representatives of this Keynesian explanation of the economic miracle, such as Shonfield, Maddison, Roskamp, Reuss, Vogt, and Hopp, overlook the fact that despite a high rate of unemployment in West Germany before the middle of the 1950s, Keynesian economic policies were not implemented until the middle of the next decade. Moreover, as will be shown later, the state did not play an important role in increasing aggregate demand during the postwar period.

A third position is taken by political economists in West Germany. This school, represented by Mandel, Janossy, Huffschmid, Altvater, Hoffman, and Semmler, among others, maintains that the success of the West German economy after World War II was exceptional. It was based originally on a very unequal income distribution, low level of consumption, and high profitability of investment—the result of the war, the postwar situation, and the dissolution of the labor movement during fascism.[6] However, these favorable conditions for capital accumulation after World War II have deteriorated since the middle of the 1960s, and the German economy has become increasingly unstable, especially since the crisis of 1974 and 1975. If we look back on the postwar period, we can analyze three factors that are responsible for the long and successful upswing of the West German economy.

First, the social and technical conditions (as mentioned above, a result of the war and the postwar situation) were quite favorable for a capitalist market system. These favorable conditions included the following:

1. The labor movement was almost destroyed after World War II, and a compromise between capital and labor (as in the United States) was not necessary.[7]

2. In spite of the general destruction during the war, the capital stock was only partially destroyed. The capital stock had increased by 20 percent between 1936 and 1945, and after World War II plants were repaired with quite low investment costs.[8]

3. The excess supply of labor and the dissolution of the labor movement made very low wages possible until the end of the 1950s (see Figure 3.1). The unit wage cost in West Germany did not catch up with the international level until 1958.[9]

4. A highly qualified, skilled, and disciplined labor force allowed for high rates of economic growth without any labor supply bottlenecks.

FIGURE 3.1

Trends of Output per Unit of Capital, Wage Share, Growth Rate of
Capital Stock, and Rates of Return on Investment
(nonfarm business sector, in current prices)

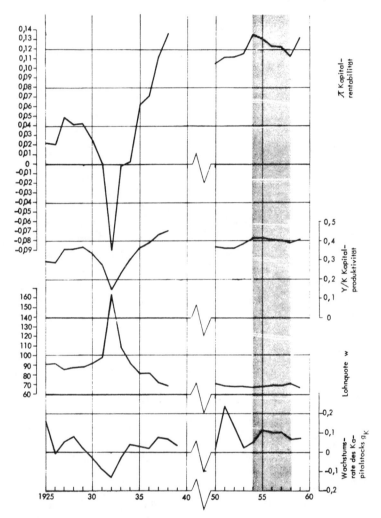

Y/K = output per unit of capital
w = wage share in value added
g_K = growth rate of capital stock
π = rate of return on investment

Source: Elmar Altvater, Jürgen Hoffmann, and Willi Semmler,
Vom Wirtschaftswunder zur Wirtschaftskrise: Ökonomie und Politik
in der Bundesrepublik (Berlin: Olle und Wolter, 1979), p. 75.

These exceptional social and technical preconditions allowed for a high profit share in value added and for a high profit rate on investments. As shown in Figure 3.1, the profit share in value added had already risen during the prewar period and remained high after the war. The output per unit of capital also went up in the prewar period and remained at a high level after the war. Both of these factors— the high profit share and the high level of output per unit of capital— contributed to a high profit rate and high growth rate of the capital stock in the postwar period. Indeed, owing to these exceptional preconditions, production in manufacturing rose even before the reform of the currency system in 1948 and before the Marshall Plan became effective. [10] Only some bottlenecks in the production of raw materials, intermediate products, and especially in transportation had to be overcome in order to increase production and to accumulate capital rapidly.

A second factor that allowed for a rapid expansion of the West German economy was the expansion of the world market and the specific structure of West German exports. Owing to its special structure, which was marked by a huge and expanding manufacturing sector (see Table 3.1), the West German economy rapidly grew to be very productive on the whole, and its industrial sector in particular became highly competitive.

With its special structure of exports and its highly export-oriented industries, West Germany had a considerable advantage over other countries during the long upswing after World War II. Exports in West Germany consisted mainly of manufactured products, and 80 percent of the exported goods consisted of producer and investment goods (machines, electrical products, cars, chemical products, and steel). The long upswing in other countries created a demand for producer and investment goods that the economy was structurally well-suited to fill. The export share in leading industries, such as cars, machines, and chemical and electrical products, went up from 10 percent to 15 percent in 1950 to, in some cases, more than 40 percent. This can be seen in Table 3.2. This structure of industry has been typical for the West German economy since the end of the nineteenth century and became a very decisive factor in the postwar development.

A third factor has to be mentioned. This is the specific role of the state in West Germany. In fact, there was a tough monetary and fiscal policy, as is accurately noted by neoliberal writers; the state did not pursue a Keynesian demand-oriented policy at all. The public management of the private economy was very limited until the middle of the 1960s. However, contrary to the view of the neoliberal authors, state policy was not limited only to Ordnungspolitik ("providing a general framework for the market system"), but rather, it

TABLE 3.2

Export Shares for Selected Industries, 1950-75
(percentage of total sales)

	1950	1958	1967	1970	1974	1975
Cars	11.5	36.3	40.7	40.6	46.1	41.5
Machines	20.3	30.2	38.0	35.5	43.5	43.7
Iron-producing industry	16.4	17.8	30.3	24.0	35.2	34.0
Chemical industry	12.3	22.5	29.0	31.1	36.0	33.0
Nonmetal industry	11.4	14.9	24.4	18.3	22.9	21.6
Mining	27.3	20.8	22.7	22.8	27.8	28.4
Manufacturing	8.3	15.1	18.7	19.3	24.2	23.6

Source: Statistische Jahrbücher der Bundesrepublik Deutschland, Annual (Wiesbaden: Statistisches Bundesamb, 1951-76).

intervened massively in favor of the formation of capital.[11] Thus,
the economic policy of the state was neither liberal nor demand-side-
oriented; instead it emphasized a supply-side approach (which has
become well known in the United States since the Reagan administration). The first chancellor, Konrad Adenauer, said in 1949 in parliament, "The primary function of the state is to encourage capital
formation." This quotation makes the supply-side-oriented policy
of the state quite clear.[12] The share of consumption in the GNP was
very low and decreased from 1950 to 1960 from 64.1 percent to 56.6
percent. The share of the state consumption in GNP decreased also
from 15.2 percent in 1950 to 12.8 percent in 1956 and 13.5 percent
in 1960. At the same time the share of investment in GNP increased
from 19.1 percent in 1950 to 24.2 percent in 1960. These data make
clear that the increase in the GNP went neither to private consumption
nor to state consumption, but to private investment.

These three factors—the social and technical conditions after
World War II, the strong export-oriented manufacturing sector, and
the role of the state—help explain the high profitability of investment,
the high growth rate of capital stock, and the high growth rate of productivity in the West German economy. Figures 3.2 and 3.3 show
the basic trends in the West German economy from 1950 to 1977.
They show the output per unit of capital (Y/K), the wage share (w),
the profit share $(1-w)$, the capital/labor ratio (K/L), the productivity

FIGURE 3.2

Rate of Return on Investment and Capital Accumulation in West
Germany, 1950-77
(manufacturing sector, in 1962 prices)

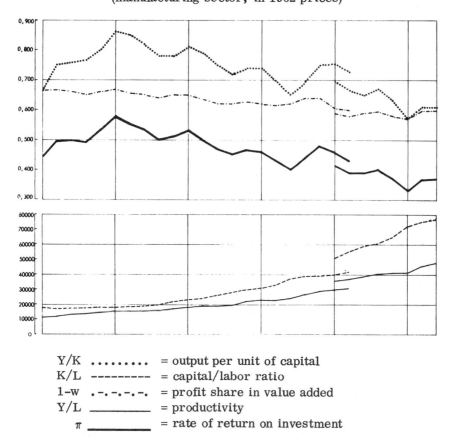

Y/K	....	= output per unit of capital
K/L	---------	= capital/labor ratio
1-w	.-.-.-.-.	= profit share in value added
Y/L	_____	= productivity
π	_____	= rate of return on investment

Source: Elmar Altvater, Jürgen Hoffmann, and Willi Semmler,
Vom Wirtschaftswunder zur Wirtschaftskrise: Ökonomie und Politik
in der Bundesrepublik (Berlin: Olle und Wolter, 1979), pp. 86, 87.

(Y/L), the share of investment in total profits (I/P), the growth rate
of the capital stock (ΔK/K), and the profit rate on investment (π).
(All data refer to manufacturing production.) All basic data on growth
and accumulation show that West Germany experienced a strong upswing from the end of the 1940s to the beginning or middle of the
1960s, followed by a period of slower rates of growth, output, productivity, and capital formation.

FIGURE 3.3

Capital Formation in West Germany, 1950-77
(manufacturing sector, in 1962 prices)

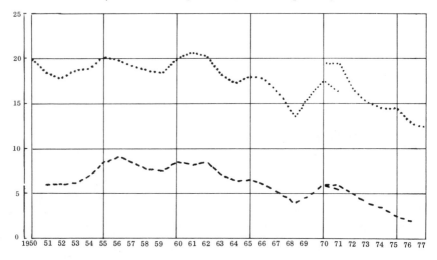

I/P   ..-..-..- = investment out of profit
ΔK/K --------- = growth rate of capital stock

Source: Elmar Altvater, Jürgen Hoffmann, and Willi Semmler, Vom Wirtschaftswunder zur Wirtschaftskrise: Ökonomie und Politik in der Bundesrepublik (Berlin: Olle und Wolter, 1979), pp. 86, 87.

As shown in Table 3.3, the German economy after World War II showed a high rate of unemployment. An excess supply of labor was available until 1957-58, and the wage share in value added was very low. Only at the end of the 1950s did the West German economy approach the situation of full employment, and since that time there has been an influx of foreign workers. The scarcity of labor since the beginning of the 1960s allowed for an increase in real wages, a rising level of consumption for West German workers, and an increasing wage share. The rate of unemployment increased in the middle of the 1970s again and remained essentially constant at a high level until the present.

Owing to the extraordinary initial conditions, one can see two stages of growth and capital accumulation in West Germany (see Figures 3.2 and 3.3). The first stage, beginning with the 1950s and ending in the middle of the 1960s, shows a very high growth rate of capital stock (much higher than in the U.S. economy [see Figures

TABLE 3.3

Development of Total Employment, Foreign Workers, Hours per Week, Unemployment, Rate of Unemployment, and Wage Share in the FRG, 1950-77

Year	Total Employment	Foreign Workers (in thousands)	Hours per Week	Unemployment (in thousands)	Rate of Unemployment	Wage Share
1950	13,674		49.0	1,580	10.4	33.6
1951	14,286		48.5	1,432	9.1	33.5
1952	14,754		48.5	1,379	8.5	33.9
1953	15,344		48.8	1,259	7.6	35.0
1954	15,968	73	49.5	1,221	7.1	33.8
1955	16,840	80	49.8	928	5.2	33.3
1956	17,483	99	49.0	761	4.2	34.5
1957	17,992	108	47.2	662	3.5	35.0
1958	18,188	127	46.4	683	3.6	35.6
1959	18,508	167	46.3	476	2.5	34.7
1960	20,257	279	46.3	271	1.3	34.9
1961	20,730	507	46.2	181	0.9	36.5
1962	21,032	629	45.6	155	0.7	37.8
1963	21,261	773	45.4	186	0.9	37.7
1964	21,484	902	44.9	169	0.8	37.1
1965	21,757	1,119	45.1	147	0.7	37.9
1966	21,765	1,244	44.7	161	0.7	38.4
1967	21,054	1,014	43.0	459	2.1	37.6
1968	21,183	1,019	44.0	323	1.5	36.0
1969	21,752	1,366	44.8	179	0.8	35.9
1970	22,246	1,807	44.8	149	0.7	39.1
1971	22,396	2,128	43.9	185	0.8	39.9
1972	22,340	2,284	43.6	246	1.1	40.7
1973	22,500	2,425	43.5	273	1.2	40.2
1974	22,092	2,323	42.7	582	2.6	42.0
1975	21,329	2,061	40.5	1,074	4.8	42.7
1976	21,233	1,925	41.6	1,060	4.7	39.8
1977	21,271	1,848	41.7	1,030	4.6	40.0

Source: Elmar Altvater, Jürgen Hoffmann, and Willi Semmler, Vom Wirtschaftswunder zur Wirtschaftskrise: Ökonomie und Politik in der Bundesrepublik (Berlin: Olle und Wolter, 1979), p. 100.

3.4 and 3.6]), a high growth rate of the capital/labor ratio (also much higher than in the United States), rates of growth in productivity even higher than the growth rates of the capital/labor ratio, and declining terms of trade. One can also see, since the end of the 1950s, decreasing unemployment, increasing real wages, and an increasing wage share (see Table 3.3). Since the beginning of full employment (the end of the 1950s), the West German unions were able to push for higher wages and have increased the wage share.

From the middle or end of the 1960s onward one can observe a second stage of growth in the West German economy, with slightly declining rates of capital formation, declining growth rates of output and productivity, scarcity of labor, increasing wage share, and more and more capital-intensive production. Moreover, especially since the beginning of the 1970s, the terms of trade have tended to rise, and input costs have tended to increase. On the whole, one can see a declining profitability of investments and a slowing down of capital accumulation (see Figures 3.2 and 3.3). In sum, the initially quite favorable conditions for rapid capital accumulation and high growth rates have deteriorated since the 1950s and 1960s. The West German economy faced new internal and external conditions of growth in the 1970s, showing higher rates of unemployment, higher inflation rates, and more unstable development than before. However, before discussing this problem, one should compare the U.S. postwar development with the West German one in order to see why growth rates differed and why the U.S. economy lost the comparative advantage it had at the end of World War II.

ECONOMIC GROWTH IN WEST GERMANY
AND IN THE UNITED STATES: A COMPARISON

The most interesting and recently the most discussed aspect of the decline of the U.S. economy has been the slowdown in productivity. This has been the most important topic of economic research in the United States during the 1970s and the most important aspect of economic policy in the United States. Most orthodox empirical studies of U.S. industries show that the decline in productivity is caused by declining capital accumulation, low growth rates in the capital/labor ratio, and the decline in the growth rate of technical progress.[13] Marxist authors maintain that the decline of productivity and the decline of U.S. capitalism is due to a declining profit rate, caused by an increase in wage share, an increase in nonproduction, a decrease in production labor, an increase in waste in U.S. capitalism, or an increase in the social wages of workers accompanied by a worsening of the terms of trade for the United States

TABLE 3.4

Gross Profits and Rates of Return: Industry Plus Transport, 1955-76

		1955	1956	1957	1958	1959	1960	1961	1962	1963	1964	1965	1966	1967	1968	1969	1970	1971	1972	1973	1974	1975	1976
Canada	P/Y	38.0	38.4	36.7	36.3	36.8	36.4	37.0	37.7	38.5	39.4	38.0	37.1	35.8	36.6	36.1	35.2	35.0	36.1	37.9	38.2	36.4	36.1
	Y/K	33.3	33.8	32.0	29.4	29.5	28.5	27.9	28.1	28.4	29.1	29.0	29.2	28.7	29.1	28.7	27.3	26.8	26.9	28.6	28.2	26.0	25.9
	P/K	12.6	13.0	11.7	10.7	10.8	10.3	10.3	10.6	10.9	11.5	11.0	10.8	10.3	10.7	10.4	9.6	9.4	9.7	10.8	10.8	9.5	9.4
United States	P/Y	35.3	34.1	33.9	33.5	34.4	33.8	33.8	33.6	33.8	34.2	34.6	34.2	33.4	33.1	31.8	30.6	31.2	31.3	30.7	29.3	31.6	32.0
	Y/K	55.7	54.0	51.9	48.1	51.4	51.4	50.7	52.5	53.4	55.1	56.4	57.4	55.3	55.3	53.7	49.9	48.7	49.1	50.2	48.0	45.7	47.6
	P/K	19.7	18.4	17.6	16.1	17.7	17.4	17.1	17.7	18.0	18.8	19.5	19.6	18.5	18.3	17.1	15.2	15.2	15.5	15.4	14.3	14.4	15.2
Japan	P/Y	41.2	42.3	45.9	43.6	43.8	47.9	48.9	46.7	46.8	46.6	44.3	44.7	46.2	47.8	48.1	48.1	45.5	44.3	41.4	37.4	37.8	
	Y/K	31.7	33.2	35.3	35.7	38.0	42.6	44.4	43.9	44.8	46.0	43.9	44.5	46.5	48.9	49.2	49.9	48.5	47.5	45.1	38.4	39.8	
	P/K	13.1	14.0	16.2	15.6	16.6	20.4	21.7	20.5	20.9	21.5	19.4	19.9	21.5	23.3	23.7	24.0	22.0	21.1	18.7	14.4	15.1	
Germany	P/Y	47.2	46.7	46.9	46.3	47.1	46.8	45.0	43.8	43.2	43.1	43.5	42.9	43.9	44.9	43.7	42.5	41.9	41.6	40.5	40.2	40.6	41.7
	Y/K	51.4	51.5	51.8	51.7	53.3	54.7	53.1	51.3	48.8	48.5	49.1	47.8	45.3	47.6	47.3	47.6	46.2	45.6	45.8	44.7	42.5	44.0
	P/K	24.3	24.1	24.3	23.9	25.1	25.6	23.9	22.5	21.1	20.9	21.4	20.5	19.9	21.4	20.7	20.2	19.4	19.0	18.6	18.0	17.2	18.4
Italy	P/Y	46.0	45.3	45.8	45.8	46.8	45.8	45.1	42.7	38.6	37.5	40.5	41.7	39.8	40.7	40.9	36.5	33.3	33.6	33.2	33.1	26.9	
	Y/K	37.4	36.9	35.8	35.6	36.8	38.4	39.6	40.4	40.5	39.0	37.7	39.0	40.8	39.7	41.2	41.7	38.5	38.2				
	P/K	17.2	16.7	16.4	16.3	17.2	17.6	17.9	17.3	15.6	14.6	15.3	16.2	16.2	16.2	16.9	15.2	12.8	12.9				
Sweden	P/Y	34.5	35.3	35.7	35.5	36.6	35.2	34.3	32.5	31.3	32.4	33.1	31.2	31.1	31.5	32.2	32.6	28.6	29.1	32.9	34.0	27.4	22.4
	Y/K	31.4	30.8	30.9	30.7	30.1	29.8	29.6	29.3	28.5	29.3	30.0	29.3	29.2	29.8	29.8	29.8	27.0	26.6	25.9	26.1	25.8	25.1
	P/K	10.8	10.9	11.0	10.9	11.0	10.5	10.2	9.6	8.9	9.5	9.9	9.2	9.1	9.3	9.6	9.7	7.7	7.8	8.5	8.9	7.1	5.6
United Kingdom	P/Y	30.7	29.8	29.4	29.2	30.1	31.7	29.7	28.8	30.5	31.0	30.3	29.1	29.7	30.8	30.9	28.6	28.9	30.1	30.7	27.5	24.7	26.7
	Y/K	28.9	28.9	28.8	28.3	29.1	30.9	30.4	29.7	29.8	30.7	30.8	29.9	28.8	29.0	28.6	27.9	27.1	26.7	26.4	24.6	24.1	23.0
	P/K	8.9	8.6	8.5	8.3	8.8	9.8	9.0	8.6	9.1	9.5	9.3	8.7	8.6	8.9	8.9	8.0	7.8	8.0	8.1	6.8	5.9	6.1
Australia	P/Y	29.6	30.1	31.7	33.1	34.1	34.5	34.0	34.1	36.4	36.6	36.5	35.9	35.9	36.5	37.1	37.7	35.7	35.3	35.8	33.3	28.9	
Denmark	P/Y	44.2	44.7	46.2	45.2	46.7	47.6	46.7	46.9	46.4	47.7	47.0	46.1	46.6	46.1	45.6	45.0	44.3	45.1	44.6	42.2	41.9	
Netherlands	P/Y	45.4	44.5	43.7	41.8	43.9	44.7	41.6	39.7	37.7	37.5	37.4	36.1	37.4	38.3	38.2	36.7	36.2	37.4	37.2	37.2	34.4	37.3

P = gross operating surplus
Y = gross value added
K = gross capital stock

Source: T. P. Hill, Profits and Rates of Return (Paris: Organization for Economic Cooperation and Development, 1979), p. 124.

—causing the rate of profit to fall.[14] Other authors maintain that the profit rate of U.S. industries has shown a long-term tendency to decline, especially since the middle of the 1960s.[15] Although the profit rate in other countries in the Organization for Economic Cooperation and Development (OECD) has been falling since the middle of the 1960s, the profit rate in the United States is below the level of the profit rates of most of the other OECD countries. As we can see from Table 3.4, the profit rates in industry and transport have declined for almost all countries since the middle of the 1960s and only the United Kingdom and Canada show a lower profit rate than the United States. Most U.S. political economists assume that U.S. capitalism, as well as the world capitalist system as a whole, entered a stage of a long downswing during the 1970s and continuing into the 1980s.[16]

The relative decline of the U.S. economy since World War II can be most dramatically demonstrated by comparing the developments in the United States with those in the West German economy during the postwar period. If one looks at the sources of economic growth one can differentiate three factors that may explain the differing growth rates of the West German and U.S. economies.

First, one can see (see Figures 3.4 and 3.6) that the growth rate of the capital stock and the growth rate of the capital/labor ratio differ considerably between the United States and West Germany. In the 1950s and 1960s, the growth rates of capital stock in West Germany were 6 percent to 9 percent.[17] The average growth rate of the capital stock of the U.S. economy was always below 5 percent. From the end of the 1950s to the middle of the 1970s, it was 3.5 percent, but it fell to 2.5 percent to 3 percent by 1975-78. The growth rates of the capital/labor ratio also showed a similar tendency. The growth rates of the capital/labor ratio in the United States are always below those of West Germany. In the United States the growth rates were 2.5 percent to 3 percent in the 1950s and 1960s, and they declined from 2 percent in the beginning of the 1970s to 1 percent at the end of the 1970s; in West Germany the growth rates of the capital/labor ratio were always above 5 percent and, in fact, increased in the 1970s.[18]

A second cause for the low and declining rate of productivity seems to be the high level of unproductive expenditure. The ratio of unproductive to total labor employed was already extraordinarily high in the United States after World War II and increased in the 1950s. Whereas in West Germany the share of unproductive labor to total labor employed was 38.3 percent in 1960, 41.5 percent in 1970, and 44.5 percent in 1975, the share of unproductive labor to total labor employed in the U.S. economy was 60.0 percent in 1952, 64.0 percent in 1961, and 64.0 percent in 1972.[19] Another indicator for the high level of unproductive expenditure in the U.S. economy is the share of

FIGURE 3.4

Data on the U.S. Economy, 1945-80, Part 1

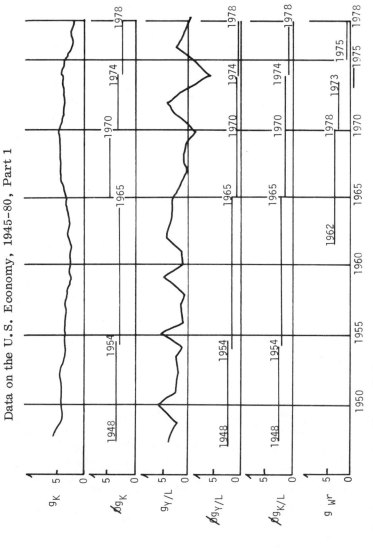

Sources: See sources for Figure 3.6.

35

FIGURE 3.5

Data on the U.S. Economy, 1945–80, Part 2

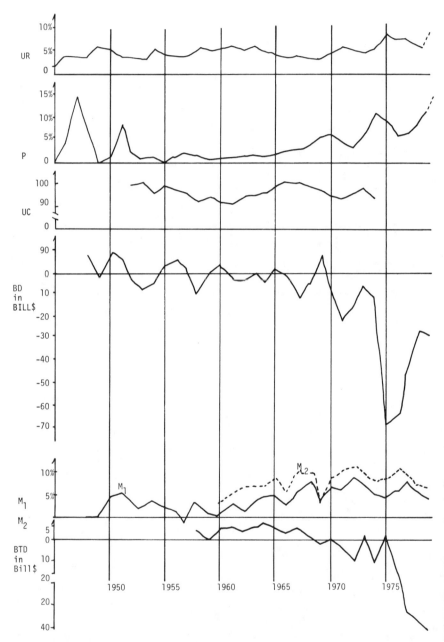

Sources: See sources for Figure 3.6.

36

FIGURE 3.6

Data on the West German Economy, 1950-80

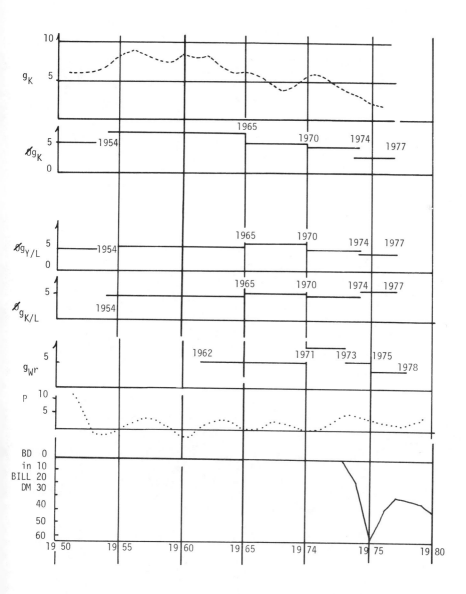

(continued)

FIGURE 3.6 (continued)

Sources: See References at the end of chapter for complete citations of sources referred to below.

		For U.S. Data	For West German Data
g_K	Growth rate of capital stock	Denison, p. 51; weighted average of gross and net capital stock in prices of 1972 (nonfarm business sector)	Altvater, Hoffmann, and Semmler, p. 96; gross capital stock, manufacturing sector in prices of 1962
ϕg_K	Average growth rate of capital stock	Denison, p. 51	Altvater, Hoffmann, and Semmler, p. 96
$g_{Y/L}$	Growth rate of productivity	Denison, p. 9; actual national income per person employed	Altvater, Hoffmann, and Semmler, p. 88; net production per person employed
$\phi g_{Y/L}$	Average growth rate of productivity	Denison, p. 10	Altvater, Hoffmann, and Semmler, p. 88
$\phi g_{K/L}$	Average growth rate of capital/labor ratio	Denison, p. 52; capital per person employed	Altvater, Hoffmann, and Semmler, p. 88; capital per person employed
g_{wr}	Growth rate of real wages	Sachs, p. 273; real hourly compensation for the aggregate economy	Sachs, p. 273; real hourly compensation for the aggregate economy
p	Price index	U.S., Department of Commerce, Bureau of the Census	Altvater, Hoffmann, and Semmler, p. 183
UR	Unemployment	Economic Report of the President, p. 239	—
UC	Utilization of capacity	Knight, p. 99	—
BD	Budget deficit	Economic Report of the President, p. 288	—
M_1, M_2	Money supply	Economic Report of the President, p. 271	—
BTD	Balance-of-trade deficit	Economic Report of the President, p. 318	—

manufacturing output as a proportion of the gross national product (GNP). In West Germany the share of manufacturing output is very high and has been rising from 31.0 percent in 1950 to 43.2 percent in 1975. In the United States it was very low and fell from 28.2 percent in 1950 to 26.0 percent in 1975 (see Table 3.1). Since unproductive expenditures generally do not contribute to the development of productivity, this factor may also explain the difference in growth rates.

Third, the declining internal capital accumulation in the United States is accompanied by an increase in the foreign investments of large U.S. corporations. In 1951 U.S. corporations owned a share of foreign investment with a value of $6 billion. By 1973 it had increased to $73 billion. The share of foreign investments in the GNP was 4.5 percent in 1951, and it increased to 7.5 percent in 1978.[20] In comparison with the United States, in 1950 the share of foreign investments in GNP was almost zero for West Germany and increased to only 3.5 percent in 1973.[21]

Although the declining international competitiveness of the U.S. economy was mitigated in the 1970s by the devaluation of the dollar, nevertheless this long-term decline in productivity produced the following results for the United States in the 1970s (see Figures 3.4 and 3.5):

1. European competitors caught up and closed the productivity gap during the 1970s. In 1977 France showed a level of GNP per capita that was 88 percent of the U.S. level. West Germany had a level of GNP per capita of 95 percent of the United States and surpassed the United States in the beginning of the 1980s.[22]

2. The United States lost, as mentioned above, its leading role in world trade and was replaced by West Germany. From the end of the 1940s to the end of the 1970s, the U.S. share in world manufacturing production dropped from 60 percent to 30 percent, and its share in the production of goods and services dropped from 40 percent to 20 percent.[23]

3. The declining growth rates of productivity; the increase in the unemployment rate to 8.0 percent in 1975, 7.0 percent to 7.5 percent in the second half of the 1970s, and back to 8.0 percent at the beginning of the 1980s; and the increasing rate of inflation (in 1974 it was already 11 percent) caused a decline in the real wage of U.S. workers. Between 1973 and 1975 the real wage of U.S. workers decreased by 0.3 percent. Today, the living standard of U.S. workers is lower than 10 years ago, and for many factions of the U.S. working class their living standard is below that of European workers.

4. The declining international competitiveness of U.S. capitalism caused an increasing balance-of-trade deficit, which began dur-

ing the 1960s (the balance-of-payments deficit started earlier). The dollar lost its leading role as the international medium of circulation and store of value at the end of the 1960s. Consequently, in 1971 President Nixon abolished the convertibility of the dollar into gold, and in 1973 he canceled the fixed-exchange ratios of the currency. The loss of the leading position of the U.S. economy in the world market expressed itself in the loss of the hegemony of the U.S. dollar over other currencies.

5. The most severe problem of the U.S. economy became the double-digit inflation rates (see Figure 3.5). The double-digit rates of inflation at the end of the 1970s cannot be explained by wage increases, deficit spending, or the money supply, let alone by the increase in the price of oil (see Figures 3.4 and 3.5). More important than these factors as causes for the high rate of inflation in the 1970s and beginning of the 1980s was the slow increase in productivity. Intertemporal and cross-sectional studies show that price changes were negatively correlated in a significant way with the growth rate of productivity. [24] The lack of development of productivity in U.S. capitalism seems also to explain the difference between the United States and its European or Japanese rivals in terms of the rate of increase of price levels.

6. During the process of deterioration of the competitiveness of the U.S. economy in the last 15 years, the internationalization of capital and international capital mobility have increased drastically. The increased international mobility of productive capital, as well as of speculative capital, became the main disturbing factor for a nationally oriented monetary and fiscal policy. Demand-side-oriented economists conceded that the regulation of a national economy became more and more difficult in the 1970s. The theory as well as the practice of economic policy shifted from the demand side to the supply side. [25]

In comparison with the United States, the West German economy was relatively better off in the 1970s. As mentioned before, it reached a high level of productivity; increased the share of the manufacturing sector in GNP; continued to increase its export share despite the continuous appreciation of the deutsche mark since the end of the 1960s; and improved its position in world trade, especially for manufacturing goods. Moreover, even with a relatively high rate of unemployment since the economic crisis of 1974-75 (see Table 3.3), the growth rate of real wages was always positive (see Figure 3.6) and the inflation rate dropped to 4 percent to 6 percent, especially in the years after the crisis of 1974-75. Nevertheless, in spite of this better performance in comparison with the United States, West Germany also faced changes in internal and external conditions of economic growth in the 1970s. Of course, the period of lower growth rates in Western countries, declining capital accumulation, decreasing world trade, higher rates of unemployment, changing terms of trade between developed capitalist countries and the OPEC countries, and the higher rates of inflation in the 1970s affected other Western countries, such as the United States, the United Kingdom, France, and Italy, much more than West Germany. Nevertheless, the West German economy was not exempted from the downswing in the world market and the increasing international instability in the 1970s. The West German market system had undergone considerable internal changes in the period just before the 1970s and showed considerable problems adjusting to the changed international environment in the 1970s.

DECLINING GROWTH, INCREASING
INTERNATIONAL INSTABILITY IN THE 1970s,
AND THE WEST GERMAN ECONOMY

Although the economic problems of the United States became more severe than the West German ones in the period of declining growth in the world economy and increasing international instability that began in the 1970s, changes in the internal and external conditions of the West German economy also gave rise to higher instability, a deteriorating trade position, higher rates of unemployment, higher rates of inflation, radicalization of trade unions and greater labor troubles, and an increasing public debt. The West German market system, so successful in the 1950s and 1960s, has shown many difficulties in adjusting to the new conditions that have been created in the postwar period, especially since the end of the 1960s. This has created more problems for the stability of the political system and has led to a change in the economic policy of the state. By referring to the current West German discussion, one can summarize the increasing difficulties of the West German economic and political system in four points.

First, since West Germany has a very open economy (with an export share of manufactured goods of 25 percent, 36 percent of the working population depending on exports, and 20 percent of the world trade in manufactured products), the economy is very sensitive to changes in external conditions. External changes, such as the instability of the international monetary system, capital flows, fluctuations of exchange rates, and change of terms of trade, have affected growth rates of industries, income, employment, productivity, and inflation very drastically. In the 1950s and 1960s, exports had always been a means to overcome internal recessions, but with increased international instability in the 1970s and the slower growth of world trade, exports can no longer function unambiguously as an outlet to prevent recessions. Exports face more severe international competition, especially because of the appreciation of the deutsche mark (up 150 percent from 1972 to 1980). Moreover, as with most of the developing countries, West Germany faces a worsening of the terms of trade.[26] Owing to the rapid process of growth and accumulation in previous years, the prices for raw materials, minerals, oil, and other inputs have gone up.[27] The increase in input prices could be partially matched by the above-mentioned appreciation of the deutsche mark, but in the last two years, the West German economy has been facing a deficit in the balance of current accounts and in the balance of payments, in part owing to a rise in the value of inputs (see Figure 3.7). Moreover, since the middle of the 1970s (see Figure 3.8), the outflow of capital also increased. In the postwar period, foreign firms invested in West Germany more than West German firms invested abroad. This trend has been changed since the recession of 1974-75.

Second, in spite of the upswing in domestic investments in the second half of the 1970s (see Figure 3.7), the rate of return on investment has been falling (see Figure 3.2) and the rate of unemployment remained quite stable at between 3.5 percent and 4.0 percent. As a recently published OECD study has shown, the growth rate of productivity in West Germany (also in the United Kingdom) was higher than the growth rate of output.[28] This was true for the second half of the 1970s. Owing to the very capital-intensive production already employed, less workers are needed to produce a constant or an increasing amount of output. Econometric studies have shown that in the 1950s and 1960s, 50 percent to 60 percent of the growth rate of productivity can be explained by the growth rate of output; in the 1970s, it is almost 100 percent. Thus, the increase in labor force employed became zero or negative. If one considers the relation between the increase in labor force, productivity, and output, one can see how the new trends create a problem for employment policy. It can be said that the growth rate of output is determined by the growth rate of productivity and the growth rate of the employed labor force $(g_y = g_y/L + g_L)$. If the growth rate of productivity is almost the same or higher than the growth rate of production, then the employed labor force will be constant or even decline. In this case, a high growth rate of productivity leads to a problem in employment. This can be seen from Table 3.5, where the data for West Germany and for the United Kingdom show that in the period from 1973 to 1980 the growth rate of productivity (g_y/L measured as GNP employment) was quite high and the growth rate of employment (g_L) was zero or even negative. From Figure 3.7 it can further be seen that a positive growth rate of output was accompanied by a declining rate of employment.

FIGURE 3.7

Data on the West German Economy, 1975-80, Part 1

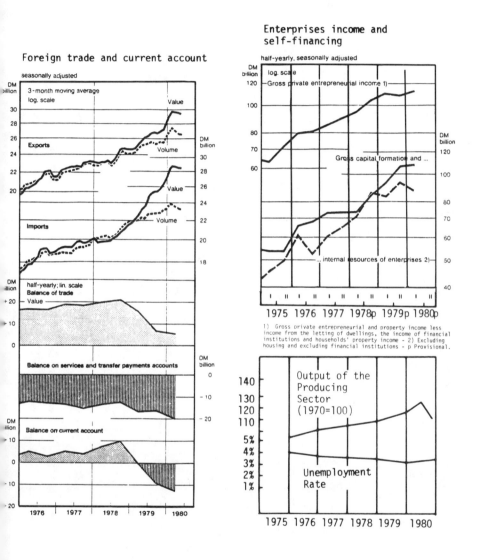

Sources: Deutsche Bundesbank, Monthly Report (Wiesbaden), September 1980, p. 12; and October 1980, p. 13.

43

FIGURE 3.8

Data on the West German Economy, 1975–80, Part 2

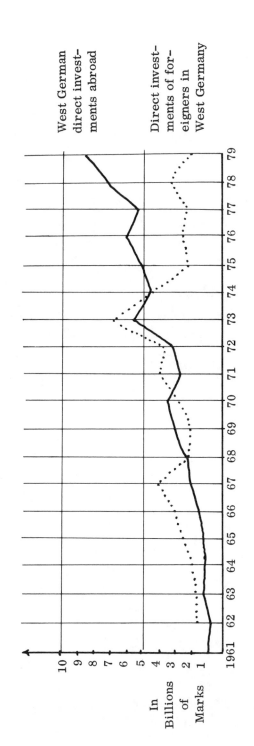

Source: Elmar Altvater, Jürgen Hoffmann, and Willi Semmler, Vom Wirtschaftswunder zur Wirtschafts-krise: Ökonomie und Politik in der Bundesrepublik (Berlin: Olle und Wolter, 1979), p. 168.

TABLE 3.5

Employment and Productivity

(total economy percentage changes, seasonally adjusted
at annual rates)

	Average		From Previous Year		
	1963–73	1973–80[a]	1978	1979	1980
United States					
Employment	2.2	2.1	4.2	2.8	0.25
GNP/Employment	1.9	0	0.1	-0.4	-1.25
Japan					
Employment	1.4	0.8	1.2	1.4	1.00
GNP/Employment	8.7	3.5	4.7	4.5	4.50
West Germany					
Employment	0	-0.7	0.3	1.3	0
GNP/Employment	4.6	3.1	3.3	3.1	2.00
France					
Employment	0.9	0.1	0.4	-0.1	-0.25
GDP/Employment	4.6	2.7	3.0	3.3	2.25
United Kingdom					
Employment[b]	-0.1	-0.1	0.4	0.2	-1.00
GDP/Employment[c]	3.0	0.4	2.3	0.8	-1.50
Italy					
Employment	-0.6	0.8	0.5	1.1	0.75
GDP/Employment	5.4	1.9	2.1	3.8	2.50
Canada					
Employment	3.3	2.7	3.3	4.0	2.50
GNP/Employment	2.4	0	0.1	-1.0	-2.25
Major seven countries					
Employment	1.1	1.1	2.2	1.7	0.50
GNP/Employment	3.8	1.4	1.9	1.7	0.75

[a]Forecast values for 1980.

[b]Great Britain employees only.

[c]Based on GDP growth, excluding the contribution from North
Sea oil.

Source: Organization for Economic Cooperation and Development, National Accounts of OECD Countries, 1952–79 (Paris: OECD, 1980), p. 22.

In the West German economy this has happened particularly since the crisis of 1974-75. From this period, the growth rate of productivity tended to be higher than the growth rate of output. Production went up without any increase in employment. This explains the constant rate of unemployment since the middle of the decade. Thus, one can see that even the successful and efficient West German economy increasingly faces the problem of permanent unemployment. Internal resources and investment of firms went up in the 1970s (see Figure 3.7), but the bulk of these investments was used for rationalizing the production process. The application of microprocessors, industrial robots, and microelectronics in the production process allowed for a replacement of labor, including the replacement of skilled labor, by new machines. Productivity and output went up, but the unemployment rate has remained almost the same since the middle of the 1970s.

Third, the change in the economic situation of West Germany led to new problems and issues for the unions and the West German labor movement and, in part, led to the new radicalization of the trade unions, to a collaboration between the unions and the New Left, and to a rise in labor troubles. In former times the West German unions were well known in Europe for their lack of militance vis-à-vis the corporations and for their collaboration with the state. But this has changed. Actually, one can see four periods in the development of the trade unions in West Germany. Initially, the West German unions showed considerable resistance to the reconstruction of the West German economy as a Western-oriented market system. Immediately after World War II the unions, rebuilt as a strong Einheitsgewerkschaft (unitary trade union movement), fought for industrial democracy, nationalization of basic industries, macroeconomic planning, and a full-employment policy. But they lost most of these struggles, especially the struggles for industrial democracy and nationalization after the war. But owing to rapid economic growth and full employment since the end of the 1950s, the unions became more and more integrated into the West German economic and political system. They supported the new Keynesian-oriented demand management introduced by the "Grand Coalition" of the Christian Democrats and the Social Democrats in 1967.

In a third stage, at the end of the 1960s, the confrontation of labor and capital increased. Owing to full employment, rapid growth, and scarcity of labor, the bargaining positions of the workers and unions increased; many strikes—partly wildcat strikes—for higher wages and better working conditions broke out in the period from 1968 to 1972 (see Figure 3.9). The unions became more militant, too, but this militance was based on a prosperous economy. Beginning with 1974 and 1975, a fourth stage occurred in the development

FIGURE 3.9

Strike Activities of West German Workers

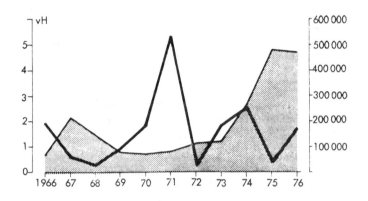

Workers on strike
(in thousands) ■■■■■■■   Rate of
                               unemployment

Source: Elmar Altvater, Jürgen Hoffmann, and Willi Semmler, Vom Wirtschaftswunder zur Wirtschaftskrise: Ökonomie und Politik in der Bundesrepublik (Berlin: Olle und Wolter, 1979), p. 353.

of the unions. With higher rates of unemployment, changed external conditions for the West German economy, and the restructuring of industries and firms, the main issues concerning the workers and the unions changed, and they became less powerful. Although centered more around the questions of unemployment, working conditions, nationalization of factories, unemployment in declining industries, social services, and environmental problems, the militance of the unions continued to be an important factor in the economic system. [29] It can be said that the West German unions are no longer unequivocally a stabilizing factor in the economic and political systems. Much militance and resistance has been built up in former times and continues to exist, at least in some of the more radical unions, like the metal and steelworkers union (IG Metall) and the printers union (IG Druck und Papier).

A fourth problem that the West German economy has been facing, beginning with the declining growth rate and high rate of unemployment in the 1960s, is the state debt. As in all Western countries, the public sector and state expenditures increased during the period of prosperity. But growth rates in the private economy, and hence the revenue of the state, decreased (see Figure 3.6). The problem was further compounded as the social cost of the private economy went up when the full employment economy turned into an economy with lower growth rates and higher rates of unemployment. Attempts have been made since the crisis of 1974-75 to improve the process in adjusting the West German market system to the new external and internal conditions through cutbacks in state expenditures and a new type of economic policy (structural policy and a policy to modernize the economy). Since the middle of the 1970s, the public management of the private economy or Keynesian demand-oriented policy has not been the prevailing economic policy of the West German government; rather, the government has followed a policy of selected measures to restructure industrial production toward industries that are more competitive on the world market.[30] These measures aim to control and stimulate the supply side (control the unit wage cost, selective measures to stimulate capital formation and productivity increases, research and development subsidies). The new policies are oriented more toward the goal of improving the competitiveness of West German manufacturing industries than toward the goals of a stabilization policy. Full employment does not seem to be a goal of the present West German government. The change of economic policy from a demand-side-oriented policy, which began in the middle 1960s, to a more supply-side-oriented policy in the 1970s only reflects increasing national and international instability, where the supply conditions once again became the most important factor in international competition.

CONCLUSIONS

This chapter has developed the hypothesis that the main causes of the so-called West German economic miracle go back to the war and the postwar situation. The preconditions for a rapidly growing, Western-oriented market system were created after World War II and to a certain extent were maintained by policy measures. These preconditions were unique, and during the long process of rapid growth and capital accumulation they have deteriorated. As with other Western market systems, the West German economy has faced increasing internally, as well as externally, created difficulties since the middle of the 1970s. The internal and external conditions for growth and capital accumulation have changed, and economic policies have been developed to attempt to hasten the process of adjustment to the new economic environment. To what extent the policies will be successful depends not only on a possible further consensus of capital, labor, and the state, but also on the further development of the international economy. Yet, most theorists in West Germany agree that a process of successful economic growth, like the one the West German economy experienced in the 1950s and 1960s, cannot be repeated in the 1980s, and that Model Germany, with its strong manufacturing sector and export-oriented industries, its specific structure of the labor movement, and its stable capital-labor relationship (at least in its successful times) cannot be transferred to other countries.

NOTES

1. Helga Majer, Die technologische Lücke zwischen der Bundesrepublik Deutschland und den Vereinigten Staaten von Amerika: Eine empirische Analyse (Tübingen: Mohr, 1973).
2. N. M. Kamrany and D. M. Chereb, "Productivity Performance in the United States," in Economic Issues of the Eighties, ed. N. M. Kamrany and R. M. Day (Baltimore: Johns Hopkins Press, 1979).
3. Edward F. Denison, Accounting for Slower Economic Growth: The United States in the 1970s (Washington, D.C.: Brookings Institution, 1979).
4. U.S., Department of Commerce, Bureau of the Census, Statistical Abstracts (Washington, D.C.: Statistical Abstracts of the United States, 1978).
5. Henry C. Wallich, Mainsprings of German Revival (New Haven, Conn.: Yale University Press, 1960); Charles P. Kindelberger, Europe's Post-War Growth: The Role of the Labor Supply (Cambridge, Mass.: Harvard University Press, 1967); Frederick G. Reuss, Fiscal Policy for Growth without Inflation: The German Experiment (Baltimore: Johns Hopkins Press, 1963); Edward F. Denison, Why Growth Rates Differ: Post-War Experience in Nine Countries (Washington, D.C.: Brookings Institution, 1967); Andrew Schonfield, Modern Capitalism: The Changing Balance of Public and Private Power (London: Oxford University Press, 1969); K. W. Roskamp, Capital Formation in West Germany (Detroit: Wayne State University Press, 1965); Angus Maddison, Economic Growth in the West: Comparative Experience in Europe and North America (New York: Twentieth Century Fund, 1964); Walther G. Hoffman, Das Wachstum der deutschen Wirtschaft seit der Mitte des 19 Jahrhunderts (Berlin and New York: Springer Verlag, 1965); Rüdiger Hopp, Schwankungen des wirtschaftlichen Wachstums in Westdeutschland 1954-67 (Meisenheim/Glain: A. Hain, 1969); Ferenc Janossy, Das Ende der Wirtschaftswunder: Erscheinungen und Wesen der wirtschaftlichen Entwicklung (Frankfurt am Main: Verlag Neue Kritik,

1969); Jörg Huffschmid, Die Politik des Kapitals: Konzentration und Wirtschaftspolitik in der Bundesrepublik (Frankfurt am Main: Suhrkamp, 1970); Ernest Mandel, Late Capitalism (London: New Left Books, 1975); Elmar Altvater, Jürgen Hoffman, and Willi Semmler, Vom Wirtschaftswunder zur Wirtschaftskrise: Ökonomie und Politik in der Bundesrepublik (Berlin: Olle und Wolter, 1979); Marianne Welteke, Theorie und Praxis der sozialen Marktwirtschaft (Frankfurt am Main: Campus Verlag, 1976); Winfried Vogt, Makroökonomische Bestimmungsgründe des wirtschaftlichen Wachstums der Bundesrepublik Deutschland von 1950 bis 1960 (Tübingen: Mohr, 1964).

6. Wallich, Mainsprings.

7. Samuel Bowles and Herbert Gintis, "The Crisis of Liberal Democratic Capitalism" (Unpublished manuscript, 1980).

8. Werner Abelshauser, Wirtschaft in Westdeutschland 1945–48: Rekonstruktion und Wachstumsbedingungen in der amerikanischen und britischen Zone (Stuttgart: Deutsche Verlags Anstalt, 1975).

9. Kindelberger, Europe's Post-War Growth; K. W. Schatz, Wachstum und Strukturwandel der Westdeutschen Wirtschaft im Internationalen Verbund (Tübingen: Mohr, 1974).

10. Abelshauser, Wirtschaft in Westdeutschland 1945–48.

11. Altvater, Hoffman, and Semmler, Vom Wirtschaftswunder zur Wirtschaftskrise; Roskamp, Capital Formation in West Germany.

12. Hans H. Hartwich, Sozialstaatspostulat und gesellschaftlicher Status-quo (Köln: Westdeutscher Verlag, 1970).

13. Denison, Accounting for Slower Growth; Kamrany and Chereb, Productivity Performance of the United States; Martin Feldstein, "Tax Incentives, Corporate Saving and Capital Accumulation in the United States," Journal of Public Economics 2 (1973): 159–72; John R. Norsworthy, Michael J. Harper, and Kent Kunz, "The Slowdown in Productivity Growth: Analysis of Some Contributing Factors," Brookings Papers on Economic Activity 2 (1979): 388–421.

14. David Gordon, "Stages of Accumulation and Long Economic Cycles," in Processes of the World System, ed. Terence K. Hopkins and Immanuel Wallerstein (Beverly Hills: Sage, 1980), pp. 9–45; Raford Boddy and James Cotty, "Class Conflict and Macropolicy: The Political Business Cycle," Review of Radical Political Economics 7 (1977): 1–20; Paul M. Sweezy, "Productivity Slowdown: A False Alarm?" Monthly Review 31 (1979): 1–13; Bowles and Gintis, "The Crisis of Liberal Democratic Capitalism"; Thomas Weisskopf, "Marxian Crisis Theory and the Rate of Profit in the Post-War U.S. Economy," Cambridge Journal of Economics 3 (1979): 341–77.

15. A. Shaikh, "Profit Rate in the U.S." (Unpublished manuscript, New York, 1979).

16. Gordon, "Stages of Accumulation and Long Economic Cycles"; Ernest Mandel, Long Waves in Capitalist Development: The Marxist Interpretation (New York: Cambridge University Press, 1978).

17. Altvater, Hoffman, and Semmler, Vom Wirtschaftswunder zur Wirtschaftskrise.

18. Ibid.

19. A. Shaikh, "National Income Accounts and Marxian Categories" (Unpublished manuscript, New York, 1978); Altvater, Hoffman, and Semmler, Vom Wirtschaftswunder zur Wirtschaftskrise.

20. Rick Seltzer, "The Development of Crisis in the United States," in U.S. Capitalism in Crisis (New York: Union of Radical Political Economists, 1978), pp. 35–45.

21. R. Jonas, "Auswirkung des weltwirtschaftlichen Strukturwandels auf die Arbeitsmarktenwicklung der Bundesrepublik Deutschland," in Wirtschaftsstruktur und Beschäftingung, ed. H. Heidermann (Bonn/Bad Godesberg: Verlag Neue Gesellschaft, 1976), pp. 9–28.

22. U.S., Department of Commerce, Bureau of the Census, Statistical Abstracts.

23. Thomas Ferguson and Joel Rogers, "The Reagan Victory: Corporate Coalition in the 1980 Campaign," in The Hidden Election: Politics and Economics in the 1980 Presidential Campaign, ed. Thomas Ferguson and Joel Rogers (New York: Pantheon Books, 1981), pp. 3–65.

24. Arthur M. Okun and George L. Perry, eds., Curing Chronic Inflation (Washington, D.C.: Brookings Institution, 1978).

25. Willi Semmler, "Zu neueren Tendenzen in der Theorie und Praxis der amerikanischen Wirtschaftspolitik," Prokla 42 (1981): 57–76.

26. Sachverständigenrat zur Begutachtung der gesamtwirtschaftlichen Entwicklung (SVR), 1980/81.

27. Ibid.

28. Organization for Economic Cooperation and Development, Economic Outlook, 1980 (Paris: OECD, 1980).

29. Jürgen Hoffman, "Einheitsgewerkschaft oder Korporatistische Blockbildung," Prokla 43 (1981): 6–26.

30. Sachverständigenrat zur Begutachtung der gesamtwirtschaftlichen Entwicklung (SVR), 1980/81.

REFERENCES

Altvater, Elmar, Jürgen Hoffmann, and Willi Semmler. Vom Wirtschaftswunder zur Wirtschaftskrise: Ökonomie und Politik in der Bundesrepublik. Berlin: Olle und Wolter, 1979.

Denison, Edward F. Accounting for Slower Economic Growth: The United States in the 1970s. Washington, D.C.: Brookings Institution, 1979.

Deutsche Bundesbank. Monthly Report (Wiesbaden), September 1980, p. 12; and October 1980, p. 13.

Economic Report of the President. Washington, D. C. : U. S. Government Printing Office, 1980.

Hill, T. P. Profits and Rates of Return. Paris: Organization for Economic Cooperation and Development, 1979.

Knight, E. Economic Policy and Inflation in the United States: A Survey of Development from the Enactment of the Employment Act from 1946 through 1974. A study prepared for the use of the Joint Economic Committee of the Congress of the United States, Paper no. 2, April 7, 1975.

Organization for Economic Cooperation and Development. Industrial Production, 1950-71, 1971-73, and 1973-75. Paris: OECD, 1972, 1974, and 1976.

_____. National Accounts of OECD Countries, 1952-79. Paris: OECD, 1980.

Sachs, Jeffrey D. "Wages, Profits and Macroeconomic Adjustment: A Comparative Study." Brookings Papers on Economic Activity, no. 2.

Statistische Jahrbücher der Bundesrepublik Deutschland. Annual. Wiesbaden: Statistisches Bundesamt, 1951-76.

U. S. , Department of Commerce, Bureau of the Census. Statistical Abstracts. Washington, D. C. : Statistical Abstracts of the United States, 1979.

4

ALTERATIONS IN THE DESIGN OF MODEL GERMANY: CRITICAL INNOVATIONS IN THE POLICY MACHINERY FOR ECONOMIC STEERING

JEREMIAH M. RIEMER

STABILITY AND WELFARE

From Marx through Keynes and down to thinkers of the present day, a central problem for critics and exponents of capitalism at all of its stages has been the relationship between stability and welfare. Marx put the problem of unstable growth at the center of his investigations into the nature and dynamics of capitalism. As he observed in the afterword to the second edition of Capital, any nineteenth century businessman could see how accumulation (as growth was called in those days) had a tendency to be interrupted by periodic crises. "The contradictions inherent in the movement of capitalist society impress themselves upon the practical bourgeois most strikingly in the changes of the periodic cycle, through which modern industry runs, and whose crowning point is the universal crisis."[1]

The neoclassical economists who came after Marx imagined having disposed of the conflict between welfare and stability by defining it away. The neoclassical concept of equilibrium was something that described the exemplary ability of market mechanisms to create wealth and distribute resources with a minimum of friction. Although, like Marx, the neoclassical tradition assigned a systematic function to the periodic crises that interrupted the process of growth, the function was corrective rather than destructive. If crises had to happen at all, and if they were not induced by noneconomic forces (intrusions of nature or politics upon the marketplace), then they

For their help with various versions of this paper, I would like to thank Peter Katzenstein, Isaac Kramnick, Andrei Markovits, Wendy Mink, and Bill Tetreault.

served the positive purpose of signaling departures from equilibrium. Equilibrium meant not only a pathway of steady accumulation but an optimal allocation of resources. Efficient resource allocation had become the new ideological yardstick of capitalism. In the less philosophical, more operational approach of marginalist economics, the utilitarian management of scarcity became the distinctive feature of market economies. Utility displaced classical political economy's preoccupation with the question of value and value's origin in the productive antagonism of social classes. By definition, markets at equilibrium balanced the general welfare (a sum of countless individual utilities) against the productive utilization of scarce resources.

With Keynes and the Great Depression, the possibility of a fundamental conflict between welfare and stability reappeared as a problem for what had become the special discipline of macroeconomics. Stability was now seen as compatible with a perversely optimal employment of all resources save one—labor. It was possible, Keynes demonstrated theoretically, to have equilibrium at underemployment. The neoclassical ideal of equilibrium at full employment was but a special (and probably unlikely) possibility within a larger, general theory that accounted for the probability of mass unemployment. The practical application of John Maynard Keynes' General Theory to macroeconomic planning after World War II resulted in a long, impressive hiatus in the history of conflict between welfare and stability. Lingering memories of depression (or inflation) were still too strong for complete trust in the neoclassical model of a pervasive market equilibrium to be restored. Yet, in the postwar period faith in political and social engineering supplemented faith in the market; supplemented—not replaced—because the neoclassical tradition lived on in microeconomics. In that subdiscipline, the outstanding virtue of the market (resource allocation) was the baby that most Keynesian economists refused to throw out with the bath water (market failure in the aggregate). Leaving microeconomics to the market, government assumed responsibility for engineering the resolution of conflicts among macroeconomic goals.

Such was the confidence of modern capitalism's planners in the 1950s and 1960s that economists in the Organization for Economic Cooperation and Development (OECD) countries codified the relationship between stability and welfare in terms of manageable trade-offs and watertight fixed-target models. The famous Phillips curve expressed the simplest such relationship of policy choices between stability (as measured by price levels) and the welfare goal emphasized most by Keynes (that is, employment). Following the example of the Dutch economist Jan Tinbergen, other theoreticians of economic policy broadened the Phillips curve to include more welfare goals. With the addition of balanced trade (an essential target for the open economy typical of postwar Europe) and growth, the Phillips curve became a magical rectangle, as the politically most popular of the fixed-target models was known. Even as the Phillips curve was extended to become a magical polygon,[2] the new welfare economics of Tinbergen and others reflected Keynes's original insight about the fundamental conflict between the general welfare, no longer guaranteed by equilibrium, and the preoccupation with stability that Keynes had once called the "Treasury view."[3] As one theoretical economist noted, the fixed-target model "generalized . . . the Keynesian full employment model."[4]

The Keynesian revolution lasted at least as long as the engineers of macroeconomic welfare were able to maintain their juggling act of balancing the welfare aims that made up the magical polygon. As early as the 1950s, there were signs that the outer edges of the polygon (to shift the metaphor just slightly) were becoming frayed. A balance-of-payments deficit might lead to at least one kind of monetary instability (a decline in the value of a currency) and induce a political response (credit restriction) that harmed another goal, like growth. This was the classic pattern of "stop and go" (together with the reverse process: growth, credit expansion, and an imports binge) that hampered the U.K. economy under Tory leadership throughout the 1950s. But troubles like "stop and go," while they inhibited growth, were entirely compatible with the stability of prices and did not seem to destroy employment prospects for roughly the first two decades of the postwar period. Only later—and especially in the 1970s—did the magical polygon start to unravel along its most important angle, the two axes defining the Phillips curve.

Economists had long anticipated that Keynesian economics would be unprepared to cope with higher levels of inflation. The Keynesian prescription for macroeconomic planning, written in the Great Depression but applied to postwar affluence, seemed to ask, After recovery and growth, then what? Filling in the blank part of the prescription—countercyclical steering at the peak of the business cycle—depended on what turned out to be a questionable assumption. It was optimistically assumed that one could break a rise in prices without curtailing production drastically. Conversely, it was assumed that classic Keynesian deficit spending could create a "quantity cycle" in which the quantity effect of economic stimulation (that is, more goods) would precede the price effect (that is, more inflation). The price effect could then, in theory, be contained. A smoothly engineered quantity cycle leading to an upswing was, of course, the prerequisite for a successful price cycle (deflation without recession) toward the downswing side.[5] The noninflationary stimulation of demand, if it could be achieved, would mean that one did not have to make the effort later on of bringing an overheated

economy down from a high price plateau. It would suffice to stem
price rises when the first inflationary warning signs appeared, and
to do this with the clear conscience that comes from dealing with an
economy at close to full employment every step along the way.

The unexpected phenomenon of stagflation made already difficult policy engineering of this sort next to impossible. At the same
time that stagflation frustrated the most skillful maneuvers of the
most adept technocrats, it called simple Keynesian economics into
question. For at its most fundamental level—a level of analysis
deeper than technical discussions of price effects and quantity cycles
—Keynesian economics assumed that positive acts of government
could hold the unstable tendencies of capitalist accumulation within
acceptable limits. What, however, if it turned out that the trend of
capitalist growth over time was toward accelerating instability, a
tendency away from equilibrium so fundamentally powerful that
neither self-correction (on the neoclassical model) nor political cor-
rection (on the simple Keynesian model) could lastingly contain it?
The possibility of such a basic disequilibrium—suggested most dramatically by stagflation but supported by other evidence on business
cycles gathered from some three postwar decades[6]—indicated that
yet another revision of views on the relationship between stability
and welfare was overdue.

Such a revised view would have to be closer to Karl Marx and
the more radical implications of John Maynard Keynes than to the
neoclassical view or to the softened textbook synthesis of Keynes
with the neoclassical tradition. Even without the classical trappings
of orthodox Marxism, without the labor theory of value as the only
guide to exploitation, and without the predictions of collapse associated with the law of the tendentially falling rate of profit, a post-
Keynesian "logic of disequilibrium" might still depend on Marx's
central "character reading" (thus Leontief[7]) into the internally contradictory system he examined a century ago. The path by which
capital (or abstract wealth) is accumulated and whereby mass welfare (or compensation to the dependently employed for their labor
and renunciation of rights to control what they produce) is created
may yet be an unstable path.[8] Progress in capitalism and the science
that studies it has not abolished the conflict between welfare and stability that has been with us since this basic tension was uncovered.

Owing to the lateness and intensity of the Keynesian revolution
in West Germany, the conflict between welfare and stability has been
posed there with a special clarity. However, the history of economic
thought and policy in Germany was never quite in step with the Anglo-
American transition from Manchester liberalism to the Keynesian-
inspired welfare state. Germany's development in the nineteenth
century did not follow the English "story," as Marx had told the

German readers of Capital to expect.[9] Instead of copying the most advanced economy of the time, the steel industrialists, East Elbian nobles, and Prussian civil servants who dominated Bismarckian Germany perceived Manchesterism either as an inappropriate model for a late industrializer or as anathema to an agrarian state. Weimar's stalemate between the forces of the old order and social democracy never produced a dominant economic ideology, while Hitler's construction programs and war economy confirmed the insights of Keynes without legitimating the Keynesian philosophy.

Only after the collapse of the Third Reich did the western half of the divided nation heal the wounds of defeat and promptly recover ideological self-righteousness vis-à-vis its eastern "other" by orienting its economic doctrine around the values of the major capitalist power, namely, the United States. It was this ersatz national identity, shaped by the cold war and prosperity during 27 years of unbroken conservative rule, that allowed one part of Germany to assimilate the entire liberal capitalist tradition, which Germany's development had never allowed the whole nation to digest. The philosophy of neoliberalism took over as the uncontested economic ideology. Significantly, the authors of the neoliberal doctrine (the "Freiburg School" of economists) interpreted the traumatic Great Depression as the outcome of experimental tinkering with the market order, not as the result of market failure à la Keynes.[10]

When Christian Democratic dominance came to an end in 1966, the rapid assimilation and adaptation of liberal and then Keynesian ideas and policies continued at an unprecedented pace. West Germany's belated Keynesian revolution (1967) was quickly followed by conservative retrenchment (1973) and a recession (1975) that made stagflation and intractable instability nagging problems for this most prosperous and stable of the world's economies. The conflict between stability and welfare, expressed as a conflict between austerity and growth, was brought into focus by two recessions that pitted the political guardians of stability against the social classes (sometimes capital, but always labor) and their public representatives who depend on growth for economic and political rewards. However trivial by international standards, West Germany's two recessions were perceived as acute systemic crises because they were defined not just as minor interruptions of growth but as stabilization crises. That is, the recessions were seen to have resulted in no small part from the efforts of the Bundesbank to restore monetary stability; though economically caused, they were politically induced.[11]

The political dimension of each stabilization crisis has made each crisis seem preventable. Each stabilization crisis has drawn attention to the fact that the most influential—and therefore most culpable—agent of policy in the FRG is the country's central bank. The

West German preoccupation with monetary stability is usually explained by reference to Germany's experiences with hyperinflation
in this century, but the obsession has an institutional component as
well. The Federal Republic of Germany has had low inflation rates
not only because of attitudes toward the priority of price stability:
such institutional features of the economy as a tight monetary constitution, the power of a few private banks, and the restriction of access to credit have helped make it that way.

Each stabilization crisis has driven home another point besides
the institutionalization of monetary stability: while stable prices may
be compatible with growth much of the time, the pursuit of monetary
stability may also lead to welfare losses at critical moments. Even
before the recession of 1966–67, sympathetic critics of the Bundesbank warned that an economic policy based chiefly on the institutional
resources of the central bank was bound to be one-sided. Unaided by
instruments for fiscal policy (or demand management), foreign economic policy, and incomes policy, the Bundesbank alone could not
pursue all four goals of the "magical rectangle" with success. Somehow, the welfare goals of the magical polygon had to be instrumen-
talized in the same way that the single goal of price stability already
had its institutional guardian. In the age of politically engineered
growth, the conflict between stability and welfare goals had to be
managed with a larger model of what the West Germans call their
"economic policy machinery" (wirtschaftspolitisches Instrumentarium).
Effective policy could only be made with a full "box of tools" (Instru-
mentenkasten).

MODEL GERMANY IN CRISIS?

Throughout the course of its economic and political development, Germany has rarely followed the example of the most advanced
capitalist economy and most liberal state. But during the decade-
long "restoration" of West German capitalism (which quickly followed
the postwar period's brief intimation of a vaguely socialist consensus),
the United States did enjoy a certain model character for the Federal
Republic of Germany's (FRG) neoliberal order. Fueled by the cold
war at its divided frontline and facilitated by the discrediting of German nationalism, the identification with the United States was subtle
and ideological. What happened was an American penetration of
West German consciousness rather than of West German institutions.
As one of the characters in Wim Wenders's movie King of the Road
remarked, "The Yanks have colonized our subconscious." In economic terms, the influence of the "American Friend" (as in the title
of another Wenders film) showed up in the popularity of ideological

values that would have made any Chamber of Commerce Republican proud to be German. The market was held in high esteen in spite of growing economic concentration. Before World War II, the philosophy of the German Left had emphasized the primacy of production, while the German Right had favored a "cartel of the productive orders." But now, like their U.S. cousins, West Germany's neoliberal conservatives preached consumer sovereignty. Membership in the Rotary Club and other U.S. connections became marks of prestige. As late as 1966, Ludwig Erhard tried (unsuccessfully, as it happened), to flatter Lyndon Johnson with the thought that the Great Society served as the model for Erhard's own "integrated society."

By the mid-1970s, the tables had turned in the game of economic and political emulation among the advanced capitalist countries. Whereas the United States was suffering from both high inflation and considerable unemployment, the West German economic profile stood out in international comparisons for its enviable prosperity and stability. Little America had become Model Germany. Although most West Germans were by no means satisfied with the state of their economy in the mid-1970s, Chancellor Helmut Schmidt was able to turn the sad shape of the world economy to his party's favor in the 1976 election. Measuring West Germany's economy by the standard of its own past performance or by future hopes, some backers of the Social Democratic-led government (the unions and the Young Socialists) found a little or a lot to criticize in Schmidt's style of conservative crisis management. But the Social Democratic party (SPD) won a third chance to head the government running on the campaign slogan "Let's continue working on Model Germany." Schmidt's emphasis on Germany's enhanced international stature drowned out the complaints of domestic groups, complaints Schmidt was known to disdain as small-minded and provincial.

The governing Social Democrats' emphasis on the model character of the FRG's institutions has served to galvanize electoral support, disorient the Christian Democratic opposition, deflect internal criticism from the SPD's more radical younger members, and bring the party's core labor constituency back into line. Yet, Model Germany has had more than a partisan character. The SPD has put its stamp on West Germany's model institutions during two stabilization crises (1966-67 and 1973-75), an intervening period of prosperity, and throughout the last half of the 1970s when "structural" problems in the economy came to the fore. Yet the party's sponsorship of policy innovations—sometimes progressive, though more recently conservative—has not radically altered the fundamental design of the West German political economy. The Social Democrats and their liberal coalition partners built Model Germany on the foundations of the "CDU state" (as the political and economic order dominated by the Christian Democrats was called). The Social Democratic era has ushered in several changes in monetary and exchange rate policies, a strengthening of the executive's fiscal powers, and an attempt to include the peak associations of business and labor in the "preformation" of cyclical policy. But the new, concerted economy has only coordinated public and private actions in an informal way. The SPD in power has avoided any sort of formal corporatism or policies that would confer official status on actions carried out by the participants in the concerted action of capital and labor. Successive Social Democratic governments have avoided making their decisions binding on the private sector. Even thinking out loud about an incomes policy that might set ceilings on wages and prices has been taboo. The central thrust of Social Democratic-sponsored innovations has been to provide both public and private institutions with a short-term, flexible orientation toward stability and growth. The aim has been to strengthen parametric planning (the setting of boundary conditions for the economy). So far, the SPD has not tried to replace parametric planning—often criticized as short-term and reactive[12]—with the sort of long-term, active approach that Scandinavian planning has used to link welfare with growth.

If the aim of Social Democratic reforms (during periods of progressive innovation) and consolidations (in periods of conservative retrenchment) has been to strengthen model institutions, it remains to be seen how these institutions have functioned in a way that has demanded only marginal improvement so far. What is the institutional core of Model Germany that has weathered two stabilization crises and more with only minor modifications of design?

The best place to begin looking at the fundamental institutional strength underlying West German economic policy is the Deutsche Bundesbank, the country's central bank headquartered in Frankfurt. Operating under its current name since 1957, the Bundesbank grew out of the Bank deutscher Länder, a creation of the Western allies in 1948. Though its associated network of regional banks (Landeszentralbanken) was partly modeled on the more decentralized U.S. Federal Reserve system, the reserve bank in Frankfurt has always had a separate apparatus to handle central bank transactions. [13]

Generally regarded as the most independent central bank among the major Western powers, the Bundesbank has always jealously guarded its autonomy. The most recent demonstration of the Frankfurt institution's ability to capture the organizational loyalty of outside appointees and stiffen their resistance to political pressure involved the Bundesbank's current president, Karl Otto Pöhl. When Pöhl, a Social Democrat who had been an adviser to Chancellor Schmidt prior to being appointed a Bundesbank director, was selected to be president of the Bundesbank in 1979, the nomination raised eyebrows in some Christian Democratic and conservative circles. But if critics of the nomination had any reservations about this political appointment, they were undoubtedly laid to rest by 1981. Then Pöhl began urging the new Schmidt government to stop blaming high interest rates for West Germany's economic troubles and to start putting the federal budget in order.[14] Pöhl warned the government not to expect that lower U.S. rates would automatically result in lower West German rates.

Pöhl's scolding of the Social-Liberal government, though only one example of the perpetual tension between Bonn and Frankfurt, nonetheless draws attention to a significant aspect of critical change in the routine of West German economic policy. The central banker's defense of tight money and criticism of looseness in fiscal policy came at a time when policy makers expected West Germany to go through its third postwar recession. Each of the previous two recessions were stabilization crises in which the Bundesbank, as in 1981, was implicated. Late in 1966 Frankfurt's tightening of the credit reins helped bring on a recession very quickly. In the spring of 1973, when the monetary authorities tried to stop inflation rates that were shooting above the traditional West German danger zone of 3 percent, tight money did not initially stop inflation from rising to nearly 7 percent but did eventually help to induce a recession in the international crisis year of 1975. From the standpoint of West Germany's model institutions, the significant fact about these two modest (by international standards) recessions is that the Bundesbank interpreted both stabilization crises as tests of the central bank's strength. The political establishment, in turn, tailored whatever changes it engineered in the policy-making apparatus to the Bundesbank's essential mission of enforcing monetary stability.

Bonn's cooperation with the central bank was most apparent in the stabilization crisis after 1973, because the early 1970s presented the central bank with more serious problems than it had confronted before. Not only had inflation reached record levels for West Germany, the Bundesbank also had some difficulty adjusting its traditional techniques of credit control to new sources of domestic and imported inflation. Outwardly, there was the breakdown of the Bretton Woods exchange rate system and the accompanying rush of foreign funds toward the strong deutsche mark; inwardly, there occurred a liberalization of controls over bank capital, which had been eroding the central bank's capacity to contain and measure the private banks' liquidity since the late 1960s. The Social-Liberal government responded to these internal problems of the credit apparatus by cooperating with a drastic new monetary policy at the cost of full employment.

The federal government's concern for the institutional health of the Bundesbank was equally in evidence during the "fiscal revolution" that was Bonn's eventual response to the stabilization crisis of 1966-67. The first stabilization crisis differed from the second in that the central bankers had already demonstrated who was strongest in the policy-making apparatus by inducing a recession in 1966 and forcing the tottering Erhard government into a fiscal crisis. The Bundesbank, still more than a safe year away from the first revaluation crisis to have international repercussions and still exercising direct control over some domestic interest rates, was not asking the new Grand Coalition for help in 1967. But it did make certain that the government's recovery programs were financed on terms indirectly set by the central bank. The Bundesbank saw to it that the new "Stability and Growth Law" included sound provisions for multiannual financial planning. The government, for its part, accommodated the Bundesbank by implementing a very conservative kind of Keynesian revolution. The pump primers in Bonn never got a substantial direct credit line to the monetary authorities in Frankfurt. Instead, the provisions of the Stability Law forced the government to rely on a countercyclical fund, for deficit spending, to be built up in prosperous times and on whatever private funds were available. The latter source of liquidity was, of course, subject to central bank regulation, especially in 1967.[15] Another conservative aspect of the mid-1960s' fiscal innovations, intended to suit the Bundesbank's philosophy of how the government should keep its house in order, was the cautious reworking of a constitutional provision limiting government borrowing. The old provision of the 1949 Basic Law (Article 115) had specified that the government could only borrow "for productive purposes." The amended article clarified and updated this vague provision by allowing the Bundestag to authorize borrowing only so long as the government's credits did not exceed the federal budget's expenditures for investments. Exceptions to this built-in bias against government consumption were permitted only as a "defense against macroeconomic disequilibrium."[16]

These tributes to conservative sound finance tell us only that the Bonn government has helped the Bundesbank when the latter has encountered problems and appeased the Bundesbank when the central bank has been strong. It should be apparent that even liberal fiscal reforms in West Germany contained a conservative monetary core. But this basic conservatism is only an indicator, not an explanation, of the Bundesbank's strength. The Bundesbank's extraordinary position at the commanding heights of the economy derives from its links to the private sector—first to the major private banks and from the banks to an industrial structure with a distinctive orientation and recipe for successful growth. The central bank's links to the powerful organization and exceptional dynamism of the West German economy have not always been tight, however. (Witness the early 1970s, when the private banks' substantial free liquid reserves and access to the Eurodollar market—both indications that they had slipped out from under central bank guardianship—created headaches for the Bundesbank.) What is more, the links can be weak in several crucial respects, notably the ability of the trade unions to cut in on dynamic growth and the inability of weaker firms to withstand the pressure that the Bundesbank will sometimes apply to strong and weak firms alike. These contradictory aspects of the Bundesbank's connections to the rest of the economy form the background to the reform of West Germany's model institutions that began in the late 1960s.

The Bundesbank's most immediate link to the private half of organized capitalism in West Germany is, of course, to the major banks. West Germany has a variety of institutions for gathering capital. Small accounts that are not deposited with the postal system frequently end up in the municipal Sparkassen, semipublic savings banks that give out loans to local and regional governments. Organized into Girozentralen or clearinghouses, the savings banks have a peak association that has sometimes lobbied effectively for monetary policies favorable to savers but unfavorable to the immediate interests of West German industry. Savers allied themselves with the Bundesbank and the SPD in the revaluation controversy of 1969 against industry and the CDU. The savings banks have lately been branching out as part of a general trend toward universal banking. Some of the Girozentralen have recently become major financial powers with international connections—most notably the Hessische Landesbank Girozentrale and the Westdeutsche Landesbank. [17]

While the network of savings banks gives the Bundesbank a natural ally for monetary stability, it is the private commercial institutions that one associates with the "power of the banks."[18] The big three banks (Deutsche, Dresdner, and Commerz) are tied in to the Bundesbank as customers of the "lender of last resort" in Frankfurt. The usual array of monetary techniques—setting of reserve requirements, discount rates, and rediscount and collateral loan (or "Lombard") contingents—are available to keep the private banks' lending activity on a tether. In theory, Bundesbank-induced variations of bank liquidity or the money supply should also affect business volume because of several sources of bank power and industrial dependence on the banks. These sources of bank power have been described by Douglas Anderson of the Harvard Business School as "the low rate of internal financing among German companies (between 30 and 45 percent) and . . . the primitive nature of the nation's stock market."[19] A third factor noted by Anderson—

"the banks' privileged positions as the depositories of the public's
equity holdings"—is the flip side of the underdeveloped stock market.
Owing to their control of large blocs of shareholder proxy votes, the
big three banks occupy strategic positions in the major West German
corporations. Anderson put the big three's voting power on the 500
biggest companies in 1960 at 45 percent.[20]

One prominent feature of the largest West German corporations,
in turn, has been their devotion to cultivating exports. The capture
of foreign markets, initially helped by cheap labor costs that lowered
West German export prices and by a long undervalued currency, was
later secured by such factors as the quality, prompt delivery, and
servicing of West German goods. Also helpful in recent years was
a remnant of earlier price advantages that derived from relatively
low inflation rates and helped compensate for the spectacular rise
of the deutsche mark in the 1970s.[21] In the classic land of export-
led growth, the sacrosanct position of foreign trade is propped
up ideologically by such clichés as the export industry's reminder
that one of every four West German jobs depends on exports. Both
public and private institutions have had a hand in promoting exports.

After the recession of 1975, the preeminent position of exports
was publicly certified when the Schmidt government refused to replace lost export demand with public orders. True to the semi-Key-
nesian conservatism of the Social-Liberal government, Bonn prac-
ticed a strict kind of "compensatory finance": the federal government would compensate for temporary export losses but would not
stimulate the economy as much as a full-blooded Keynesian would
have done for fear of ousting or distorting the export market more
permanently.[22] But the special sensitivity to exports goes back far
beyond 1975.

Wilhelm Hankel, an economist with wide personal experience
in West German public finance, has described the system of export
promotion as "neomercantilistic." It was originally provided by a
"multi-tiered system of long-term export finance" whereby the central bank provided private banks with cheap credit lines for export
accounts, the banks established their own consortium in the Export
Credit Company (Ausfuhrkreditgesellschaft [AKA]), the federal government cooperated via the Reconstruction Loan Corporation (ex-
ecutor of Marshall Plan funds), and the HERMES Credit Insurance
Company ("a private insurance company operating on contract to the
federal government") provided loan guarantees for risky foreign
ventures.[23]

Although this system of concerted export promotion dates from
the 1950s (when it was easier for the rebuilding country to rationalize such mercantilistic policies, to avoid the alternative international responsibility of spending more on development aid, and gen-

erally to escape foreign criticism), traces of the system are still in
evidence. Most recently, a consortium of West German banks relying on AKA helped to save a major natural gas and pipeline deal
with the USSR that was running up against the obstacle of high international interest rates. The deal was saved when the consortium
guaranteed delivery credits on favorable terms so that the USSR
could buy pipes from Mannesmann and compressors from AEG and
Salzgitter.[24]

From the Bundesbank's point of view, the orientation of private banks and industrial clients toward exports is advantageous because it gives both sectors a stake in monetary stability. Low inflation rates keep West German goods competitive. But since an
export-oriented economy with a chronic balance-of-payments surplus
(which, until quite recently, the FRG enjoyed year in and year out)
"gives away" resources that might be put to use at home, one might
well ask whether West German workers would have the same stake in
export-led growth. Would not West German workers be better off if
West German industry devoted even more of its production to the
home market? Here, perhaps, another model institution has helped
reconcile the domestic labor force to the international concerns of
West German business. Codetermination, the practice whereby labor appointees sit on the supervisory board (Aufsichtsrat) of West
German companies, has helped to quell potential militance in West
Germany's industrial unions and to make organized labor accept
business leadership. Another factor undoubtedly working in the
same direction is the trade union federation's control of a major
bank, the Bank für Gemeinwirtschaft.

Until the 1970s, it is safe to say, the Deutscher Gewerkschaftsbund (DGB), West Germany's trade union federation, did not have any
strong position on foreign economic policy. Even where, as in the
revaluation debates, workers' interests might have been at stake,
the unions left it up to the SPD to determine when it was safe enough
to take a stand against business. In the 1970s, structural problems
in some sectors (steel, chemicals, textiles), the energy crisis, and
the changing international division of labor heightened the DGB's
consciousness on foreign economic issues. The expansion of the
federations' research staff, the Wirtschafts- und Sozialwissenschaftliches Institut (WSI) has also given the DGB a greater capacity for
articulating policy positions distinct from those of business. But
the unions' new awareness remains just that—a more certain knowledge that the interests of capital and labor do not always coincide
and a greater forthrightness about saying so. The verbal militancy
continues to fool only conservative commentators who have yet to
learn that rhetoric is the very substance of class consciousness for
organized labor in West Germany and that such talk rarely reflects

deeper antagonisms with a potential for threatening business-labor collaboration.

These, then, have been the institutional components of Model Germany: a highly independent central bank that has already put the economy through two recessionary wringers in the fight against inflation; a government whose exercise of fiscal power at its most Keynesian has respected the Bundesbank's priorities; a few large banks interlocked with concentrated businesses whose heavy export trade gives them a stake in monetary stability; and unions that have generally behaved with moderation and respected the prerogatives of the capitalists whom they face not only at the bargaining table but in the corporation boardroom and at bankers' lunches. How could this congeries of peak associations allied on behalf of stability possibly be in need of reform?

The answer to this question is best stolen from the title given to a history of the United States in the 1920s—"the perils of prosperity."[25] In the West German economy of the 1960s, affluence had become a danger to the management of stability under conservative auspices. It is fair to say that Chancellor Ludwig Erhard, the principal architect of the Christian Democratic policies that fostered the so-called economic miracle, was worried about the prospects for West German capitalism in a social climate where prosperity was taken for granted. The federal parliamentary campaign of 1965 had demonstrated that the Bundestag was vulnerable to prosperity, too, and had little compunction about distributing election gifts (Wahlgeschenke) to interested constituencies. It was criticism of Bonn's overspending, combined with Erhard's inability to retrench in 1966 without violating his coalition partner's election promise not to raise taxes, that formed the background to Erhard's fall from power. Some have seen irony in the successful economist who stumbled over an economic issue. But there is less irony when one considers that a minister of reconstruction does not necessarily make a good chancellor of affluence. Erhard, who started to cut a bad economic figure in television appearances where he urged West Germans to tighten their belts, tried to come up with a comprehensive program for reconciling the wealthy Germans to stability. This was the chancellor's project for an integrated society (formierte Gesellschaft). But this ineffective, programmatic appeal to prudence was no more than jawboning in search of a vision. Erhard refused to let West Germany's increasingly self-conscious interest groups, and especially the unions, have much of a say in his integrated society. The really remarkable irony of Erhard's fall was that he brought his party into trouble by failing to acknowledge in practice the ruling ideology of Christian Democratic West Germany—pluralism. By contrast, Erhard's rival, Karl Schiller, showed that Social Democrats made better pluralists when Schiller embraced the liberal doctrine of interest group participation with a frankness and optimism that helped the SPD establish its image as the more modern party.

At a less personal, less ideological level the "perils of prosperity" resulted from deeper changes in the postwar economy. These changes had to do with the prospects for economic growth and with the mechanisms for resolving distributive conflicts after the end of reconstruction. Some economists have described the change in West Germany's economic constellation as a shift from an extensive to an intensive phase of growth. The phases had to do with changes in industry's capital stock and its relationship to productivity and labor. Productivity increased during the 1950s via expanding plant equipment and a swelling labor force. After 1959, and then especially after the sealing off of East German refugee labor in 1961, productivity could only increase by intensifying capital investment. While capital intensity increased, labor and capital productivity declined. Although foreigners and women were taken into the work force in increasing numbers, these additions to the labor reserve could not compensate for higher wages and shorter hours. Average weekly working hours went from 46.3 in 1960 to 44.8 in 1970. The wage quotient rose from 60.6 percent to 66.7 percent in the same period.[26] Capital productivity, which rose by 6 percent or more in three of the ten years from 1951 to 1960 and went below zero only once during that decade (to -2 percent in 1958), did not register a positive figure again until 1968 after a low of -5.4 percent in 1967.[27]

In the words of the theoretical economist Hajo Riese, "West German society gradually became, as it was called back then, growth-conscious."[28] Economic growth in the 1950s, according to Riese, had combined a "profits inflation" with an "incomes deflation." The latter trend was concealed from wage earners by what Riese has called a productivity illusion: productivity increases were high, so unexpectedly high that workers did not immediately calculate them into their anticipations of wage demands. The combination of high profits and low relative wage shares guaranteed price stability and growth. Since real wages were rising, too, the productivity illusion concealing the incomes deflation went unnoticed for some time.[29] But as West German society became growth-conscious, wage earners caught onto the fact that productivity increases could be anticipated. In the 1960s economic growth was characterized (again, according to Riese) by "a tendentially rising investment quotient, accompanying advances in productivity, and export surpluses, but above all rising inflation rates—with the consequence of a money illusion that braked the increase of the wage quotient" and led to a "hidden instability."[30] In other words, Model Germany continued to grow much as before, but with the crucial new strain of latent inflation. (The "advances in productivity" to which Riese refers also did not necessarily translate into annual rates of productivity increase.) The changing distributive pattern—from "profit-securing" in the 1950s to what Riese has characterized as "income (distribution) securing" in the 1960s[31]—had serious consequences for the functioning of the Bundesbank's model partnership with the private sector for stability.

A good diagnosis of the breakdown in the alliance for stability can be gleaned from the first few reports of the Council of Experts (Sachverständigenrat) that was created in 1963 to evaluate the economy every year. For it was the council, joined by Karl Schiller and the SPD, that initiated an active and creative search for ways to restore stability. The council's diagnosis amounted to this: in trying to curtail the inflation typical of the intensive phase of growth, the Bundesbank had to restrain credit with the available monetary instruments. This monetary apparatus could be counted upon to brake inflation, but at a substantial cost to the weaker participants in West Germany's economy and to the ultimate detriment of the entire West German model. With bank finance increasing in significance relative to internal company finance,[32] a credit squeeze was bound to be felt in the early 1960s. Employers feeling the pinch would be less inclined to grant generous wage concessions; unions would have to reckon with the possibility of a decline in employment. But whereas the export-oriented larger businesses were in a strong position to survive the pinch, workers and small businesses were less well situated.

Furthermore, the council doubted that a little unemployment would suffice to tame workers who had become accustomed to growth. The amount of unemployment "would certainly have to be larger than what was conducive to an increase in labor productivity."[33] The council appreciated that Riese's productivity illusion—the growth trick of the 1950s—had come to an end in the new period of capital-intensive investment. "The notion that, among our workers, one does not have to reckon with reactions against labor-saving innovations or with an attitude that makes cooperation with productivity-enhancing measures dependent on hefty wage increases—this is nothing more than a questionable extrapolation of favorable experiences from periods of powerful economic expansion."[34]

The council dwelt on the issue of productivity because productivity differences were at the heart of what was wrong with the Bundesbank's old approach to new problems. The council felt that the traditional monetary approach to stability would be one that ended up discriminating against employment in domestic-oriented sectors, although the Bundesbank's actions were intended to slow the inflationary pace of the dynamic, export-oriented sector. Such a traditional stabilization policy "would have to throttle domestic demand

so that—in spite of additional foreign demand—the export-intensive
sectors (as wage leaders) would not be able to guarantee wage increases any more powerful than whatever corresponded to the overall level of productivity gains. But this presupposes a very percep-
tible underemployment in the domestic sectors."[35] What the council
looked for was sophisticated productivity bargaining that could strike
a balance between employment for the thriving export market and
employment for the less dynamic domestic market. The inability of
indiscriminate monetary measures to strike such a balance aroused
another fear. Productivity-oriented and cost-oriented wage bargaining might collapse entirely, giving way to the sort of bargaining that
could set off a price-wage spiral. "The old purchasing power theory
of the wage, which attempts to justify an aggressive wage policy on
grounds of employment policy, would soon find more and more adherence."[36]

The breakdown of the old unified coalition for "growth without
inflation" (as one economist has described the Erhard era)[37] had two
related implications. The component parts of Model Germany had to
be rearranged so as to restore the Bundesbank's confidence in the
antiinflationary potential of the private economy and of public spending
habits. The rearrangement of Model Germany demanded skillful political leadership, largely provided by the SPD, both to manage an
incomes policy and to mobilize latent support for issues that ran contrary to the business lobby's sometimes narrow perception of its interests. Long-range financial planning and the concerted action—an
incomes forum initiated by the Council of Experts, endorsed by Karl
Schiller, and written into the Stability and Growth Law (1967)—helped
to convince the Bundesbank that it could afford to phase out the stabilization crisis it had induced in 1966. (However, by the early 1970s,
the Bundesbank felt obliged to intervene again in a manner similar to
that of 1966 and in spite of the 1967 Stability Law's promise.)

The orchestrated mobilization of support for an alternative
stabilization policy was more protracted than the passage of the Stability Law in its Social Democratic version. The Council of Experts
started the process of regrouping the antiinflationary coalition by
proposing greater flexibility on foreign economic policy as an alternative to Bundesbank pressure. Upward revaluations of the deutsche
márk (DM), the council suggested, might keep inflation from reaching
the point where it required central bank intervention. The Bundesbank
would not have to act then for several reasons. With a higher DM
parity, West German businesses could not export as much and would
not grant such generous wage concessions in the rush to take advantage of flourishing markets abroad. Revaluations would have all the
advantages of credit restraint without its discriminating side-effects
against smaller, domestic-oriented businesses. Imported goods

bought with cheaper foreign currency would also lower cost pressures on West German industry and help maintain a standard of living that might forestall a wage-price spiral. Finally, there would be less imported inflation owing to speculative inflows of foreign capital betting on a change in the undervalued deutsche mark. Karl Schiller endorsed the spirit of the council's new economic diplomacy and got new powers for a more flexible foreign economic policy written into the Stability Law. But it took until the election of 1969 before Schiller and the SPD were willing to mobilize organized labor for a joint effort with the savers' lobby on behalf of the first upward revaluation since 1961—a cause secretly supported by the Bundesbank but opposed by the CDU and West German business.

Since 1969, the conservative wing of the antiinflationary alliance, bruised but partially restored under the Social-Liberal coalition, has learned to live with far more spectacular revaluations. But it took a process of adjustment, with Social Democratic presence and prodding, to make Model Germany adjust to the international perils of prosperity. The special international danger was West Germany's vulnerability (as an "open economy" with a stake in free trade but with little interest in taking on the responsibilities of a reserve currency) to inflationary pressures imported from abroad. In a sense, Model Germany had to be reformed under Social Democratic sponsorship because the SPD was best suited to deal with a fundamentally stable economy that could no longer be insulated from two sources of instability: domestically, the peril of growth-conscious workers; and internationally, the peril of trying to remain a relatively stable island inextricably bound up with an increasingly unstable world.

CHANGES IN THE DESIGN OF POLICY:
STEERING CAPACITY AND INNOVATION
BY "RED" AND "EXPERT"

Whenever the prospect of a stabilization crisis has motivated the public maintenance personnel of the policy machinery to contemplate a major overhaul, the political establishment has always sought to increase welfare only when it has proved compatible with stability. No public figure would dare to challenge the fundamental duties and operating methods of the Bundesbank without risking a short-lived career in Bonn. Just as Keynesianism tried to supplement the market without replacing it, the Keynesian revolution in West Germany tried to combine the pursuit of stability with the pursuit of other goals. Institutional innovation at its most progressive was meant to create new mechanisms that would allow policy makers to "steer" other macroeconomic aggregates aside from the traditional monetary ones. Reformers of the policy machinery have tried not to oust the priority of monetary stability, nor even to relativize that goal, but to forge a less one-sided steering device than the control of credit.

The search for a more comprehensive steering mechanism has had a political and social dimension, as well an an economic side. If it were possible, the reconciliation of stability with welfare would do much more than solve the central legitimation problem of modern capitalism. Solving the economic problem would also enhance the steering capacity of government to concentrate on more inspiring tasks, such as the pursuit of peace and social equality. For this reason, the resolution of the tension between welfare and stability has held a special attraction for social democracy, the reformist heir to the traditions of the labor movement and internationalist solidarity. West German Social Democrats, whose stated political commitments are to egalitarian reforms at home and détente abroad, have therefore had an overwhelming stake in improving the state's economic steering capacity. The Social Democratic constituency, still based in organized labor despite the SPD's broadening into a "catch-all" party, ought to have made social democracy the natural champion of welfare in any critical skirmish with stability. Yet, the SPD's interest in using business and the instruments of state for creative diplomacy and sometimes social reforms has made the party wary about risking a head-on confrontation with the guardians of stability. The party's internalization of the tension between welfare and stability has thus made the SPD an eager advocate of innovations that would strengthen the government's capacity for reconciling these two goals.

As one of the forces willing to consider innovations in the policy machinery, the SPD has always stood in principle for a less repressive resolution of the conflict between welfare and stability. Contrary to the view that has equated CDU Chancellor Ludwig Erhard's conservative vision of an "integrated society" with SPD Economics Minister Karl Schiller's contrasting program of a "mature society,"[38] at times the SPD has made a difference toward a "progressive alternative" to austerity. Without the contribution of Schiller's Social Democratic amendments, the legislative embodiment of the Keynesian revolution would have been a restrictive stability law, not the liberal Stability and Growth Law it became in 1967.

Understandably, events since 1967 have made it seem highly improbable to skeptical contemporaries that this recent "party of the state" could even have been a progressive force. By entering into a Grand Coalition with the Christian Democrats, the SPD virtually obliterated the concept of a progressive opposition. There have been far more serious compromises since then. But the abrupt end to Brandt's brief era of domestic reforms, the Social-Liberal gov-

ernment's management of a second stabilization crisis and austere
recovery, restrictions of civil liberties both with respect to the bar-
ring of radicals from public service and the curtailment of fundamental legal rights in the policing of terrorist acts, and most recently
the contemplation of welfare service cutbacks in a third stabilization
crisis—none of these developments should lead one to overlook the
SPD's objectively progressive contribution to the welfare of the West
German working class, especially in the 1960s. It cannot be denied
that the SPD has not consistently been able to deliver on the basis of
progressive principles alone. Nor has the party's reputed preference
for Keynesian solutions papered over basic contradictions in the
FRG's indisputably capitalist system. But the history of policy innovations in West Germany also shows that the extraparliamentary Left,
for all of its subjective ruminations on an alternative economic policy,
has not had an objective monopoly on progressive politics.

Owing to the SPD's assumption of governing responsibilities with
a reformist program in the 1970s, there has been a shift in the center
of policy innovation within Social Democracy. When Karl Schiller
sponsored West Germany's Keynesian revolution in the 1960s, he did
so as part of the SPD's governing team. The entire thrust of Social
Democratic and labor politics in the 1960s was to gain entry into the
Bonn establishment. Intraparty politics was subordinated to the overriding goal of proving the SPD's governing capability (Regierungs-
fähigkeit), tarnished by Christian Democratic propaganda during
Adenauer's long patriarchal reign. The trade unions, too, were
eager to achieve political participation and gain a status coequal with
big business and the middle class, who had represented economic
interests under bourgeois governments for so long that West German
usage equated business with the economy (die Wirtschaft). Under
these circumstances, any potential conflicts between the SPD's dual
roles as a governing party and as the party of labor and reform were
either nonexistent or easily suppressed. The dissolution of Christian
Democratic leadership under Adenauer and the receptivity of the
policy-making establishment to the new welfare economics of the
"magical polygon" encouraged the SPD to push for a new balance between a political establishment accustomed to stability and a political
constituency growing accustomed to new affluence.

Once Social Democrats were not only in power but also heading
successive governments, this situation changed. A ruling party could
not be expected to sponsor major policy innovations even if—or especially when—it presided over a second stabilization crisis of the
sort its earlier innovations had been designed to prevent. Even if
the SPD had chosen to acknowledge its culpability as the governing
party of austerity and then recover its identity as the center of working-class opposition to the capitalist system, the party would have

had a bourgeois coalition partner to contend with that was permanently mobilized to defend the central bank and neoliberal values. The task of self-criticism and committed (if embarrassed) partisanship for social welfare and reform therefore fell to party members lower down, further leftward, and generally younger in the Social Democratic hierarchy. In this niche of the political spectrum, stability was not always a priority of the first order. Young Socialists were instructed by their elders from the party "barrack" in Bonn that they should pay more than lip service to this conservative value. But the tendency of the Social Democratic Left was either to deny the centrality of stabilization or to redefine stability by placing it in a long-term perspective. Since the unacceptable alternative to the exhausted Social Democratic innovations of the 1960s was the toleration of new stabilization crises under Social Democratic leadership, democratic socialists preferred to view the instability of the 1970s as part of a larger structural crisis. Armed with a structural diagnosis for the economy's ills, the Social Democratic Left tried to repeat Karl Schiller's innovative accomplishments of 1967 with a new structural policy; but these democratic socialists only imitated Schiller without his accent on pragmatic, short-term crisis management and without Schiller's ritual obeisance to the guardians of stability.

The apparent significance of crisis diagnoses (such as the SPD Left's structural diagnosis) for innovations in the policy machinery points to another salient feature of changes in the government's economic steering capacity. Because of its unique ability to harness the forces of stability and affluence under the right conditions, the SPD has been a major source of innovation, but it has never been the only one. Another carrier of innovation has sometimes been the professional economist. Even a Keynesian revolution engineered by "capitalist roaders" needs the creative exchange between "expert" and "red." Needless to say, the role of the economist has been different from that of the politician, even when (as in the 1960s) Social Democrats and economists on the newly created Council of Experts worked in tandem to bring about a less repressive version of the Stability Law. The memory of establishment economists' contribution to the Keynesian revolution has been impressed on the consciousness of Left-Keynesian economists with such indelible force that the Council of Experts' subsequent conservative turn has appeared as a "monetarist" betrayal of principle.[39] But this sense of betrayal only obscures the fact that economic advisers to the Bonn establishment have sided with stability even when, like the SPD, they held out hope for the reconciliation of stability with welfare.

Since the Council of Experts (henceforth abbreviated as SVR, for the German Sachverständigenrat) was created in 1963 to advise the federal government, it has understood its statutory mission as

that of a watchdog for the enforcers of stability. Perhaps the function of the SVR is best understood by borrowing an image from the
theory of the ego in psychoanalysis: the SVR conducts "reality testing"[40] for the establishment's blind drive toward satisfying stability
in an unstable world. Precisely because the one-sided credit apparatus of the Bundesbank cannot deal with all the parameters of stability,
the central bank and its supporting fiscal institutions need an entity to
keep an eye on the economic world outside Frankfurt and Bonn. The
SVR provides the policy machinery with sensory devices to evaluate
the total state of the economy. Hence, the full name of the SVR is
Sachverständigenrat zur Begutachtung der gesamtwirtschaftlichen
Entwicklung, or Council of Experts for the Evaluation of the Total
Economic Development. (The last term may also be translated as
"aggregate" or "macroeconomic development.")

Had the stability-conscious Erhard government not expected its
board of independent advisers to provide "scientific" proof for the
chancellor's warning that the West German people were living beyond
their means, the Council of Experts might never have been created.
As things turned out, it was the conservative Erhard rather than the
Keynesians who got the first chance to be "betrayed" by the advisers.
Yet, the SVR's initial engagement for the Keynesian cause merely concealed a latent conservatism that the council's subsequent reports
made only too apparent. If the five economists who made up the SVR
initially seemed to stress growth over stability, this priority was an
illusion explicable in terms of the council's assignment to provide
reality testing for the growth-blind guardians of stability. In its first
four years, the council was convinced that the innovative application
of new instruments to untested areas (incomes policy, exchange rate
policy) would guarantee stability without the disruptions of a stabilization crisis. The commitment to strengthening the Bundesbank by taking the burden of complex fiscal problems off its shoulders is apparent just from the titles of the SVR's first four annual reports: "Stable
Money—Steady Growth" (1964-65), "Stabilization without Stagnation"
(1965-66), "Expansion and Stability" (1966-67), and "Stability in
Growth" (1967-68). The council's subsequent preoccupation with
stable wages, stable prices, the stability of expectations, the preser-
vation of the market order, and the need for a new monetary policy
was thus entirely consistent with the earlier Keynesian phase. The
exposure of the council's latent conservatism shows that the psycho-
analytic analogy to reality testing is a useful yet limited metaphor.
By testing reality for the psyche's blind drives, the ego gives the mental personality integrity; in Freud's words, the healthy ego should be
able to "appropriate fresh portions of the id" and to civilize instincts.[41]
Precisely the opposite development has overcome the SVR, which continues to be driven by the taskmasters of instinctual stability it was
commissioned to enlighten and serve.

The conservative, even repressive character of official economics, the "scientific" carrier of policy innovations that has occa-
sionally supplemented the SPD's political push for reform, draws attention to a final aspect of changes in the government's steering capacity. Crisis economics and crisis management can just as easily
galvanize the policy machinery with conservative as with progressive
results. A major change in economic planning like the new monetary
policy that was introduced in 1973, then fortified and tested in the recession of 1975, was no less of an innovation for having represented
a step backward toward austerity. Although the machinery of "global
guidance" (as the fixtures of the Stability and Growth Law were called)
was exhausted in the stabilization crisis between 1973 and 1975, the
new monetary policy was not simply a throwback to the pre-Keynesian
position of 1966. Central to the new policy was an upgrading of the
Bundesbank's institutional capabilities, its ability to link up with and
have an impact on the rest of the credit apparatus and economy. This
attempted renovation of the central bank's effectiveness was a response
to new and unusual circumstances not encountered in the 1960s:
higher inflation rates, the liberalization of capital movements both at
home and abroad, and the near collapse of the U.S.-dominated world
monetary system. Although repressive in the sense that welfare was
postponed until stability could be achieved (The Investments of Today
Are the Jobs of Tomorrow was the conservative slogan of the 1970s),
the new austerity renounced only the promise of global guidance, not
its lasting institutional framework. (Schiller had defined the promise
of global guidance as "social symmetry," a guaranteed link between
investments and jobs.) Furthermore, whatever was pre-Keynesian
about the new monetary policy was a pre-Keynesian remnant of
Keynesian global guidance, too.

Altogether, there have been three episodes of policy innovation
in the Social Democratic era, one with progressive promise (global
guidance), one the product of neoconservative disillusionment (the new
monetary policy),[42] and one with untested radical potential (structural
policy). Although both "red" and "expert" have been at work in each
innovation—rethinking and prodding for changes, or sometimes just
recording and administering them—the thrust behind these innovations
has not been party politics or the politics of economic advice. Each
innovation has been principally an institutional affair, facilitated by
subsidiary changes in the strength of the institutions making policy,
in the participation of the major interest associations constituting organized capitalism, and in the ideological division of responsibilities
between public and private institutions. These institutional factors
have stamped the changes in strategic designs for reconciling welfare
with stability. The academic designers and the partisan executors
have only helped to catalyze change.

INTELLECTUAL FASHIONS AND ACADEMIC
SCHOOLS—DESIGN BY CRISIS DIAGNOSIS?

Since professional economists have had a hand in designing
every new steering device, and since the same guild has articulated
every major change within an official forum (the Council of Experts),
it is only natural that the academic and polemical controversies surrounding economic planning should have immediately focused on the
role of advisers. It is also understandable that the systematic methods of analysis in which professional economists are trained should
give other scholars a point of departure for trying to comprehend how
policy making has changed. Economists have transmitted their professional fashions, whether Keynesian or monetarist, from the academy to government. On occasion, an influential school of thought
might even be located on home territory—not one of the two Cambridges
or Chicago, but Kiel, whose Institute for World Economics has supplied the FRG with Keynesians, monetarists, and the distinctive crisis diagnosis behind structural policy.

There is another reason why much scholarship has found it reasonable to assume that each innovation or (in the case of structural
policy) prospective innovation has begun with a crisis diagnosis
straight out of an identifiable school. Each contemplated change of
the policy machinery has been associated with some central aspect
of an economic doctrine. Global guidance originally emphasized demand management, while the new monetary policy stressed indicators
of the money supply. Structural policy seemed to go along with the
emphasis on selective competitiveness, increased research and development, and a new international division of labor articulated by the
Kiel school. Moreover, the crisis diagnosis of each school has accorded neatly with a particular position on the state's responsibility
for labor's welfare. Global guidance spelled the "full employment
guarantee." The new monetary policy meant a definitive abandonment
of that guarantee, acceptance of the welfare losses entailed by a stabilization crisis, and the discipline tight money restores to the reserve
army of the unemployed. Structural policy, with its developmental
perspective on the West German economy, redefined the conservative
concept of "minimum wage unemployment" as "structural unemployment" brought on by distortions in the postwar pattern of growth.

There is much to be said for the influence of particular schools
of economic thought. But it would be incorrect to overestimate this
influence. The evidence also shows that no school of thought was ever
adopted lock, stock, and barrel. At most, there has been an elective
affinity between the central concepts of economic doctrines and the innovative features of new policy designs. What is more, each of these
innovative features has always been embedded in a larger design made

up of elements that have had more to do with structural features of organized capitalism in West Germany than with any school of thought. Sometimes these features of the FRG's mixed economy have stood in dramatic opposition to the central thrust of a new economic doctrine.

For example, the Keynesian emphasis on aggregate demand was but one component of the stabilization design jointly authored by Karl Schiller and the Council of Experts between 1965 and 1967. Maintaining moderate levels of aggregate demand was part of a package for a "concerted stabilization action" that included an informal incomes policy and a flexible exchange rate policy. The push for deficit spending by Schiller and the SVR came late, toward the end of 1967, after the Stability Law had been passed. Even then, the institutional prerequisites for classic Keynesian deficit spending had not been completed with approval of the Stability and Growth Law. The Bundesbank remained far too independent and capital markets too vulnerable to a tug of war between the state and private investors for the government to conduct "pump priming" without discouraging private investment.

Likewise, the new monetary policy of 1973 and the "monetary mantle" of 1975 were at most inspired by the renaissance of monetarist economics, not dictated by the Friedmanite persuasion. A more plausible explanation of this monetary "counterrevolution" is that it resulted from a breakdown and reformation of the Keynesian design of 1965-67. Because of flaws in the design and mishaps in the execution of Schiller's concerted action, the incomes forum failed to prevent what it had been designed to forestall—an inflationary "distributive struggle" among labor, capital, and government, which establishment economists had always deplored as "functionless." The concerted action got off to a bad start because its introduction in the recession of 1967 gave business an advantage over labor, while Schiller was unable to deliver on his promise of social symmetry for labor during the runaway profits boom following the recession. The boom led to wildcat strikes in 1969, when steelworkers and coal miners insisted on renegotiating contracts that had been concluded under the impact of the recession. Organized labor later made up for its losses from the 1967 recovery and took advantage of prosperity in the early 1970s, while businesses passed on costs into higher prices and government helped to guarantee both full employment and high capacity utilization until 1973. Under these circumstances, incomes policy lost its purpose as a prop for measured growth in all components of the GNP. The same was true of the second, foreign economic "flank" protecting stable growth. Until the bloc float of the European snake currencies in March 1973, ad hoc manipulations of the exchange rate did not suffice to keep new money off West German territory. By the time the Bundesbank was able to regain control over the process of creating money, the combined extent of domestic and imported inflation was too great for the authorities to want to try maintaining aggregate demand again. The Keynesian strategy, after all, had been designed to prevent stabilization crises by stemming inflation first.

Yet, the drastic curtailment of the money supply undertaken after March 1973 and the broadening of the monetary orientation into the monetary mantle in 1975 were not monetarist acts. The credit crunch of 1973 was probably more Draconian than was necessary, but the depletion of the private banks' free liquid reserves in that year was required if the Bundesbank was going to succeed with a new indicator, the "quantity of central bank money." This indicator did not come out of a Chicago seminar but was a supplementary replacement for an older indicator, free liquid reserves, which had lost its predictive value after Schiller liberalized controls on domestic capital and another Western finance minister (Connally) helped to shake up capital movements across national borders after devaluing the dollar in 1971. The tightening of monetary reins in 1973 was chiefly an institutional response to the domestic and international mobility of capital, not an academic response to new theories of inflation. When the new chancellor, Schmidt, consulted with authorities in Frankfurt and came up with the monetary mantle late in 1974, this new concept owed even less to academic inspiration. The idea that decisions on government spending, wage determination, and pricing be made in a climate of awareness about the monetary limits to all these decisions was fundamentally no different from the concerted action of government and the parties to collective bargaining. The monetary mantle simply took away the limelight from what had become an empty forum on incomes and gave a monetary twist to the notion of concerted restraint. What made cost controls, the linchpin of the concerted action in the 1960s, any less of an exercise in supply-side economics simply because the fundamental unit of analysis was national income rather than the money supply?

The whole story on the third prospective innovation, structural policy, is not yet in. But this much is already clear: the "scientific" contribution has gone through many more filters than either Keynesianism or monetarism did. The Council of Experts eventually proved receptive to parts of the Kiel school's structural crisis diagnosis. Interestingly, it was the same set of issues, incomes policy and West Germany's relations with the world economy, that gave the Kiel school a hearing in the advisory establishment. The policy and administrative sciences, the active or reformist heir to West Germany's traditional Staatswissenschaft, made a limited contribution to the enunciation of structural policy by Social Democratic technocrats. A third voice on behalf of an innovative structural policy, heard in the investment guidance controversy within the broader SPD, was not so much the voice of the academy as of academics. It was not economics pro-

fessors but activists with university degrees who swelled the ranks of
the SPD and kept new modes of political intervention in the economy
on the party's programmatic agenda. The advocates of structural
policy as a form of investment guidance did not really represent a
school (not even an identifiable Marxist tendency) or subscribe to a
single crisis diagnosis. To the extent that these mostly young democratic socialists took a scholarly position, it was more or less Left-
Keynesian. Their advocacy of more deficit spending and criticisms
of the Bundesbank showed how incomplete the Keynesian revolution
remained after more than ten years.

The relevant branches of the policy-making establishment har-
vested what they could from all these academic sources of structural
policy with even greater selectivity than they had distilled Keynesian
and monetarist doctrine. The SVR took the liberalism of the Kiel
school seriously—the Kiel economists' commitment to free trade and
the doctrine of comparative advantage. But the conclusion that
West Germany in the 1970s confronted more serious structural change
than the market had resolved successfully in earlier decades was discarded by the SVR's official economics. By contrast, the interventionist and technocratic implications of the Kiel analysis were just the
things recommending the structural diagnosis to the Social Democratic
Research Ministry. The Liberal Economics Ministry adopted a wait-
and-see posture. Economics Minister Lambsdorff has stressed an
older, neoliberal tradition of structural policy that combines a low
government profile with sponsorship of more research on the market's
own structural trends.

One thing that stands out about all three episodes of policy innovation is the significance of incomes policy and foreign economic policy. These two supporting "flanks" of economic planning show up in
every policy design, almost as if to demonstrate that every innovation has involved more than the translation of textbook doctrines into
public policy. The original form of global guidance was the Keynesian
stabilization of aggregate demand plus hopes for the concerted action
and a flexible exchange-rate policy. The new monetary policy was a
turn away from demand management toward control of the money supply minus the belief that a short-term incomes policy could be balanced by short-term manipulations of the currency. Structural policy
was a redefinition (or creative evasion) of stabilization (the structural
crisis) and growth (now qualitative growth) plus a defense of West Germany's high-wage levels and a new approach to the international division of labor.

Why always these two supporting flanks in every policy design?
Karl Schiller answered this question in a way by saying that economic
planning would be a "table with two legs" if Erhard's Stability Law did
not include an incomes policy and fortifications of the weak Foreign

Economic Policy Law, an outdated piece of statutory dirigisme from 1961.[43] But the suggestion that a creative incomes policy and foreign economic policy would somehow round out the "magical polygon" provides only a metaphoric answer and continues to beg the question. A better clue was given further on in the same speech where Schiller urged the Bundestag to revise the Stability Law.

> The example of Great Britain has been referred to. Yes indeed, we do not want Draconian measures of incomes policy via the wage freeze and the price freeze as in Great Britain. We want to spare this from the German population; and precisely for this reason, we—of all people, we —urge the introduction of orienting measures and therewith a light-handed incomes policy. [Emphasis added][44]

The "we" (gerade wir) Schiller meant was the SPD. Schiller's remark raises yet another set of questions: What interest could the party of organized labor have in advocating wage restraint? Why should the major party of business be initially opposed to an incomes policy if price freezes were categorically ruled out?

The answer is that an incomes policy promised to give the trade unions participation, or at least a nominal voice, in what was called the preformation of policy. The concerted action made the unions part of economic planning's clearinghouse. "Co-opting" the unions allowed the SPD to delegate direct responsibility for reconciling stability with the growth of wages to the party's major organized constituency. But wage restraint would never have been acceptable to the DGB (West Germany's trade union federation) unless the entire stabilization design contained an escape valve making severe repression of workers' previous income gains unnecessary. Such a safety mechanism was provided by exchange-rate diplomacy. Again, the lineup of political forces is unusual, but from an ideological point of view, why should a Social Democratic party be promoting trade liberalization (as Schiller's party did by coming out for revaluation of the deutsche mark in 1969), while the party of neoliberalism resisted the free play of market forces?

Again, the answer has to do with the balance between welfare and stability that innovators try to achieve in progressive new policy designs. Schiller and the SVR, who eventually lined up with the Bundesbank in support of revaluation, hoped to restrain the inflationary stimulus of the export-led recovery in 1968-69 and expose the West German economy to import competition that would dampen domestic supply costs while alleviating cost-of-living pressures. The new foreign economic policy would thus obviate the need for repeated central bank intervention while it enhanced the concerted action's prospects for achieving cost controls.

The SPD's advocacy of market forces and basic distrust of protectionism go deeper than the party's conversion to the market economy with the Godesberg Program. Although the task of governing has since compromised the SPD's positions on business concentration and consumerism, in Adenauer's day the Social Democratic opposition was often a more reliable supporter of strong anticartelization legislation and marketplace competition than most Christian Democrats save Erhard. The party's stands on market issues show that there have always been two sides to economic liberalism in West Germany. One side is what the economist and public banker Wilhelm Hankel calls the liberal consciousness of the FRG's neomercantilist being. In spite of export-oriented practices that frequently have had little to do with liberal economics, West Germany's policy makers like to think that their economy's success has resulted from strict adherence to the liberal rules of the game, free trade and competition. This side of West German economic liberalism is more theological than practical; it is the civil religion of Model Germany's economist-preachers. The more practical side of liberalism is the one always emphasized by the SPD—the concrete benefits (such as they are) of free trade and the market for workers who save and spend their take-home pay.

INSTITUTIONS, INTERESTS, AND IDEOLOGIES OF INTERVENTION

Two things ought to be evident about innovations of the policy machinery. First, academic fashions, schools of economic thought, and crisis diagnoses have contributed to changes in macroeconomic steering mechanisms only after the ideas of professional economists have gone through a political filter fitted to the peculiar structure of the West German economy. Second, the centerpiece of every progressive innovation contemplated by economists and politicians (global guidance with its original fiscal emphasis, the "active" structural policy) has been "flanked" by supportive props from incomes policy and foreign economic policy. In the case of the single conservative innovation (the new monetary policy), the policy machinery took in its damaged supportive wings (the concerted action weathered by distributive conflict, an exchange-rate policy battered by the debris of the collapsing Bretton Woods system) to concentrate on repairing the core motor of stabilization.

These two characteristics of policy innovation do not explain changes in the design of economic planning; they only redefine them. Since one facile type of explanation (changing crisis diagnoses) must be discarded for explaining the wrong things (a Keynesian revolution that never happened in textbook fashion, a monetarist counterrevolution that owed little to the Friedmanites, and industrial policy innovations that never got off the ground in response to a structural crisis diagnosis that may not even be very accurate), how can one account for the vagaries of economic planning in the Social Democratic era?

Three factors tangential to party politics and the politics of economic advice best explain these vagaries.

1. The potential of prospective innovations for strengthening the institutions of the policy-making establishment,
2. The prospects for interest-group consensus and conflict on divisive distributive issues, and
3. The ideological task of justifying new political powers to intervene in the economy (both commodity and labor markets) and of redefining the division of responsibilities between the public and private sectors of organized capitalism.

The policy innovations of the 1960s had less to do with Keynesianism than with these other factors, more specifically:

1. The institutional fortification of the policy machinery to lessen the burden of stabilization hitherto placed on the Bundesbank alone and to fulfill the agenda of the new welfare economics (the "magical polygon"),
2. The interest-group politics of including peak associations in what the founders of global guidance hoped would be a new consensus on concerted stabilization, and
3. The ideological packaging of increased governmental powers to intervene in the economy as part of a new division of responsibilities that preserved the sanctity of the market and the "autonomy of collective bargaining."

Similarly, the exhaustion of global guidance and the new economics had less to do with monetarism than with the breakdown of the components listed above.

1. International monetary turmoil and the inflation that accompanied the Brandt government's full employment policies led to a restoration of Bundesbank primacy within the policy machinery. The central bankers also wanted to regain control over links to the private banks and the rest of the economy, which had been lost because of capital liberalization starting in the late 1960s.
2. A "distributive struggle" took the place of the artificial consensus that, while still strong enough to uphold West Germany's reputation for "social peace," failed to deliver "social symmetry" (distributive fairness) to workers and the trade union apparatus at critical moments.

3. The official economic ideology reverted an emphasis on conservative basics: less government, more trust in market forces, and
a distrust of organized economic power (especially the power of organized labor).

The picture of policy reform that emerges in these two episodes
is a picture of continuity in the establishment's stabilization strategy
interrupted by occasional crises that galvanize the policy machinery
with progressive or conservative results. Structural policy poses a
more complicated set of causes and outcomes for changes in the design
of policy. Because the center of innovation moved leftward while the
political establishment moved toward the Right, the enthusiasts of
structural policy have often seemed antagonistic to the guardians of
stability. This institutional antagonism may explain why attempts
to find a new direction for macroeconomic planning in the late 1970s
were frustrated even when it was evident that global guidance and its
conservative revision had been tried and found wanting.

The barriers to an "active" structural policy had less to do with
the acceptance or accuracy of any structural diagnosis than with institutional considerations, interest-group politics, and ideologies of intervention. These barriers may be examined by looking at what happened to political initiatives on structural policy, chief of which was
the work of an SPD committee on the subject chaired by Wolfgang Roth.
The three factors explaining the fate of the SPD Left's would-be socialist innovations related to structural policy in the following way:

1. The institutional impulse for a change of macroeconomic
steering mechanisms from cyclical to structural policy has not come
from inside the policy-making establishment but from reformers in
the SPD. The movers behind structural policy, who have tried to
build a bridge between the "reform" and "state" party segments of
the SPD, have remained outsiders to the establishment run by Schmidt
and liberal economics ministers since 1974. Indeed, the reformers'
very interest in bending the federal machinery to suit partisan and
reformist ends suggests the difficulty of their enterprise in a political
establishment that likes to have its institutions strengthened, not
challenged, by innovations like the Stability Law.

2. The interest-group politics of structural policy would institutionalize West Germany's informal corporatist arrangements to a degree that neither doctrinaire parliamentarians nor market ideologues
—the major spokesmen for the Bonn establishment—would tolerate.
Although the Roth Committee and several party congresses made a
Young Socialist-DGB coalition on behalf of structural councils possible within the SPD, this innovation carried the principle of codetermination too far for everyone except the unions and the Social Democratic

Center-Left. To the rest of West Germany's political establishment, the interest-group arrangements for structural policy sound too much like the early Weimar Republic's "syndicalist" experiments.

3. Finally, the extension of state intervention envisioned by the most vocal of structural policy's advocates carries the stigma of "investment guidance," an ideologically loaded controversy thrashed out between Young Socialists and the Social Democratic Center-Right to the alarm of everyone further to the Right.

Yet, there have also been a few practical instances where the Social-Liberal government has found it safe enough to implement something the coalition has called structural policy. In 1977 the coalition was willing to sponsor research on structural trends and to initiate a four-year, DM16 billion program of investments in the future. The 1981 energy program, announced in anticipation of West Germany's third stabilization crisis, also has elements of the Social-Liberal compromise on structural policy. Both programs have been in line with the austerity course held since 1975 (with some departures toward a half-hearted Keynesianism after 1977). Both have also shown how strong the resistance remains to Keynesian spending that would allow the public sector to overcompensate for lost export demand.

In a way, the younger Social Democrats on Roth's committee have tried to duplicate and outdo Karl Schiller's past innovations by arguing that structural policy will do for the current structural crisis what global guidance did for cyclical problems in the late 1960s. The parallel has not worked out as Roth and his colleagues might have hoped. But the Young Socialist economists have kept the way open for a fundamental debate on economic planning in the 1980s. The debate has been kept open by two developments that reveal a growing strategic maturity on the part of the former Young Socialists now in the Bundestag.

First, within the SPD young party members like Roth managed to keep the lines of communication open to the unions for a Young Socialist-DGB alliance on behalf of structural councils and some other specific proposals. This is significant because the Young Socialists' general attempt to gain union support for direct investment guidance schemes failed at the Mannheim party congress in 1975. Party stalwarts like Herbert Ehrenberg (now labor minister) beat down the Young Socialists by appealing to trade union fears that investment guidance might mean wage controls and an outbreak of syndicalist rivalries. At the same time, however, the chemical workers union (IG Chemie) developed an interest in ad hoc branch committees to solve a concrete problem—overcapacity in the chemical fibers sector and a possible industry solution to that problem via cartelization, something that might have left the unions out in the cold. Initially, the largest DGB union (IG Metall) distrusted the idea of setting up structural councils in the form of branch committees. The DGB organization was also afraid that these branch councils might leave little room for union influence via codetermination at the level of the firm. However, IG Metall and IG Chemie patched up their differences by 1975, when IG Metall received assurances that structural policy would supplement codetermination, not replace it. Roth's committee built on this new problem-oriented consensus and made several proposals (some adopted at the SPD's 1977 congress in Hamburg) that avoided the controversial aspects of direct investment guidance.

Second, with respect to the SPD's liberal coalition partner, Roth has also learned how to establish distinctly Social Democratic positions within the limits set by coalition politics. He has entered Bonn's favorite game—posturing. Practitioners of posturing keep partisan options open by interpreting Social-Liberal compromises in a fashion that lets each party strike the pose on economic issues most compatible with its view of the liberal economic order. The Liberal Economics Ministry, for example, has interpreted the competitive structural policy research of the five economics institutes as a way of avoiding official pronouncements on structural trends, which ought to be determined by the market. Roth has used the same idea of scientific competition to attack the Council of Experts' monopoly on economic wisdom, and he has ridiculed the idea that money would be spent on research if the researchers' conclusions were not going to be used in some kind of government forecast. [45] It is entirely possible that this sort of posturing will degenerate into short-sighted squabbling as the Social-Liberal coalition tries to survive a third austerity crisis. Only the coming decade will tell whether the politics of structural policy will lead to genuine innovations in the design for steering the economy.

As of December 1981, the Schmidt government's response to West Germany's third stabilization crisis appears to fit the pattern of crisis management in the previous two recessions (1967 and 1975). The fiscal crisis that began soon after the reelection of the Social-Liberal coalition looks like a new round in West Germany's peculiar mixture of pre-Keynesian and mildly Keynesian economics. Early in 1981 the government committed itself to cutbacks in defense and social welfare spending. At the same time, Schmidt arranged to have the Kreditanstalt für Wiederaufbau (the West German arm of the old Marshall Plan) finance an investment program concentrating on energy conservation. The investment program, which included a project for "district heating" that had overtones of structural policy, was meant to reassure the Social Democratic constituency that an austerity-minded government in Bonn would not go the way of Thatcher and Reagan. By creating business orders for small construction firms, a Liberal clientele, the program also satisfied the Free Democrats.

By the end of 1981, the government was preparing more cutbacks and a Budgetary Structure Law (Haushaltsstrukturgesetz) similar in spirit to a measure from 1975. Yet, while the austerity budget of 1982 was being prepared, the government was under pressure to come up with a new recovery program. The major difference between 1981 and either 1975 or 1967 seems to be the longer time gap between cutbacks and spending. Previous governments managed to combine both sorts of measures in package deals that took less time to work out. This time the amount of leeway seems smaller and the strains of coalition politics seem greater than in the previous two austerity periods. The Christian Democrats have greater opportunities to woo the FDP away from its alliance with the SPD.

One interesting feature of the third stabilization crisis is the apparent nostalgia of Bonn's politicians for the days when Model Germany seemed to work. Such nostalgia is expressed with a great deal of rhetorical posturing. The Liberal economics minister, Count Lambsdorff, has urged the West Germans to work as hard as they did just after the war. Social Democrats like Wolfgang Roth (now economic spokesperson for the SPD parliamentary caucus) have countered that the spirit of postwar reconstruction would be incomplete if it did not include a great deal of investment guidance by such agencies as the Kreditanstalt für Wiederaufbau. Thus far, verbal exchanges such as these, hard coalition bargaining, and short-term political considerations have prevailed in the absence of long-term, strategic perspectives on West Germany's economic future. A serious debate on the role of the state in the economy seems unlikely as long as the Schmidt government cautiously tests the uncertain new climate of economic decline and international tension. The 1980s may, therefore, offer the first real test of Model Germany without a serious new examination of the model's fundamental strengths and weaknesses.

NOTES

1. Karl Marx, "Capital, Volume One," in The Marx-Engels Reader, ed. Robert C. Tucker, 2d ed. (New York: W. W. Norton, 1978), p. 302.

2. Michael Bolle, "Magisches Mehreck," in Wörterbuch zur politischen Ökonomie, ed. Gert von Eynern and Carl Böhret, 2d ed. (Opladen: Westdeutscher Verlag, 1977), pp. 272-76.

3. Herbert Stein, The Fiscal Revolution in America (Chicago: University of Chicago Press, 1969), p. 138.

4. Hajo Riese, Wohlfahrt und Wirtschaftspolitik (Reinbek: Rowohlt, 1975). Riese wrote that the fixed-target model is "a model that is inappropriate because it generalizes the Keynesian full employment model in an inadmissable manner."

5. Michael Bolle, "Vollbeschäftigung: Theorie und Politik," in Arbeitsmarkttheorie und Arbeitsmarktpolitik, ed. Michael Bolle (Opladen: Leske, 1976), p. 29.

6. See Gernot Müller, Ulrich Rödel, Charles Sabel, Frank Stille, and Winfried Vogt, Ökonomische Krisentendenzen im gegenwärtigen Kapitalismus (Frankfurt am Main: Campus, 1978).

7. Wassily Leontief, "The Significance of Marxian Economics for Present Day Economic Theory," in Marx and Modern Economics (New York and London: MacGibbon and Kee, 1968), p. 98.

8. Müller et al., Ökonomische Krisentendenzen, pp. 15, 17.

9. Marx, "Capital, Volume One," pp. 295-96.

10. Bolle, "Vollbeschäftigung," p. 28; and Hajo Riese, "Ordnungsidee und Ordnungspolitik: Kritik einer wirtschaftspolitischen Konzeption," Kyklos 25 (1972): 24-48.

11. See Gudrun Lindner, "Die Krise als Steuerungsmittel: Eine Analyse der Bundesbankpolitik in den Jahren 1964-66/67," Leviathan 3 (1973): 342-81.

12. Erhard Blankenburg, Günther Schmid, and Hubert Treiber, "Von der reaktiven zur aktiven Politik? Darstellung und Kritik des Policy Science-Ansatzes," in Handlungsspielräume der Staatsadministration, ed. Peter Grottian and Axel Murswieck (Hamburg: Hoffman und Campe, 1974), pp. 37-51.

13. Hans Möller, "Die westdeutsche Währungsreform von 1948," in Währung und Wirtschaft in Deutschland 1876-1975, ed. Deutsche Bundesbank (Frankfurt am Main: Fritz Knapp, 1976), p. 453.

14. John Tagliabue, "Bonn Fiscal Policy Reviewed," New York Times, August 4, 1981, p. D1.

15. Dietrich Dickertmann, Die Finanzierung von Eventualhaushalten durch Notenbankkredit—Erfahrungen aus der Rezessionsbekämpfung des Jahres 1967 (Berlin: Duncker und Humblot, 1972).

16. Karl-Heinrich Hansmeyer, Der öffentliche Kredit, 2d ed. (Frankfurt am Main: Fritz Knapp, 1970), pp. 55, 69.

17. The Landesbank Girozentrale should not be confused with the Landeszentralbank. The former is a regional clearinghouse for the savings banks; the latter is a regional member of the federal reserve system.

18. On this subject, see Ulrich Jürgens and Gudrun Lindner, "Zur Funktion und Macht der Banken," Kursbuch 36 (June 1974): 121-60; see also Wilhelm Hankel, "Über die sogenannte Macht der Banken (I and II)," in Wettbewerb und Sparerschutz im Kreditgewerbe: Perspektiven für eine moderne Bankpolitik, ed. Wilhelm Hankel (Stuttgart: W. Kohlhammer, 1974), pp. 13-45.

19. Douglas Anderson, Germany (B): The Uncertain Stride of a Reluctant Giant (Boston: President and Fellows of Harvard College, 1980), p. 15.

20. Ibid.
21. Wilhelm Hankel, Der Ausweg aus der Krise (Düsseldorf: Econ, 1975), pp. 122-24; see also Hajo Riese, "Strukturwandel und unterbewertete Währung in der Bundesrepublik Deutschland," Konjunkturpolitik 24 (1978): 160. Riese points out that the release of the DM's exchange rate in the early 1970s did not constitute a break with mercantilistic policies.
22. See Schmidt's address to the Bundestag on September 17, 1975, "Erklärung der Bundesregierung zur Finanz- und Konjunkturpolitik," ed. Presse- und Informationsamt der Bundesregierung, Bulletin, no. 114 (September 18, 1975), pp. 1117-28.
23. Hankel, Ausweg, pp. 117-18; see also Hans-Eckart Scharrer, "Die Rolle der Banken," in Handbuch der deutschen Aussenpolitik, ed. Hans-Peter Schwarz (Munich: Piper, 1975), p. 221.
24. Heinz-Günter Kemmer, "Das kleinere Übel: Finanzierungstricks sollen das Erdgasgeschäft mit den Sowjets retten," Die Zeit, August 7, 1981, p. 12.
25. William E. Leuchtenberg, The Perils of Prosperity, 1914-1932 (Chicago: University of Chicago Press, 1958).
26. Marianne Welteke, Theorie und Praxis der sozialen Marktwirtschaft: Einführung in die politische Ökonomie der BRD (Frankfurt am Main: Campus, 1976), p. 113.
27. Ibid., p. 114.
28. Hajo Riese, "Theoretische Grundlagen stabilitätspolitischer Kontroversen," Kyklos 32 (1979): 226.
29. Ibid., p. 225.
30. Ibid., p. 229.
31. Ibid., p. 235.
32. Sachverständigenrat zur Begutachtung der gesamtwirtschaftlichen Entwicklung, Stabilität im Wachstum (Stuttgart: Kohlhammer, 1967), sec. 486.
33. Sachverständigenrat, Expansion und Stabilität (Stuttgart: Kohlhammer, 1966), sec. 285.
34. Ibid.
35. Ibid.
36. Ibid.
37. F. G. Reuss, Fiscal Policy for Growth without Inflation: The German Experiment (Baltimore: Johns Hopkins University Press, 1963).
38. Jörg Huffschmid, Die Politik des Kapitals: Konzentration und Wirtschaftspolitik in der Bundesrepublik (Frankfurt am Main: Suhrkamp, 1969), pp. 111-21.
39. But for a stimulating skeptical view about these "paradigm shifts" in economic policy, see Heinz-Peter Spahn, Die Stabilitätspolitik des Sachverständigenrates (Frankfurt am Main: Campus, 1979).

40. Sigmund Freud, New Introductory Lectures on Psychoanaly-sis (New York: W. W. Norton, 1965), p. 75.

41. Ibid., p. 80.

42. The term neoconservative is used here in the same way that Peter Steinfels employs it in The Neoconservatives (New York: Simon and Schuster, 1979)—as a disillusioned liberal.

43. See Schiller's speech before the Bundestag on September 14, 1966, reprinted in Im Deutschen Bundestag—Wirtschaftspolitik, ed. Otto Graf Lambsdorff, vol. 2 (Bonn: Bertelsmann/az studio, 1974), p. 26.

44. Ibid., pp. 26-27.

45. See Wolfgang Roth, "Strukturpolitik zwischen Notwendigkeit und Möglichkeit," in Wirtschaftspolitik kontrovers, ed. Diethard B. Simmert (Cologne: Bund, 1980), pp. 441-42.

5

MODELL DEUTSCHLAND AND THE INTERNATIONAL REGIONALIZATION OF THE WEST GERMAN STATE IN THE 1970s

CARL F. LANKOWSKI

WEST GERMAN EXPORT
STRATEGY AND WESTERN EUROPE

By now it is commonplace that the remarkable degree of social cohesion prevailing in West Germany throughout most of the postwar period is attributable in large part to the high rates of economic growth enjoyed by that country. Perhaps slighly less well known is the increasing contribution of West German industry's export performance to this impressive record of expansion. The recent, excellent work of Frieder Schlupp, Christian Deubner, and Udo Rehfeldt[1] documents in explicit detail how West Germany's export position in key manufacturing sectors, but above all in machinery and machine tools, was extended in the 1970s. The statistics compiled by these authors reveal a hypertrophic share of manufacturing in gross national product (GNP) compared with other advanced capitalist countries, measured at over 40 percent in 1973 (at current prices), which corresponds to a steadily rising share of foreign trade in the GNP, starting at 8.5 percent (imports = 11.5 percent) in 1950 and reaching 22.8 percent (imports = 19.8 percent) in 1976. Comparable figures for 1980 show that exports accounted for 23.3 percent (imports = 22.7 percent). West German manufacturers of capital goods exported an average of 43.8 percent of their production each year between 1972 and 1976. The comparable figure for basic materials and production goods is 40.2 percent; for consumption goods, 23.7 percent. The centrality

---

The arguments presented in this chapter are developed at length in the author's Ph.D. dissertation, "Germany and the European Community: Anatomy of a Hegemonial Relation" (Columbia University, 1981).

of the West German capital goods industry is underlined by the fact that in 1976 the foreign sales of this sector accounted for 54. 0 percent of total West German export value. Of this sector, electrical and non-electrical machinery and automobiles alone accounted for 43. 5 percent of total West German export value in 1976. Some idea of the competitiveness of West German producers in this area is given by data on world market shares. Although West Germans produced only 12. 5 percent of nonelectrical machinery in 1976, they exported 23. 2 percent of total exports in that industry in that year. This compares with 36. 5 percent of world production and 24. 6 percent of world exports. For Japan the figures were 11. 0 percent and 7. 7 percent, respectively. From these figures one must conclude that West Germany's political formula cannot be considered in isolation from its foreign trade position.

As interesting as the magnitudes just cited is the regional destination of West German production. In 1970, 83. 6 percent of West German exports went to developed capitalist countries. Over 40 percent went to the European Community (the Benelux, Italy, and France). Six years later, 76. 6 percent of West German foreign trade went to the developed capitalist countries and 45. 7 percent to the European Community (enlarged by the inclusion of the United Kingdom, Denmark, and Ireland). Of the members of the enlarged European Community (EC), the Federal Republic of Germany (FRG) was the number one exporter to six (seven if one includes Greece, which became a member in 1981) and ranked as second largest exporter to the United Kingdom and third largest to Ireland in 1975. Referring again to nonelectrical machinery exports, the data show that West Germany was the first rank exporter to Western Europe and Eastern Europe in 1976. It was the second rank exporter to the United States, Japan, Latin America, and Africa; third rank to Canada and Asia. Given the fact that 42 percent of all nonelectrical machinery exports in 1976 went to Western Europe, it is clear that the basis of West Germany's capacity to penetrate other areas is contingent upon its ability to hold onto its market share in Western Europe.

Holding market shares in key industries became problematic for West German industrialists in the 1970s. Not only did labor costs in the metalworking industries rise rapidly after 1968, but a major premise of West German export success (the Bretton Woods fixed-rate international monetary system) came undone. The latter occurrence, in particular, threatened the West German export industry in its own heartland, Western Europe.

The unusually widespread and intense wave of strike activity in West Germany's metalworking industries in the autumn of 1969 launched a period of rank-and-file labor militancy that coincided with the apogee of postwar, worldwide capitalist expansion. As a result, workers were able to increase the ratio of wages to national income. West Germany's captains of industry responded with a wave of investment designed to raise labor productivity while simultaneously reorganizing the labor process and lessening the need for labor itself. The key machine-tools and capital-goods industries, along with the electronics, automobile, and chemical industries, also rapidly expanded their overseas production and marketing operations and increased the numbers of <u>Gastarbeiter</u> ("foreign workers") in their work forces. In this situation, the Social Democratic party (SPD) and trade union strategists' chief task was the maintenance of high levels of employment. From this point of view, the heterogeneous reform program initiated by the coalition government between the SPD and the Free Democratic party (FDP) in October 1969 can be interpreted as a way of taking pressure off wages by offering the working class compensation through public spending and institutional innovation in the form of extending worker participation at the point of production. [2] This strategy resulted in a substantial expansion of West Germany's public sector "social budget" before the economic recession of mid-decade. The West German Ministry of Economics places the magnitude of social expenditure at 24.6 percent of German GNP in 1965, 25.7 percent in 1970, and 27.4 percent in 1973. [3]

From October 1969 to June 1972, the government's macroeconomic policy was aimed at improving the production costs picture of the West German export industry by attacking inflationary pressures with monetary policy. Since West Germany's balance-of-payments position forbade a policy of high interest rates, deutsche mark (DM) appreciation against other currencies was proposed and, in fact, carried out. The strategy to reorient demand to the domestic market was finally abandoned when it came under attack from both the Confederation of German Industry (BDI) and the left wing of the SPD. Elements of the latter had proposed deliberate job creation through some sort of investment planning as the necessary flank of the policy of demand reorientation. However, the minister of economics and finance at this time refused to countenance the increase in public spending that this plan arguably implied, consistent with his position on inflation. Meanwhile, industrial capitalists argued through the BDI that the main effect of DM revaluations was not cheaper production costs (through a reduction of "imported inflation") but arbitrarily higher prices for West German products on world markets. The only option that remained for a government and trade union leadership that desired to maintain employment levels overall, therefore, consisted in consolidating and expanding the export sector. Recognition of this fact led quickly to a fundamental reconceptualization of the government's accumulation strategy and the installation of a new minister of economics and finance in July 1972. In light of Helmut Schmidt's continual preoccupation with inflation, only the assumption of such a reconceptualization allows one to make sense of his remark during this period that "5 percent inflation is better than 5 percent unemployment."

Essentially, the strategy developed in the summer of 1972 reversed Minister Schiller's policy of insulating the West German economy from liquidity effects of rapidly expanding economies in Europe and elsewhere and rather took as its basic premise appeasement of the West German export industry's demand for stable rates of exchange between the DM and other currencies. This was the only guarantee that West German exports would not be priced out of the market, and hence, was the best protection against displacement of West German production abroad. Further insinuation of West German production in the world market offered the government the hope of continued growth, which could provide the fiscal means for realizing the domestic reform program.

The leading difficulty with this strategy consisted in the divergent rates of inflation among the economies of the EC. Fixed exchange rates among EC countries implied imported inflation for West Germany, since its inflation rate was consistently on the lower end of the EC inflation spectrum. This situation may not have been problematic for West German exports to EC countries, but since the majority of West German exports were absorbed outside of the EC, some way had to be found to fix rates of exchange at low rates of inflation. I will argue that West Germany's program for a zone of "stability and growth in Europe" in the 1970s made the SPD/FDP government the steward of a planned capitalist crisis orchestrated at the regional level. The aim of this induced crisis of the mid-1970s was nothing other than the creation of the conditions of existence for West Germany's accumulation strategy, and its main target was the social wage (wages, fringe, and public-sector spending directly benefiting the working class) in other EC countries. The strategy was implemented by reorganization of international monetary relations and refocusing these relations on Europe, as well as through the orchestration of pressure on wages at the regional level, operating directly through EC member states' trade union organizations. It was carried out both by promising substantial financial support for compliance and by a series of vetoes over counterproposals inconsistent with West German strategy. Insofar as this strategy was orchestrated through the institutions of the EC and insofar as its unfolding accounts for most of the programmatic development of the EC in the 1970s, one cannot escape the conclusion that Modell Deutschland is inextricably bound up with the regional extension of the West German state.

CRISIS MANAGEMENT FROM THE
ECONOMIC AND MONETARY UNION TO
THE EUROPEAN MONETARY SYSTEM

A general transformation of production, trade, and monetary
relations in the capitalist world economy shaped the political landscape within which the Economic and Monetary Union (EMU) was
placed on the EC agenda. Starting as a dialogue over maintenance of
the EC customs union in a period of foreign exchange disruptions,
the EMU talks soon became the focus of deliberations over the future
of the EC in general. As it turned out, this dialogue was refracted
through the prism of nationally defined interests and ultimately provided a cover for mechanisms that served the interest of West German economic dominance in the region.

Following the Hague Summit Conference of December 1969,
the EC Commission presented a memorandum to the EC Council of
Ministers outlining a three-stage plan for the establishment of organs
for the purpose of defining and implementing a coherent economic
policy at EC level by 1980. This document led to a series of negotiations between economics and finance ministers, which quickly revealed a major difference of opinion on how to proceed. The French
government, eager to protect the Common Agricultural Policy (CAP)
and to undermine the privileged position of the U.S. dollar in the
Bretton Woods international monetary order, desired the immediate
establishment of an intra-European monetary regime featuring fixed
rates of exchange among EC currencies. The West German government, wary of any commitment that might result in inflationary finance communicating itself to West Germany, argued that the introduction of fixed rates along with unlimited support by EC institutions
drawing on national reserves could only come at the end of a period
of economic adjustments between countries. The compromise worked
out in February 1971 favored the French position in that EC monetary
authorities were invited to collaborate immediately to maintain the
rates of exchange between their currencies within a margin of 2.5
percent around a central rate defined by the U.S. dollar value expressed in gold. If the plan worked, at the end of three years a European Monetary Cooperation Fund would be established as the embryo
of a system of pooled reserves and unlimited rate support. The final
stage in this progression would be the creation of a European central
bank and other instruments of economic policy coordination. In return
for its willingness to embark on the first stage of this experiment,
the West German government obtained an important concession. The
principle of "parallelism" between progress in monetary policy and
progress in "real" adjustments through control over public spending
and incomes policies was to be observed. The West German govern-

ment was particularly eager to avoid adjusting the West German economy to economies exhibiting a higher level of inflation. To underline this concern, the West German government also obtained an escape clause, which authorized the discontinuation of the entire EMU effort if the principle of parallelism were not observed.

The willingness of the West German government to allow this scheme to be launched despite the strong resistance of the Economics and Finance Ministry is indicative of the degree to which West German EC policy at that time derived from considerations having little to do with macroeconomic stabilization policy. EC policy during the first Brandt-Scheel government was dominated by ardent courtship of the French government, the support of which was a sine qua non of the coalition's Ostpolitik. An additional, although distinctly secondary, element of West Germany's position was the appointment of a few committed European "federalists" to key posts in the upper echelons of the government, including the chancellory. As might be expected, the consequence of the coexistence of such opposing positions in the West German government was a reactive and, to some extent, incoherent EC policy. This situation was to characterize West German EC policy until the summer of 1972, at which point a major change in EC policy was introduced.

Less than three months after the initial decision to bind intra-EC exchange rates, the West German government floated the DM in the face of large speculative inflows of dollars. This measure was soundly criticized by the French government, which demanded dollar adjustment within the fixed-rate framework. However, in August 1971 U.S. authorities unilaterally abandoned the monetary system they had called into existence in 1944 by announcing the suspension of gold-dollar convertibility between national monetary authorities and ceased to defend the exchange value of the dollar against other currencies. A modified fixed-rate system was introduced in December 1971 when agreement was reached to widen the margin of fluctuation of currency rates around the dollar to 4.5 percent. In addition, the dollar was devalued against gold, and several other major currencies were slightly revalued.

It was within this transitional monetary framework that the EC monetary experiment was finally launched in February 1972. The EC Council of Ministers invited the member states' central banks to manage their currencies so that their market value would not deviate more than 2.25 percent on either side of the central rate. This the banks were able to do until June, when continued strong export performance in West Germany attracted another wave of speculation in favor of the DM. Confronting the choices of imposing capital controls or revaluing the DM, the minister of economics and finance argued for revaluation. However, the Bundesbank sided with the Foreign

Office and the West German export industry in arguing for controls; not only would exports be damaged by continual DM appreciation, but West Germany would also lose what influence its government had over French economic policy. The chancellor, facing the erosion of the government's Bundestag majority over his policy of normalizing relations with Eastern Europe, needed French support for Ostpolitik to undermine domestic opposition. Hence, capital controls were adopted and a cabinet reshuffle resulted in the installation of a new minister of economics and finance.

In retrospect, the events described above were the occasion for a fundamental reversal of Bonn's tactics in the EC. Instead of maintaining a basically defensive posture vis-à-vis the EMU discussions and monetary cooperation in particular, the government would offer monetary cooperation as a reward for policy adjustments, which would close the gap between monetary developments in EC member states. West German economic performance would provide the point of reference for the adjustment process.

For this approach to work, however, the remnants of the dollar-led system of international monetary relations had to be broken, for it was the overvalued dollar that was identified as the main source of inflation in Europe. The dissolution of the Smithsonian Agreement, which extended the life of the Bretton Woods system by allowing more rate flexibility, was perceived to be the prerequisite for attracting EC governments to follow West Germany in establishing a European "zone of stability and growth." Since it was no longer in the interests of the U.S. government to support the Smithsonian Agreement either, West Germany and the United States were able to bring about its demise. In the context of U.S. "benign neglect" of the international dollar rate, West Germany had only to engineer a sudden improvement of its trade balance to precipitate another massive wave of speculation that could be mobilized as the pretext to bring the system down. This result was accomplished with the introduction of fiscal austerity in West Germany in the autumn and winter of 1972/73. The predictable speculative movements occurred in February and March 1973. The exchanges were closed in Europe, and when they reopened, they did so in the context of a de facto system of freely floating exchange rates. However, the genius of West German diplomacy is expressed in the fact that the onus for the transition to floating was made to rest on the U.S. administration instead of on West Germany. Thus was the French government out-maneuvered on the monetary front.

The main condition for effecting a general realignment of economic policies around West German priorities within the legitimizing rubric of EC institutional development was then assured. The Bundesbank and the West German government pursued tactics that would consolidate the export position of West German industry. The bank, freed for the first time from the necessity of maintaining rate parity with the dollar, pursued a monetary policy designed to absorb purchasing power, which had appeared as a result of the recent dollar inflows. At the same time, taxes were raised, mortgage subsidies were cut, and other forms of fiscal retrenchment were introduced. Given the political significance of the reform program announced in 1969, these measures could only have been pursued by virtue of the unusually close relationship between the West German trade union movement and the government. Trade union leaders had to be convinced that these measures would ensure that the foreign competitiveness of West German exports would be enhanced, ultimately providing the fiscal base for future reform spending and full employment.

The other side of this tactic was the strong deutsche mark. A strong DM was perceived as a decided advantage, insofar as the raw materials West German industrialists imported for fabrication and export would be cheaper for them than for industrialists operating elsewhere. But the expensive DM was only an attractive goal of policy to the extent that West Germany's foreign customers could afford West German products. Specifically, an expensive DM helped West German exports outside of the EC more than it hurt them, since the cost of raw materials to West German producers fell by a greater rate than the rate of price increase implicit in DM appreciation. Within the EC, West German authorities were impelled, therefore, to induce a maximum number of states to manage their currencies in a stable relationship to the DM. Importers in countries with depreciating currencies would find it difficult to maintain imports from West Germany. It was particularly important to attempt to stabilize exchange rates with the larger EC member states. If that could be accomplished, the others would be pulled along in their wake, since the costs of remaining outside of the system of stable rates would be even greater than the costs of managing currencies at high rates of exchange. At least the latter option carried with it the possibility of continual negotiation with West German authorities over the actual operation of the system. In any event, the trick for West German tacticians was to define a level for the DM that was high enough to preserve the cost effects mentioned above while at the same time low enough to induce other EC states to adhere to stable rates.

On the other hand, there were good reasons why governments of other EC states would feel compelled to follow West Germany's lead. First, a sizable portion of EC countries' imports from West Germany were investment goods. A stable relationship to the DM would thereby improve the investment climate, or at least not establish a further roadblock to investment. Increasingly intense international competition among producers of consumer goods made investment for rationalization an urgent priority in Europe. Second, adherence to the West German scheme carried the promise of balance-of-payments support and short-term support operations carried out by the Bundesbank, a not inconsiderable matter in light of the enormous resources at its disposal following an uninterrupted series of trade surpluses since 1951. Finally, an important inducement to close ranks behind the West German tactic was the appreciation EC currencies would experience against the dollar. Within limits, this was advantageous to European governments, since it implied cheaper raw material and energy costs for manufacturers in these countries, too. This was a consideration of great importance following the quadrupling of the price of crude oil between October 1973 and January 1974.

If successful these arrangements would make the West German state the mediator of European capital vis-à-vis the other major centers of state power in international capitalism, the United States and Japan. The EC as a whole would strengthen its position as a net exporter of commodities with high value-added content, namely, sophisticated semifinished and finished manufactures. Meanwhile, the goal of West German policy consisted in ensuring continued West German preeminence in capital goods. It was presumed that the scope for establishing stable worldwide trading rules would be increased, thus favoring a continuation of West German postwar economic penetration of Latin America, Southeast Asia, and Africa. If such a pattern could be sustained, the fabric of a solution to incipient conflicts between the EC, United States, and Japanese "influence zones" over trade and investment could emerge. [4]

The success of this ambitious program required prior tactical success with West Germany's EC partners, however. West German support for conservative governments in France, Italy, and the United Kingdom was premised on adoption of domestic policies synchronized with the West German "game plan." In using the recently contrived, embryonic EC monetary system as a cover for demanding that the other EC governments adopt policies that would adjust their economic performance to that of West Germany, the West German government was actually asking for the initiation of austerity policies throughout Europe. Governments were being asked, in effect, to prevent the expansion of spending on consumer goods from abroad within the context of free trade. The only way to accomplish this was to rein in purchasing power through increased taxation and/or by maintaining relentless pressure on wages as well as by paring down public spending. Under these circumstances, the West German government was willing to support the external value of the currencies of its EC partners with its enormous foreign exchange and gold reserves. In so doing, Bonn was inducing an economic crisis in the EC area and setting itself up as the International Monetary Fund of Europe. This would become clear in the aftermath of the international monetary disruptions of February and March 1973.

Wrapping itself in the cloak of the champion of European integration, the West German government proposed a joint float of EC currencies against the dollar in March 1973. This proposal was accepted by all but the British and Irish governments. The international monetary system that resulted has been sustained with occasional modifications up to the present time. Overall, however, such modifications as have been carried out are easily interpreted as tactical adjustments fully in conformity with the requirements of West Germany's export strategy. In general, the stabilization policies of other EC member states was geared to West German priorities. When the Bundesbank brought about a severe contraction in the domestic money supply in the months immediately following the constitution of the "snake," as this West German-led regional monetary system was called, other snake members were compelled to do likewise. Those that did were forced to arrest public spending and resist demands for wage increases, as well as raise taxes. Those that did not found that their steadily depreciating currencies placed severe limits on imports of necessary commodities. Italy and Denmark finally were compelled to appeal to the EC Council of Ministers for balance-of-payments support loans to check the dramatic increases in import prices—above all, but not limited to, fuel oil—caused by their depreciating currencies. Owing to the growing strength of the Italian Communist party, the Italian government dared not assume direct responsibility for imposing austerity measures. It therefore shifted the responsibility to the EC Council of Ministers by imposing trade restrictions in clear contradiction to the Rome Treaty. The council promised sizable balance-of-payments support in return for finding an alternative to import controls. West Germany provided the lion's share of the EC loan and advanced substantial additional funds on a bilateral basis some months later. Under cover of the EC, the Italian government then revoked its trade controls and mandated cuts in public spending and increased taxation.[5]

The key country for the success of the West German monetary tactic was France. As the largest economy next to West Germany's in the EC, French participation would make it much easier for other member states to participate. Hence, West Germany's task was to determine a level for the DM that was low enough to attract the French government while still dear enough to achieve the main aims of the tactic. In early 1974, the force of West Germany's domestic austerity program had strengthened the DM to the point where the French government faced serious political trouble in France if it adhered to the scheme, despite the West German offer of generous support operations from the Bundesbank. Less than two years after the conclusion of the historic "union of the Left," which allied the French Communist party with the Socialist party, the death of President Pompidou forced a presidential election in May 1974. Facing a unified Left, the Gaullist government could not afford to risk increases in unemployment through the introduction of austerity measures implied by the requirement to maintain franc-DM parity in the snake. The franc did rejoin the system under the austerity government of Gaullist Jacques Chirac and his minister of trade, Raymond Barre, who, in fact, was soon to replace Chirac.[6] In recognition of the closeness of the 1974 French presidential election (Mitterrand lost by less than 1 percent of the vote), when it was time to prepare for another election—this time for the National Assembly—the French government again cut the franc free from the EC currency snake.

Member states did attempt to change the shape of the monetary serpent by altering the conditions of adhesion but without effect until 1978. Upon French reentry in July 1975, the government requested a modification of snake guidelines, which would have enabled currencies to vary more against one another, but the request was denied.

The snake was eventually modified under the impact of a precipitous and erratic decline in the dollar in 1977-78, subsequent to the Carter administration's reflation program. A series of high-level delegations from Washington did nothing to dissuade Bonn from joining the reflation party, even when the matter was forcefully raised by the U.S. delegation at two successive trilateral summit meetings in London (May 1977) and Bonn (July 1978). Instead, the Europeans lined up behind the West German government in demanding that the United States commit itself to lowering its imports of oil and developing other, domestic energy sources, disingenuously sidestepping the fact that a major source of the U.S. trade deficit was declining market shares in key industries, such as machine tools. In this respect it would appear as if the increasing specialization of production, which was the premise of Bonn's official vision of world economic harmony, had already approached its limits.

The effect of U.S. policy upon the European economies was critical. Not only did the dollar's gyrations upset calculations for industrialists between Europe and the dollar area, thus undermining a key function of money (facilitation of commodity circulation), but its continual depreciation placed tremendous pressure on members of the Organization of Petroleum Exporting Countries (OPEC) to raise the price of oil in anticipation of still further erosion of the international value of the dollar. The French conservative government explicitly laid the blame for the failure of its stabilization program (and its eventual defeat at the polls by the socialists in 1981) to the resulting "second oil shock."

The European reaction to this situation was to modify the snake regulations sufficiently to permit participation by the Italian and Irish governments. Whereas, the Italian government had, like France, formally participated in the snake at an earlier time, the Irish government had not and undertook to sever the longstanding formal link between the Irish and British currencies in order to become a member. This move was necessitated by the fact that the British government found it politically impossible to accede to the scheme, so negative a symbol had the EC become in the United Kingdom. However, the Thatcher government did indicate that it would undertake to manage the pound sterling as if it were a member.

In addition to forming a two-tiered structure, wherein weaker currencies were permitted a wider band of fluctuation than stronger currencies, the European Monetary System (EMS), launched officially in March 1979, created a deeper common reserve pool than that which was established with the creation of the European Fund for Monetary Cooperation in 1974. Moreover, a substantial gold component was included in the reserve fund, and intervention rules were proposed so as to retard the expansion of the deutsche mark as an international reserve currency.[7] West German monetary authorities have expressed the belief that such a process could undermine West Germany's tactical flexibility in economic policy, drawing lessons from both the United Kingdom and the United States.

It is important to point out, however, that the main lines of West Germany's monetary tactic, generated by the necessity to preserve the coherence of the EC customs union, remain intact. West German flexibility has not been significantly affected. It is symptomatic of West Germany's role in the system that in 1981 it vetoed the transition to a common reserve fund authorized to grant unlimited support to EC member states. Neither in 1974 nor in 1981 was the position of the Bundesbank affected by irreversible commitments of any sort. In this case, then, it appears that EC programmatic development is an expression of West German dominance at the regional level.

TRIPARTITISM: EUROPEAN CONCERTED ACTION

Lest it be thought that the EC was a tabula rasa for West German authorities to write on, it is useful to point out that other alternative policies were at least partially articulated in EC arenas, although they were outmanuevered by West German statecraft and overwhelmed by West German resources. Nevertheless, the existence of alternatives does suggest points of resistance to West German hegemony.

This situation becomes clear if we briefly examine another area of EC institutional innovation in the 1970s, which, at the end of the day, was molded to conform to West German designs. The initiation of tripartite meetings of representatives of trade union organizations, confederations of industry, and government officials was a response to the recognition that medium-term planning in the EC was a dead letter unless and until the trade unions were involved and some sort of incomes policy at EC level could be worked out. In order to get trade union participation, however, unions had to be assured that any discussion of incomes would include income to capital as well as wages. The timing and the substance of the tripartites, however, strongly suggest that this participation was managed with great finesse and to good effect, at least from the point of view of West Germany's accumulation strategy.

To win trade union confidence for the project, a study group on inflation was constituted in 1974 by the commission. Its members had a decidedly socialist/social-democratic cast. It happened that the group completed its report in the period just preceding the first tripartite conference (November 1975). Coming at that moment, and from the pens of individuals respected in the trade union movement, one might have thought that the commission would ensure the widest possible circulation of the document on which it pinned so much hope and that the agenda of the Tripartite would reflect its views.

This was not to be the case. The reasons are amply clear from the documents. [8] The study group found, inter alia, that the root of inflation is not primarily wages but, rather, the current structure of industry itself. Inflation was primarily attributable to the monopolistic position of firms and exacerbated by the multinationalization of production. Thus, if inflation were truly the major target of economic policy, then government would have to devise ways of monitoring pricing and investment decisions of large multinational firms. The next step would be to direct the state to intervene in order to channel investment where it was socially useful. That would require the establishment of political authorities requisite to that purpose—something like a general planning organ possessing effective powers.

It was not exactly a conspiracy of silence that greeted the Maldague Report, as it was called. The report was the object rather of aggressive suppression. At the height of the European economic crisis in 1975-76, the widespread circulation of such a document could only spell trouble for the orchestration of an EC-wide monetarist tactic. The commission did its part by taking two unusual steps. For the first time in anyone's memory in commission circles, the completed report was not unveiled at a press conference organized by the commission. Moreover, for the first time, the commission specifically repudiated the contents of the report in a new-fangled disclaimer attached to the document. Finally, the commission kept the document internal (that is, classified) until just prior to the convocation of the June 1976 Tripartite (it is dated March 3, 1976).

The unions did their part, too. There was little discussion of the report, despite its leakage to the press through Agenor, a Left-leaning periodical published in Brussels. The stenographic report of the European Trade Union Confederation (ETUC) congress, whose major business was to prepare for the Tripartite conference (in April 1976), does show signs of Maldague language, but ETUC intervention at the Tripartite conference itself is devoid of traces of the Maldague arguments.

Instead, what emerged at the June 1976 meeting was a declaration that cited unemployment and inflation as the two policy concerns of the moment. Unemployment was to be taken care of by "coordinated growth." But that growth had to be carefully orchestrated so that inflationary pressures might be contained. Targets were established for unemployment and inflation: national governments undertook to reduce inflation to below the 5 percent level by 1980 and unemployment to below 5 percent of the labor force by the same date. The document suggested no means to realize these goals. This, however, is understandable in light of West Germany's orchestration of economic policy, which has already been discussed.

One might question how deliberate the outcome of this crucial Tripartite was. Interviewing in EC circles has disclosed that the Maldague Report's suppression was at least discussed at the highest levels of West German government. Circumstances of EC staffing suggest a link, since the commissioner in charge of Tripartite preparation at the time, Wilhelm Haferkamp, is an old SPD trade union man appointed by the SPD government in the 1960s to his position in Brussels. It would have been Haferkamp's responsibility to decide on the publication of the report and on the usual press conference. Second, the ETUC was chaired by the Federation of German Trade Unions (DGB) chairman, Heinz Oskar Vetter. It would have been up to Vetter to make something of the Maldague arguments in the Tripartite meeting. He did not (although he had to be aware of the report's contents, since the director of the DGB research institute was the West German delegate to the group). Finally, the author of the Tripartite declaration was a West German SPD commission appointee. In light of the close relations between the West German government and the DGB, it seems highly improbable that the agenda of the Tripartite was not cleverly manipulated to achieve the result desired by the West German delegation, namely, fortification of the policy already being pursued under West German aegis in the EC rubric.

What can be said about the result of this episode? The effects are probably several. In the first place, the Tripartite was never in-

tended to resolve anything. It rather seems quite clear that its purpose was to transmit information about a matter that was already resolved. The audience for this message was quite clearly the working
class through its leaders. In passing it should be noted that one of
the significant coups of the 1976 Tripartite is that it was attended by
both the Italian General Confederation of Labor (CGIL) (which had
just recently joined the ETUC) and the French General Confederation
of Labor (CGT) (although the CGT representatives reportedly left
early).

A second notable aspect of the political process surrounding the
Tripartite is the intensive and detailed coordination of the West German delegation acting as a single team with a single purpose.

The third interesting aspect was the format itself. Is it not
ironic that the one institutional innovation in the EC that appears to
depart from the national patterns discussed above is a direct import
from West Germany? West German government officials, trade
unionists, and industrialists were meeting regularly between 1967
and 1977 in precisely this format (the "concerted action") and with
the same intentions and results. The irony of ironies here consists
in the fact that at the very moment that this West German import had
been introduced at EC level, the DGB had decided to withdraw its representatives from the one back home because of the constitutional
challenge to the extension of the West German codetermination law
just passed in the West German legislature, lodged by the German
Employers Association, in the person of Hanns Martin Schleyer.

BREAKTHROUGH IN NORTH-SOUTH RELATIONS

The significance of the EC as an arena in which West German
authorities could orchestrate an economic policy reflecting West German interests also extends to relations with the Third World. After
the oil boycott organized by OPEC in October 1973, a diplomatic offensive to establish institutions for the purpose of redistributing wealth
among the advanced capitalist and developing countries (without, however, implying major changes in the capitalist logic governing the
creation of that wealth) was launched by leaders of the Third World.
Of all the specific proposals that ultimately were brought forth in the
UN system, the one that most directly impinged on West Germany's
accumulation strategy was the so-called Corea Plan, the United Nations Conference on Trade and Development's (UNCTAD's) proposal
for an integrated commodity price support scheme. The essential
principle of the Corea Plan consisted in following the example of
OPEC by significantly raising the prices of basic agricultural and mining products in order to increase revenues to Third World countries.

Any such scheme would require significant control over supplies and would have established the precedent for widening the scope of the application of its operations. [9] The Corea Plan threatened to circumvent West Germany's policy of low prices for raw materials, perceived as a prerequisite for continued export success. On the other hand, since the developing countries were, taken as a whole, substantial importers of West German manufactures, West German diplomats were loath to confront Third World leaders directly over this and other related issues.

The resolution of this dilemma came out of negotiations between the EC and the United Kingdom's former colonies in Africa and the Caribbean, begun in 1973 and culminating in the Convention of Lomé in February 1975. Ostensibly, the overriding purpose of the negotiations was to adjust the EC's relations with the Third World to accommodate the accession of the United Kingdom to the EC on January 1, 1973. Briefly, West German negotiators supported including a maximum number of countries in any new scheme of trade, aid, and investment relations. Any significant multiplication of the 18 African states related by special convention to the EC in 1973 would serve West German interests in three complementary ways. In the first place, finding a substitute for the British system of preferences would cement the United Kingdom more firmly to the EC, a traditional desideratum of West German EC policy. Second, it would help dilute French control over the EC bureaucratic apparatus, which regulated relations between the EC and those former French colonies in Africa covered under Title IV of the Rome Treaty. Substantial widening of EC aid schemes would almost necessarily diminish their distinctiveness from other multilateral programs. Hence, despite West German EC membership, the logic of widening was to increase the chances of West German economic penetration both in Francophone Africa and in the rest of the Third World. Finally, a larger scheme would make it possible to propose a program to a large group of developing countries aimed at meeting their demand for increased export receipts for the basic commodities they exported, which differentiated itself from the Corea Plan. If EC negotiators could win over the associated states to such a program, the ardor with which they supported the Corea Plan might be dampened.

The outcome of the negotiations constituted a victory for West German diplomacy on each of these key issues. Initially, 52 members of UNCTAD's Group of 77 adhered to the Lomé Convention. The number has increased to 61 under the first renegotiation of the treaty, completed in 1980. The EC offered the developing countries a scheme of price stabilization of export receipts whose central operating principle was prevention of erratic movements in the prices of basic commodities produced in the Third World. Hence, it differed in principle

from the Corea Plan in that it operated to guarantee income instead
of prices. Meanwhile, as this volume goes to press, the Corea Plan
has been successfully resisted. Moreover, other Third World demands
were also bent to serve West German interests through the Lomé
Convention. Raw material supplies to West Germany were dependent
on investment in the primary and extractive sectors, and the overall
absorptive capacity of developing countries depended on their own industrial development. To meet both these needs, West Germany
sponsored the establishment of an EC Center for Industrial Development. The center acts as a "marriage counselor" between developing countries and European capital looking for investment outlets.
It should be obvious that its guiding principles are a far cry from the
sort of global investment planning called for in some UNCTAD documents. Direct foreign investment would require the cultivation of a
"sound investment climate." The operation of the center functions in
a manner consistent with West German strategy, ideologically, politically, and in narrower economic terms.

To summarize, West German diplomacy in the EC was able to
increase the chances of continued British membership by accommodat-
ing the United Kingdom's excolonies while simultaneously opening up
Francophone Africa to increased penetration by West German capital
through the Lomé negotiations. In addition, the expansion of EC-
Third World relations could only deepen the convergence between EC
treatment of Lomé affiliates and EC treatment of other Third World
countries, thus supporting West Germany's "mondialist" Third World
posture. Finally, it was able to fend off threats to West Germany's
accumulation strategy by interposing a more moderate formula for
increasing Third World export earnings than that proposed by UNCTAD.

VETO POWER AND FISCAL CONTROL
IN COMMUNITY DEVELOPMENT

Relentless pursuit of its policy goals through the EC implied
that West German officials reject or at least co-opt program proposals not commensurate with the government's accumulation strategy,
which had originated in opposition to or simply without regard to the
inner logic of West Germany's position. Trade union and government
behavior in the preparatory stages of the 1976 Tripartite conference
and in the drafting of the conference communiqué demonstrate how
West German delegates shaped EC institutions to prevent or at least
modify the normal channels of distribution of information essential
to articulating policy alternatives, thereby exercising decisive influence over the definition of important issues. However, once proposals at odds with West German preferences did manage to get articu-

lated in a politically salient manner, West German delegates could and did invoke the veto in the Council of Ministers or in European Council meetings.

West Germany's power to instrumentalize the EC in this way rests upon a firmer foundation than the definition of voting rights, however. Rather, the economic success enjoyed by West Germany after the war made it, in addition to a crucial market for its EC partners, the repository of an enormous monetary reserve generated by three decades of trade surpluses. These could be deployed to subsidize EC programs. Indeed, although official statistics show the West German contribution to the EC budget at just short of 30 percent of the total in 1977, owing to the arbitrariness of EC accounting formulas an additional 5 percent of real contributions are hidden by DM revaluation effects. [10] Schlupp has estimated that over 80 percent of net international budgetary transfers in the EC come from West Germany. [11] Throughout the 1970s, nearly 80 percent of the yearly EC budget went to agricultural subsidies, but the CAP, although intensely disliked in SPD circles, could actually have been substantially less expensive were it not for the SPD's readiness to appease its governing coalition partner, the FDP. The setting of EC agricultural prices at levels above those that would satisfy the French, Italian, and Danish governments reflects the inefficiency of West German small farmers. The problem confronting the SPD in this respect consists in the limitations on domestic reform spending implied by the expensive CAP. The consequence of this situation has been extreme West German reluctance to finance additional EC programs deemed important by other EC member states. Indeed, the crystallization of this attitude came in the form of the derisive West German complaint of the mid-1970s: "Deutschland ist nicht der Zahlmeister (die Milchkuh) Europas" ("Germany is not Europe's milkcow").

Several examples will suffice to underline West Germany's ability to maintain EC policy coherence via control over financial resources. Since a central feature of EC development to date has not been homogeneous diffusion of economic benefits throughout the EC area but, rather, the precipitation of a constellation of major regions of poverty juxtaposed to nodal points of concentrated wealth, it is not surprising that EC decision-making bodies at all levels have been preoccupied with proposals for devising fiscal and economic correctives at the European level. One initiative was launched at the Hague Summit Conference in December 1969 and ratified at the Summit in Paris in October 1972. It foresaw the creation of a regional fund, the primary purpose of which would have been to subsidize production in the new intra-EC peripheries (for example, Scotland, Ireland, the Mezzogiorno, southwestern and northeastern France), thus attenuating unemployment and shoring up the tax base of those areas. This approach found its organizational expression in a very small fund, authorized in 1974, completely inadequate to the tasks for which it was created. The basic cause of this failure lay in West Germany's insistence that disbursement of funds be subject to satisfaction of stringent requirements set at the EC level where West Germany continued to hold a veto. The sole significant expansion of the fund was offered as an inducement to Italy and Ireland to join the EMS in 1979.

The fate of a more recent approach to the "regional problem" taken up in EC institutions parallels the fate of the Tripartite conference already discussed. In 1976 the commission authorized a study group supervised by the directorate-general on economic and financial affairs to investigate what role public finance might play in alleviating regional disparities in the community. The group's report, published in 1977,[12] treated the regional problem in a federal perspective, taking the U.S. experience with economic growth as its point of departure. The report suggested that the economic success of the rich areas was systemically related to poverty in other areas, but that this poverty was substantially attenuated by a massive system of interregional transfer payments from surplus to deficit areas. This system was held accountable for a high level of national identification among citizens of all regions. The authors of the MacDougall Report, as it was called, opined that this method might work for Europe as well. Moreover, beyond some threshold, such a system would attain a sufficient magnitude to serve as the fiscal basis of a European macroeconomic budget.

Seminar sessions were organized to discuss the ideas contained in the MacDougall Report, but the report's resonance in national capitals has been very weak thus far. One major reason for its tepid reception was its political impracticability. In order to have a chance of success, the main surplus country, West Germany, would have to subscribe to its basic tenets. It became clear at a very early stage of discussion that the West German government would not subscribe. The West German response shifted the focus of discussion from distribution to production. West German delegates to MacDougall seminars advocated the creation of the conditions of existence for voluntary, private-sector investment in poverty-stricken regions. West Germany, for its part, would encourage West German investment in these areas. In fact, joint business-government investment teams were dispatched in this period in order to underline West German preferences.

If the West German government remained unresponsive to proposals that would have the effect of increasing financial flows through the EC from "rich" to "poor" areas in the community, it was also adverse to proposals requiring West Germany to commit expanded EC resources to the Third World. In 1974 the West German minister for development aid, a member of the left wing of the SPD's Bundestag delegation, was dismissed because he assented to an EC contribution to the UN aid fund that was too large for West German tastes.

It would be a mistake to overlook those cases in which the West German government did commit large financial resources in the EC system, however. Medium-term, balance-of-payments loans to the United Kingdom and Italy in 1974 and 1976 are cases in point. However, these loans came with West German advice. The advice was very much like standard IMF advice to governments that come to it for loans when their countries have large balance-of-payments deficits but whose import requirements continue at high levels. Through the Council of Ministers, as well as in bilateral settings, West German authorities counseled higher taxes, lower wage settlements, and cuts in government spending. This advice did differ from IMF advice in one important particular: West Germany did not want EC members to devalue their currencies.

In summary, the pattern of EC disbursements correlates strikingly with the logic of West Germany's accumulation strategy. I have attempted to sustain the view that this was no accidental occurrence but, rather, the result of deliberate policy coordination at the highest levels of the West German government.

DILEMMAS OF SUCCESS IN THE 1980s

What were the most significant results of the West German government's successful strategy to transform the EC into an institution mainly responsive to the requirements of that government's accumulation strategy? Three areas can be fruitfully singled out: the development of West German export performance, the evolution of patterns of conflict within West Germany that can be related to the success of the export strategy, and the evolution of the EC itself.

German Export Performance

The operation of the snake, the Tripartite conferences, West Germany's position during the Lomé negotiations, and its position on the EC budget worked together to parry demands from other EC actors (governments, nongovernmental political parties, and Eurocrats, in addition to governments that are not members of the EC) for West German reflation during the worldwide economic recession it helped induce in 1973-74. Not only did this strategy prevent a fragmentation of the EC—which might have eroded West Germany's market shares in Western Europe to the advantage of the United States and Japan, both of whose governments were preparing major export drives—but

the West German strategy probably accounts in part for the maintenance of West German and EC market shares beyond Western Europe.
West German exports between 1970 and 1980 increased by a yearly
average of DM20.5 billion. The average yearly increase between
1970 and 1975 was DM19.3 billion; between 1976 and 1980, the figure
was DM28.8 billion. To the extent that West German-orchestrated
austerity raised the market shares of other EC states, they were
better able to afford imports from West Germany.

The controlled reflation strategy ratified by the 1976 EC Tripartite conference very likely enabled the West German government
to extend and formalize the EC currency snake in 1978–79 in the aftermath of a precipitous depreciation in the international value of the
U.S. dollar, which was associated with the Carter administration's
reflation program launched in 1977. The resulting European Monetary System implied greater West German control over the macroeconomic policies of Italy and Ireland. The addition of these two states
to the scheme and the readmission of France fulfilled one of West
Germany's central EC policy objectives in the 1970s.

Meanwhile, the continued deterioration of the U.S. trade position led the Federal Reserve Board to shift its monetary tactics,
ushering in a new phase of conflict between the EC countries and the
United States in October 1979. In a policy departure upheld by the
Reagan administration, the Federal Reserve Board has attempted to
place strict limits on the growth of the money supply to fight domestic inflation, hoping that less inflation will mean increased exports.
The high rates of interest that have been the consequence of this policy
have depressed the price of the deutsche mark and, through it, the
European Currency Unit (ECU), which in turn has led to a substantial
increase in the price of imported raw materials in Europe. Since a
key aspect of West Germany's strategy was an expensive DM, the government's response to this situation has been to borrow short-term
money from abroad and jack up its own interest rates. Further pressure on the West German balance of payments has come in the form
of U.S. insistence that West German outlays on military products be
substantially increased. The West German government found itself
confronted with a Hobson's choice as a consequence: either expand
military spending and cut back other forms of social spending or maintain high interest rates with a more moderate cut in spending, which
will decrease production oriented to the domestic market. This point
brings us to the second set of consequences of West Germany's successful export strategy.

Domestic Politics

Persistent adherence to the EC strategy defined in 1972 has led
to a substantial rise in unemployment in West Germany since 1974.

First, the austerity policy of mid-decade, then the high real rates of interest occasioned by Washington's monetary policy and the Bundesbank's response to it, have resulted in an unemployment rate hovering around 5 percent of the work force, by official estimates. This rate might not seem very high in international comparison, but its effects are concentrated on a highly politicized, younger generation of West Germans, many of whom are aware of the systemic implication of their plight. Thus, the defense budget is a focus of considerable controversy in West Germany at present, not only because many West Germans question the wisdom of emplacing new generations of nuclear armament on West German soil, but also because of the connection between defense spending and high interest rates. The latter have had a devastating impact on housing construction in recent years. Confronting a housing shortage and high rents, young West Germans have taken over abandoned or condemned buildings in a direct expression of social need over private ownership. In some cases, the squatters have been supported by shopkeepers who have also been adversely affected by these developments. When local governments have mobilized the police against squatters, the result has been to widen the conflict by increasing the solidarity between those immediately affected and those who learn about police violence through the mass media. There have been ramifications for the stability of the government in Bonn. At least partly as a result of squatter demonstrations and citizens' initiatives against nuclear power and nuclear weapons, Länder elections have been lost by the Social Democrats and serious breaches of party discipline have become thinkable, even probable, in the parliamentary SPD.

More ominously, one must wonder to what degree the complicity of West Germany's trade unions in the political organization of the export-accumulation strategy is linked to repression of dissident political elements within the trade unions themselves. Certainly, one of the most worrisome developments of the 1970s was the internal application of the Berufsverbot by union functionaries. The net effect of this practice and the hesitancy of the SPD hierarchy to rethink its approach to economic growth can only lead to the growth and consolidation of opposition movements outside the party-union matrix. In the West German context, however, it is difficult to see how such movements will overcome their political marginality, so concentrated are organizational resources in the Federal Republic of Germany.

EC Development

If the thesis is correct that the EC is a system of intercapitalist regulation at the regional level through which adjustments among national constellations of class relations are engineered, then it should be possible to relate national patterns of political change and stability to EC programmatic development. This alternative to viewing EC politics as politics of the lowest common denominator permits us to make sense of the juxtaposition of the striking continuity of SPD/FDP governance in West Germany and the equally striking shifts in the social bases of politics in the other EC member-states. Indeed, it is not too much to assert that the Europe-wide austerity policy orchestrated by West Germany through the EC in the 1970s has discredited the governments that followed it to the degree that they could no longer hold their electoral bases.

In the case of France, there can be no doubt that the Barre Plan, initiated in August 1976, directly contributed to the acceleration of the substantial political reorganization that has been occurring in that country since 1968. The fragmentation of the Gaullist formation and the emergence of a more or less electorally unified Left cannot be explained apart from the industrial havoc, unemployment, and downward pressure on wages that were associated with the attempts of the French government to keep the value of the franc at par with the West German DM. Nor is it surprising that the economic policy impact of the 1981 presidential and assembly elections has been a reflationary program carried out with the aid of newly nationalized firms in "lead" sectors to create more employment. It is interesting that at least the initial monetary parameter set by the French government is maintenance of a stable DM-franc rate. The major imponderable is whether West Germany will allow the EMS to carry the freight of the French expansion.

Only two directions seem possible in the short run: either West Germany will support the franc and French reflation through the EMS, or it will pull out. In the case of franc support, West Germany will be forced to reflate along with France or find a way to "sterilize" the liquidity created in the process. The latter scenario, presently supported by the Bundesbank, might lead to a further tightening of credit in West Germany, which could intensify the conflicts outlined in the preceding section. For the moment, at least, any other tactic would be difficult for the SPD leadership to embrace, since it would probably entail a direct confrontation with the FDP and the collapse of the government. But if the West German government should decide to discontinue its support of the franc, the French government would be forced into a posture that would call into question the basic premises of the EC customs union. Hence, the most likely possibility is continued franc support and continued high interest rates and capital controls in West Germany, in the hope that French export requirements will set strict limits on political innovation in France in the medium term.

The deindustrializing consequences of Thatcherism in the United Kingdom must be seen as the Anglo-Saxon correlate of the Barre Plan.

The major difference between the experiences of the two countries insofar as the EC is concerned, lies in the widespread identification of EC membership with economic malaise. It is easy to understand this attitude, given the United Kingdom's date of entry into the EC (January 1, 1973). The United Kingdom was brought into the community by the Tories, giving the new Labour government an opportunity to redefine the issue of membership in terms of the specifics of accession negotiations, rather than the more fundamental question of the price in industrial dislocation that the United Kingdom would have to pay for synchronizing its macroeconomic policy with that of West Germany. The return of a Conservative government in 1979 led to a new phase of bargaining in the EC, but the resulting budgetary modifications did nothing to alter the underlying logic of community development. Therefore, in the context of rising unemployment, intractable inflation, and union disorganization since 1979, it is not difficult to fathom the depth of hostility to the EC in the labor movement. If a Labour government is elected in 1984 (or before), a path may be followed very much like the one being pioneered by the French socialists today, albeit outside the community framework. Should a Social Democratic (SDP)-Liberal coalition emerge to govern the United Kingdom in the next general election one could expect to see a continuation of the present government's EC policy, focusing on reforming the CAP, limiting budgetary contributions, and reorienting EC expenditure patterns.

It need only be observed that political developments in Greece and Italy underline the shakiness of support for Modell Deutschland in Europe. The sweeping electoral victory of the Greek socialist party (PASOK) promises the introduction of a program of economic democratization and nationalization resembling current French socialist policies. Taken together, all these instances of rejuvenation of Western European social democracy amount to a formidable basis of resistance to West German EC policy. The danger of a general dissolution of the community that such developments portend lies in fostering the illusion that socialist responses to the advance of the international restructuring of capitalist relations in the 1980s can succeed at the national level alone. The danger consists in a missed opportunity to affect West German policy through the institution that served as the medium through which articulate political oppositions were spawned. It would be a tragedy if these oppositions let the chance for developing a regional response to Modell Deutschland slip by.

CONCLUSION

From the preceding discussion one may conclude, first, that the West German government and trade union leadership exhibited a high level of agreement over goals to be pursued through the EC and developed a sophisticated and coordinated approach to specific issues as they arose in the community context. Second, EC programmatic and institutional development in the 1970s would be unintelligible without reference to West Germany's accumulation strategy, itself a reaction to trends in economic development and negotiated by the SPD and trade unionists. Conversely, the foregoing analysis suggests something perhaps more analytically intriguing than that of EC programs being merely an expression of Modell Deutschland. It rather suggests that the elaboration of mechanisms and programs at the EC level constituted conditions of existence for the functioning of Modell Deutschland. Third, the analysis supports the Schlupp thesis that European capitalism is a hierarchical system with the Federal Republic of Germany at its apex by revealing the specific mechanisms at the regional level that sustain West German dominance in that system. It is hard to imagine the survival of such a situation without some structure within which priorities could be set and challenges arising out of its operations met. Hence, if the cooperation of unions and government in West Germany is the source of West Germany's power in the EC, the calculated exercise of this power has decisively shaped that institution to the point where it is impossible to think of the EC in any other terms than as a regional extension of the West German state.

NOTES

1. Figures cited in the first section of this chapter for the period prior to 1978 are from Frieder Schlupp, "Modell Deutschland" and the International Division of Labor: The Federal Republic of Germany in the World Political Economy," in The Foreign Policy of West Germany: Formation and Contents, ed. Ekkehardt Krippendorff and Volker Rittberger (Beverly Hills, Calif.: Sage, 1980), pp. 33-100. An extensive listing of the work of Schlupp, Rehfeldt, and Deubner can be found in the first footnote of this article. Post-1977 figures in this section are derived from the 1981 publication of the German-American Chamber of Commerce, US-German Trade 1980 (New York: German-American Chamber of Commerce, 1981).

2. For an excellent explication and analysis of these reforms, see Manfred G. Schmidt, "The Politics of Domestic Reform in the Federal Republic of Germany," Politics and Society 8 (1978): 165-200. One of Schmidt's conclusions is that the SPD/FDP reform policies were intended as a "modernization of capitalism based on conventional parliamentary politics."

3. Bundesministerium für Wirtschaft, Leistung in Zahlen '76 (Bonn: Bundesministerium für Wirtschaft, August 1977), p. 103. Significantly, expenditures on education are not included in this accounting.

4. I have adopted the term influence zone from Schlupp, "Modell Deutschland." It refers to the geographic loci of exports from metropolitan capitalist countries. In light of the early confiscation of German colonies through the political settlement after World War I and the expropriation of Germany's foreign assets during both world wars, it may be surmised that West Germany is especially vulnerable to such interzonal conflicts.

5. The irony here is that the cuts in public spending primarily affected the administration of municipalities, the most populous ones of which are virtually all governed by Communists.

6. The same Barre who drafted the initial EMU memorandums in the EC Commission. The "Eurocracy" was and continues to be a leading ground for training and testing promising candidates for upper echelon bureaucratic posts in national capitals. The SPD has made a virtual science of channeling promising personnel through the community institutions in order to prepare them for posts in key ministries in Bonn. It is difficult to imagine how the SPD could penetrate the CDU state without such a training ground.

7. Meanwhile, the use of German deutsche marks as an international transactions currency has quickly blossomed in recent years. Trade factoring in DMs now exceeds factoring in British pounds.

8. See Commission of the European Community, Report of the Study Group: Problems of Inflation (Brussels: Commission of the EC, 1976), also known as the Maldague Report.

9. This section is distilled from my unpublished manuscript, prepared for the 1977 meetings of the American Political Science Association in Washington, D. C., entitled "National Capital and the European Community: The Struggle over the Lomé Convention."

10. For an overview of West Germany's EC budgetary contributions, see Bundesministerium der Finanzen, Finanzbericht 1978 (Bonn: Referat Presse und Information des Bundesministeriums für Wirtschaft, 1977). p. 54.

11. Ibid.

12. Commission of the European Community, Report of the Study Group on the Role of Public Finance in European Integration, 2 vols. (Brussels: Commission of the EC, 1977), vol. 1, also known as the MacDougall Report.

6
ECONOMIC DEMOCRACY AS A LABOR ALTERNATIVE TO THE GROWTH STRATEGY IN WEIMAR GERMANY

DAVID ABRAHAM

For a historian even to consider Germany as a "model" a brief 35 years after Auschwitz may, at first glance, seem cruelly sarcastic. Even looking to the more noble side of German history, one can hardly come away thinking that one has stumbled upon an overlooked prototype. If anything, the literature of the last generation has tended to stress Germany's divergence from some presumably shared Western path of development.[1] In recent years, however, the continuing success of West Germany (and even of East Germany) together with the demystification of the 1960s, the disappointments of the 1970s, and the apparently inauspicious start of the 1980s in the Anglo-American world, have led both scholars and popular opinion alike to consider the possibility that the Germans, or at least the "good" Germans, may have done some things right. Further, they may have

----

From a methodological perspective, this chapter consists of two parts, each characterized by a different type of analysis. Although both seek to explore the transformative potential and limits of German social democracy, they are different in approach and grounded in unequal amounts of research. Roughly the first half of the study is based on research already concluded and represents an analysis of the path taken by the socialist labor movement during the Weimar years. The latter half is grounded in research just under way and is, perforce, more strictly conceptual and logical; further, it treats the path not taken. Of course, this is not to suggest that there are no sources for a discussion of the economic democracy program, its sponsors, opponents and fate. Indeed, as shall be noted, a very lively debate took place in the theoretical and practical journals of the SPD and unions as well as at trade union congresses, party meetings, and in numerous other publications.

done them sooner than others, so that we may see in the German past and present the institutions and practices that lie in our own future. Thus, if the model is not normative, it may at least be descriptive.

Whereas German expressionism in the fine arts and persistent quality in the practical arts have already proved the beneficiaries of our changed and more generous perspective, this new appreciation is being extended to social, economic, and political matters only tentatively. Here the tendency in recent years, among academics if not among official U.S. policy makers, has been to credit West Germany, its businessmen, bureaucrats, and trade union leaders, with introducing and developing economic and social mechanisms, structures, and attitudes designed to lessen social conflict and smoothen economic transformation. Depending mostly on their political and ideological positions, various analysts have judged these so-called corporatist tendencies to be good, bad, or inevitable. For some analysts, corporatism promises to lessen social and economic tensions by enabling representatives of capital, labor, and the state to plan together and to resolve conflicts more or less as equal partners free of the harsh glare and disruptions of "overloaded" popular and democratic procedures. For others, the equality is only illusory, and the insulation from popular, democratic debate is precisely the problem. Nearly all observers agree, however, that this corporatist arrangement is part of "Model Germany" and that it has solid roots in the history of Prussia and pre-1933 Germany—with their politically weak bourgeoisie—and perhaps especially in the Weimar Republic. [2]

As real as they may have been during the middle Weimar years, arrangements of the corporatist type were not the sole model contribution to social and economic organization to issue from Germany in that period. Though the middle years of Weimar did feature bureaucratic administration rather than parliamentary debate, class collaboration rather than class conflict and repression, integration rather than fractionalization, inclusion rather than exclusion, and the like, German political and civil society also witnessed the articulation of a more aggressive democratic and socialist-oriented program by parts of the Social Democratic party (SPD)-affiliated labor movement. Though militant reformism in league with dynamic industries—a precocious corporatist growth strategy—was the dominant motif in German labor's interwar approach,[3] it provided only one of two models. The other—"economic democracy"—was less concerned with mitigating conflict through tripartite cooperation and growth than with transforming society, with "bending" capitalism in a nonrevolutionary era. Just as the "growth strategy" of the Weimar years became encased in corporatist structures and processes prefiguring what seems to be happening in official politics today, so the economic democracy strategy of those years stands now as the chief alternative to official politics.

In Scandinavia, West Germany, Austria, among the Eurocommunists of Mediterranean Europe, and even (ever so faintly) in the United States, representatives of labor and the Left are now articulating macroeconomic and microeconomic programs very substantially prefigured by the German economic democracy program of the mid- and late 1920s.[4] All of these movements seek to insulate the labor movement and its present and future achievements from the mercies of the international economy and the built-in prerogatives of the owners of capital.

This last point is crucial because corporatist growth strategies in the 1960s as in the 1920s were always vulnerable to fluctuations and crises in the international economy, as well as to the inherent right of capitalists to withdraw from tacit or official compacts. Further, under the pressure of fiscal crises, liberal democratic states have revealed their inability to compel participation by or enforce discipline on capitalists once the economic going turned rough.[5] This was not a lesson that the leaders or theoreticians of the workers' movement learned quickly, not even in the context of Weimar's shaky political democracy. Indeed, after the abortive revolution of 1918-19 and the severe counterrevolutionary chastening of 1923, the SPD and its affiliated trade unions (ADGB) embarked on an economic and political program grounded in cooperation, direct and via the state, with the more successful, expansive, dynamic, and liberal industries and industrialists. There were political reasons for this choice having to do with the opportunities for political coalitions (personified by the liberal industrialist-turned-politician Gustav Stresemann); there were theoretical inducements and justifications for such a strategy (typified by the analyses of labor's leading theorist, Rudolf Hilferding); and even in the 1920s, there was ample economic opportunity.

THE GROWTH STRATEGY AND ITS DEMISE

Despite the series of defeats they suffered between 1919 and 1924, the SPD and ADGB remained powerful representatives of German labor—powerful not only in terms of electoral support and organizational membership, but powerful also in obtaining wage gains, social and economic legislation, and prolabor state intervention in a range of labor-management conflicts.[6] The growth strategy did pay off. It was able to do so because, despite the reality of overall economic stagnation during the 1920s, certain economically and politically pivotal German industries fared rather well. In fact, those that fared best in the interwar years were those same industries that we have come to associate with West Germany's tremendous economic recovery after World War II: chemicals, electronics, machine goods,

TABLE 5.1

Production Indices for Sample Major Industries

	Stagnant			Borderline	Expansive		
	Coal	All Mining	Iron and Steel	Textile and Clothing	Lignite[a]	Metal-Finishing[b]	Chemical
1925	70	79	70	96	158	131	133
1926	76	82	62	80	159	104	124
1927	81	88	86	117	171	143	155
1928	79	88	80	98	188	164	161
1929	86	98	86	89	197	170	186
1930	75	84	63	83	163	157	172
1931	62	70	45	77	151	120	148
1932	55	63	32	82	140	84	139

[a]Lignite was used primarily for electric power production. It was a new and booming field closely linked to those whom it supplied. The most prominent lignite industrialist was the liberal Paul Silverberg.
[b]Includes all those industries consuming raw iron or steel and producing finished products or machinery.

Note: All figures derive from a base of 1913 = 100.

Source: Walther Hoffmann, Das Wachstum der deutschen Wirtschaft (Berlin and Heidelberg: Springer Verlag, 1965), pp. 342, 343, 392, 393.

technically refined products (optics, instruments), engineered and
other highly capital-intensive products. The production indices
listed in Table 6.1 provide some indication of the differential success
of Germany's largest industries during the Weimar years.

The mid- and late 1920s, much more so than the post-1945
years, witnessed not only a substantial disparity in production and
profits between the expansive and stagnant industries but also sharp
conflicts within the economic elite, which was unable to formulate a
shared and coherent project for Germany. The industrial, commercial, and agrarian capitalist class in Weimar Germany was divided
on a number of key issues: trade and commercial policy (Handelspolitik), social welfare policy (Sozialpolitik), reparations policy
(Reparationspolitik), the fostering of capital accumulation, and the
expansion of political democracy. On the one side stood a group of
men from heavy industry, many of an older generation, who were
oriented primarily toward the domestic market or international cartels and consequently rather protectionist in orientation. These entrepreneurs were constantly opposed to concessions to labor in their
frequently labor-intensive industries while, at the same time, displaying considerable sympathy for Germany's unprofitable and non-
competitive but politically significant agrarian sector.[7] On the other
side stood representatives of more modern or dynamic industries,
as well as the most artisanal, many members of a younger generation,
who were oriented toward the export market and consequently were
free trading in orientation. These entrepreneurs wished to be more
flexible toward labor in their generally capital-intensive industries
(it was they who took the lead in reaching tacit accommodations with
labor), while consistently displaying suspicion toward the backward-
looking and capital-devouring agrarian sector.

Issues in Handelspolitik clearly split German industrialists and
rural producers into those who could or needed to compete in world
markets (supported by workers and consumers) and those who could
not. Table 6.2 indicates the importance of exports to key industries
and the growing centrality of those exports to the German economy
as a whole, exceeding one-third of the total production by 1931. Those
who could compete effectively or who had lesser labor inputs were
also generally less concerned with the cost of those labor inputs.
Reparationspolitik further divided Germany's capitalists between
those who were prepared to live with and profit from the Dawes and
Young Plans while trying to revise them and those who could not
cope and wanted instead to go to the bitter end in opposing them. And
obviously, Sozialpolitik created a cleavage between those industrialists
who could afford to live with organized labor's demands (in exchange
for labor's support on other issues) and those who simply could not
or would not.[8]

TABLE 5.2

Exports of Several Key Industries: Values, Export Prices, Volume,
and "World" Share

	1925	1926	1927	1928	1929	1930	1931	1932
Coal								
Value	311	895	660	523	590	561	466	275
Price index	140	148	155	137	138	143	123	91
Volume index	39	105	74	66	75	68	66	53
World share (1928 = 10 percent)								
Raw and semi iron and steel								
Value	457	670	589	650	781	622	531	284
Price index	127	118	127	125	129	130	123	112
Volume index	51	81	66	74	86	68	61	36
World share (1928 = 22 percent)								
Textiles[a]								
Value	1,150	1,167	1,274	1,338	1,399	1,249	1,055	526
Price index	195	183	195	196	189	190	163	133
Volume index	57	62	70	72	79	73	71	42
World share (1928 = 13 percent)								
Metal goods[b]								
Value	2,261	2,445	2,670	3,146	3,769	3,645	1,943	1,835
Price index	138	135	135	140	143	139	131	124
Volume index	77	85	91	107	126	129	112	74
World share (1928 = 30 percent)								
Chemicals[c]								
Value	953	1,173	1,277	1,396	1,460	1,257	1,036	730
Price index	133	138	143	138	129	126	115	105
Volume index	69	80	87	97	109	96	87	67
World share (1928 = 43 percent)								

[a]Figures for textiles include clothing. The export price index for clothing was some 70 or more points higher than that of cloth and fabric. In the 1920s Germany became a large importer of clothing.

[b]Figures for metal goods include machines and vehicles.

[c]Figures for chemicals include finished goods only.

Note: All figures for value denote millions of reichsmarks; export price and volume indices derive from a base of 1913 = 100; figures for world share denote percentages. "World" share here means the eight most industrialized countries of Europe plus the United States. Given the products being considered, this definition should not introduce much of a discrepancy.

Sources: Walther Hoffmann, Das Wachstum der deutschen Wirtschaft (Berlin and Heidelberg: Springer Verlag, 1965), pp. 522, 534, 604-7; Ingvar Svennilson, Growth and Stagnation in the European Economy (Geneva: United Nations Economic Commission, 1954), p. 187.

These divisions, among others, led to the absence of a clear, coherent, and indisputable leadership within German capital. Out of touch with and, indeed, resented by most of the middle strata of society (Mittelstand) because of the damage done to them by the great inflation, which had benefited industrialists and estate owners, the German bourgeoisie was handicapped by the absence of popular allies or a mass base among non-working-class groups. [9] This state of affairs enabled labor to score considerable gains; further, in many crucial respects, it was labor that provided the popular support for bourgeois democracy. As in the Bundesrepublik, the political underwriting for the private enterprise economy issued primarily from the working class through the SPD. Today, other social groups in West Germany may be as committed to liberal democracy as the working class, but during the Weimar years it often seemed that the working class alone appreciated this most advanced product of the bourgeois epoch.

Thus, a number of factors coalesced to foster a short-term tacit alliance between capital and labor grounded in a growth strategy: from the business side, relative (though uneven) prosperity and the ascendance of the dynamic industries involved in international trade and quality production; from the labor side, rank-and-file pressure for amelioration after the chastening of 1920-23 and a strategy substantially grounded in Hilferding's notion of "organized capitalism," according to which working-class participation in state planning would simultaneously further democratization of the economy and the polity while laying the groundwork for ultimate socialization;[10] and from the side of party politics, the absence of other, nonlabor political forces capable of aggregating voters and winning elections within a parliamentary democratic framework. The consequence of all this was a tacit political and economic alliance from 1925 to 1930, one which Communist and reactionary agrarian publicists both referred to as the Severing-Stresemann-Silverberg coalition, aptly named, respectively, after the SPD interior minister and party whip, the liberal foreign minister who also presided over reparations and stood close to the dynamic industrialists, and one of Germany's leading industrialists, who in the name of industry held out the olive branch to labor in 1926. [11]

As noted above, from this growth compact organized labor won relatively high industry-wide wage rates; compulsory binding arbitration of contract disputes by the Labor Ministry; a broad spectrum of social welfare measures; vastly increased state spending, especially on behalf of the working population; a generous and comprehensive unemployment insurance law; the beginnings of democratization in the education and health systems; an eight-hour day; and many other benefits. In some, though clearly not all, respects this arrangement presaged the more general, contemporary situation that Jürgen Habermas, summarizing the findings of Claus Offe and others of his students, has described in the following:

> In the monopolistic sector, by means of a coalition between
> business associations and unions, the price of . . . labour
> power is quasi-politically negotiated. . . . The mechanism
> of competition is replaced by compromises between organi-
> zations to which the state has delegated legitimate power.
> . . . Through "political wages" it has been possible in the
> capital-and-growth-intensive sectors of the economy to
> mitigate the opposition between capital and wage labour
> and to bring about a political class compromise. [12]

This Weimar version of the growth strategy lasted until early 1930, despite persistent opposition from quarters to the Right and the Left. It served as the principal sociopolitical undergirding for the democratic republic; once it collapsed, the Weimar Republic, established in a society practically without a liberal bourgeois past but now facing a difficult conjuncture, itself slid and was pushed in an authoritarian direction, ultimately to be replaced by the Nazi state. That process itself cannot be addressed here, but it commenced as soon as the growth coalitions' premises were undermined: as international trade and capital flows broke down, as the more progressive industrialists lost their hold on the industrial organizations, as conservative industrialists exerted greater pressure on the liberal political parties after Stresemann's death, as the rural sector mobilized to press its protectionist demands, and as organized labor's earlier gains became increasingly burdensome to both the treasury and the cost and profit calculations of businessmen. All of these factors were exacerbated by the SPD's relative victory in the 1928 elections, for that victory emboldened substantial portions of labor and led to greater militancy and higher expectations at the very moment that the economic situation began to deteriorate. The SPD was trapped in a dilemma: it was the party leading a responsible coalition government with bourgeois partners, but it was also the chief representative of the daily interests of the working class. Under pressure from the Communist party (KPD) and the rank and file, its leaders were compelled to accede to worker and union demands while its cabinet ministers sought to keep the treasury solvent and their restive bourgeois partners in the government. [13]

Their efforts were in vain, however. Without any real control over how the owners of the means of production could dispose of what was theirs, the unions and SPD were left entirely vulnerable to changes in the overall economic situation and political constellation. Despite their legislative gains and institutional arrangements, their success —the success of the growth strategy—had been conjunctural, not structural. Labor had benefited from the previous situation but proved unable to determine its future evolution. From 1930 on, the growth of the reserve army of the unemployed, the refusal of capitalists to invest, and the attendant fiscal crisis combined to negate the victories of the preceding years. [14] Yet, the unions and party remained strong enough to ensure that the <u>economic</u> crisis would be a <u>profit</u> crisis, too. (In the United States, with weak unions and no labor party, economic crises can be combined with record profit levels.)

The economic conflict between labor and capital was politicized by the offensive of the latter, and having banked on growth rather than control, the SPD could develop no adequate counterstrategy. The SPD rejected the Woytinsky-Tarnow-Baade (WTB) program of massive, consumption-oriented relief efforts put forward by several unionists in particular. The party's own view of the workings of the capitalist economy was too orthodox to accommodate measures of such a sort, so it never really subscribed to the WTB program, let alone did it campaign for it. [15] Defense of workers' short-run economic interests and support of the political "lesser evil" were the two chief components of SPD economic and political policy from 1930 on; that policy left organized labor and its supporters without any initiative, even during the worst moments between the breakdown of the Grand Coalition in March 1930 and the transfer of power to Hitler at the end of January 1933. The striking passivity of the Socialist Left in late Weimar itself provides the sharpest indictment of the policies it pursued during the "good" growth years.

"ECONOMIC DEMOCRACY" AS AN
ALTERNATIVE MODEL

Was there an alternate strategy by means of which the labor movement in Weimar Germany could have achieved gains and rendered those gains less vulnerable to economic and fiscal contraction? Is there any approach available to any labor movement within a capitalist democracy that might enable labor to institutionalize worker influence and power independent of economic conjunctures and transient political coalitions? The most ambitious of the economic democracy programs extant today, the Swedish Meidner Plan alluded to above, would seek to socialize or collectivize the investment function, basically by having profits turned over to workers and unions, who would use them to buy out private owners. In effect, the plan would prevent owners of industrial capital from disposing freely of what is theirs until such time as it ceases to be theirs in any case. Investment strikes and the exodus

of capital would both be made increasingly difficult, while large doses
of worker management and oversight would prevent any sabotage either
at the factory level or at the commanding heights of the economy as a
whole. This is not the place for an analysis of the Swedish proposals,
except to note that, like the program for economic democracy formu-
lated by German socialists during the Weimar Republic, this program
envisions economic democracy as a step toward socialism, as a weakening of the individual and collective rights and prerogatives of capitalists, and as a "bending" of capitalism before "breaking" it.

Beginning with the formulations of the 1920s, these programs
have all been committed to using the already-won principles of political democracy to enhance social democracy, to compel the democratic state to take part in the progressive transformation of the
capitalist economy. [16] And they have all been committed to accom-
plishing this transformation prior to or instead of any seizure of
political power by the working class or a party claiming to represent
it. Consequently, these programs have represented an alternative
not only to the growth strategy but also to Leninism, which posits a
seizure of power prior to undertaking economic and social transformation; for this reason also, economic democracy has sometimes been
described, favorably or derisively, as a "third way."[17] Further,
all programs for economic democracy have shared a belief in the ultimate incompatability of democracy and capitalism—and in the greater
power of the former. [18] As to the evolution of capitalist ownership
and exchange, all programs for economic democracy have grounded
themselves in an analysis of capitalism's self-organizing, self-con-
centrating, and self-undermining tendencies that has led them to hold
that with the virtual disappearance of competition in favor of oligopolies
and cartels, public direction of the economy in the interests of the commonweal—that is, public direction centered in the labor movement—
would become easier. This view of capitalism's dynamics lies at the
root of the difficulties organized labor has experienced in recent years
in dealing with popular youth movements, with ecologists, and with
advocates of decentralization and "small is beautiful." All forms of
economic democracy have been productivist and have stood in favor
of organization.

The advocates of a strategy of economic democracy in Weimar
Germany based their efforts on what a parliamentary republic had to
offer. For Rudolf Hilferding, the chief theorist of the period, formal
democracy was the form of state in which the class demands of workers could be carried furthest without systematic violence, while for
Hugo Sinzheimer, Ernst Fraenkel, and other labor lawyers and economists, the privileged position of the unions—guaranteed by the constitution's commitment to the parity of labor and capital in the determination of economic policy—provided a favorable basis for the further

development of society, nation, and state. This sense of emerging parity, of labor's coresponsibility for the social, economic, and political "common good" (Gemeinwohl) of society, came to be conceptualized as a pluralist democracy, in which the democratization of the state would be followed by the democratization of the conomy. [19]

Few German Social Democrats or trade unionists attempted to describe what socialism, that is, the goal of real economic democracy, would be like. In Economic Democracy: Its Character, Means and Ends, published in 1928, Fritz Naphtali and the other authors presented a plan to end the autocracy, anarchy, and injustice of capitalism; begin the democratization of the economy; and finally, strive to transform the existing economic system, step by step, into socialism. [20] The definitive program produced by Naphtali and his collaborators was the fruit of several years of discussion and debate, especially within the ranks of the trade union movement. The call for economic democracy first emerged in the ADGB in 1924 as a defensive tactic in the coalfields, where the workers were taking a beating: in place of the expected postrevolutionary socialization, the inflation and Ruhr occupation permitted the owners to lower wages, increase work hours, and otherwise reestablish their authority. At the ADGB's 1925 Breslau Congress, Herbert Jäckel articulated Wirtschaftsdemokratie ("economic democracy") primarily as a way to salvage the daily social and economic functions of the unions, halt the decline in membership, and sustain the faith of the rank and file in a period of vicissitudes. For the next three years, Fritz Naphtali and Fritz Tarnow worked at systematizing the program. In the process, economic democracy took on an offensive cast; first, because of the substantial improvement in the economy and socialist electoral gains, and second, because Naphtali's analysis compelled him to concede that economic democracy was impossible within the framework of the capitalist order and, therefore, that some struggle toward socialism was a prerequisite.

The discussions begun at the Breslau Congress of 1925 continued for the next three years, generating a series of debates that took the form of articles and polemics in the socialist, communist, and liberal press, and even in certain publications of the League of German Industry. By the time the next congress assembled in Hamburg in 1928, a program considerably more coherent, if still broad ranging, had been produced. [21]

In the broadest sense, the program encompassed all the social, economic, and cultural demands of the trade unions and the party, and there can be no question that this was a reformist or evolutionist strategy. Step by step, the unions would eliminate the domination based on the possession of capital and transform the leading organs of the economy from vehicles of capitalist class interest to organs of the public, general good for which, presumably, the organized working class was the most qualified, if not sole, voice.[22] Such a transformation was already being facilitated by the emergence of organized monopoly capitalism and planned production. Although in the short run organized monopoly capitalism strengthened the macroeconomic autocracy of capitalists, as against that enjoyed in the earlier period of free competition, the political power of organized labor, together with other developmental tendencies in capitalism, would shift the momentum in labor's favor.[23] Already, however, important aspects of the market economy were being transferred from private to state hands. No longer were labor market, workplace, or even wage conditions determined by the market. These were being politicized through the collective strength of the unions and legislation, which increasingly infringed on the rights of employers and even narrowed the definition of property rights.[24] That process that Karl Marx argued began with the passage of the Ten Hours Law in industrializing England could now be expanded and accelerated: the replacement of the political economy of capitalism by the political economy of the working class.

By 1928 German labor's spokesmen had conceptualized a strategy for moving toward economic democracy, one which may sound somewhat familiar after the experiences of both the New Left and Eurocommunism, but which was rather novel at the time. On the other hand, legislative and administrative demands were to be raised within the state, an activity for which the class-conscious political mobilization of the working class on the terrain of democracy was the prerequisite and starting point. On the other side, in civil society the chief task was seen as the nurturing of new, democratic economic forms established and operated by the working class as prototypes or germ cells for a future socialist society.[25] Together, the two facets of the strategy would strengthen public interests against private interests, narrow the freedom of operation of capital, and facilitate a new system of exchange and allocation.

Fritz Naphtali offered and the trade unions congress in 1928 adopted a catalog of 12 immediate and long-term tasks designed to pave the way to socialism: the elaboration of favorable labor laws;[26] the passage of wage- and job-protection legislation; an aggressive but planned wages policy; the expansion and autonomous administration of social insurance funds;[27] the broadening of workers' codetermination rights within the factory to include matters previously reserved to capital (for example, in regard to the organization of the shop floor and production-line authority);[28] the representation of labor, on the basis of parity, in all public bodies dealing with economic policy (such as the National Economics Council and the National Bank);[29] state control of monopolies and cartels (particularly in the extractive industries) drawing on the participation of the trade unions;[30] tripartite, entrepreneur-worker-consumer self-administration bodies (Selbstverwaltungskörper) in industries that might possibly be nationalized, especially mining—here, too, the working class would gain schooling for future control of the economy; the expansion of democratically organized, publicly owned production units and utilities, which already employed 5 percent of the labor force;[31] agricultural planning based on technical improvement and production cooperatives;[32] support for consumer cooperatives of various sorts, to which about 20 percent of the population already belonged;[33] the establishment of trade union-owned factories, insurance funds, workshops, and building and construction firms, all to be facilitated by the capital resources of a Workers' Bank;[34] and finally, the piercing of the educational and cultural monopoly of the propertied through the expansion and democratization of educational opportunity.[35]

There is little doubt that all of these measures were, would have been, or (later) proved to be, good for the working class. Certainly, they are all capable of being better anchored than the gains accruing from the growth strategy. Whatever their individual or collective efficacity, however, most of them were very dependent on labor's ability to harness the state, indeed to be integrated into the apparatus of the existing, yet improving, liberal-democratic state. These plans counted a great deal on the democratic state's ability to institutionalize class opposition over a prolonged period of time; unmediated political struggle by the working class on behalf of ultimate goals therefore took a backseat to trade union and SPD activism within the existing democratic state and in the name of all of the people.[36]

At its most optimistic, the campaign for economic democracy was designed to transcend the split between socialist labor's "politicist" strategy (ascendant from 1912 to 1918 and again from 1920 to 1925) and its "syndicalist" strategy (ascendant before 1912, at the end of 1918, and again during the rising tide of strikes between 1925 and 1928). Each strategy by itself had seemed to reach the limits of what it might achieve, and the new program presumed to incorporate the best of each. Hence, economic democracy was able to win support from the established, most mature, and cautious workers, such as those in the Woodworkers' Union, as well as from the more radical, younger, and confrontationist workers, such as those in the Metalworkers' Union. Yet, in reality, mass activism by the union rank and file, especially within the factory, was seen as less important than union representation on various planning boards, present and future. What political constellation would bring such bodies into being, and what kind of state would exercise economic control functions remained less than clear, even if one accepts the social democrats' argument that they, unlike the communists, were prepared to "begin before power is captured one hundred percent." The cartels, monopolies, syndicates, and trusts generated by monopoly capitalism might ultimately make control of the economy easier. Meanwhile, however, how were these entities to be rendered amenable to democratic administration and planning? And how was "the state" to be won over on behalf of democratic planning, investment control, and oversight, steps necessary to accelerate the way to abolition of capitalist property relations? Indeed, a question easily posed after three decades of Keynesianism was, Why should the working class expect to benefit at all from developments endogenous to the dynamics of capitalism?

These questions inevitably lead back to the central assumption of the German socialist trade unionists mentioned earlier, namely, that democracy would explode capitalism; that the democratic state, because it could be made to represent "the people" (die Allgemeinheit), would compel entrepreneurs to proceed according to principles inimical to their own survival. For most Social Democrats the core determinant in the democratic state was the competition of the political parties, itself a process mirroring class conflict.[37] So long as a numerically inferior bourgeoisie could be kept from abandoning the rules of parliamentary democracy, the power of the working class was bound to grow both because of its accumulated political successes and activism and because capitalism's own economic tendencies were creating new and larger constituencies for social democracy, precisely as Karl Kautsky had predicted in The Class Struggle. The working class, as the spokesman for the great, noncapitalist majority, would enforce the primacy of politics throughout the economy, as well as in politics per se.[38] That is, the working class's democratic politics would compel the state to overcome the limitations on its activities hitherto posed by such mechanisms as fiscal crunches and investment strikes or crises of confidence on the part of capital. Further, monopoly capitalism's increasing inability to regulate itself without major crises would force it into greater dependence on the state—the base from which socialists could democratize and transform it. Capitalism would increasingly be compelled to turn for help to an agency in which the working class might exercise decisive influence.

Thus, in this conception, the formally neutral instrumentalities constituting the state take on the character of an independent subject, capable of intervening in civil society in the direction determined by those enjoying political (that is, ultimately parliamentary) dominance. What that implies, logically enough, is that the struggle to change society and the campaign to democratize the economy are underpinned by electoral politics. The rather obvious problem, one brought home to socialists often enough, is that neither the working class nor its electoral support could be counted on to grow, even if other social forces continued to adhere to the rules of democracy and even if no major economic crises intervened to disrupt the smooth evolution of organized capitalism. The confidence in capitalism's evolutionary course appears to have been so fixed that even the trauma of the Depression did not shake their vision.[39]

At any rate, while social democracy moved to harness the power of the state, the unions would carry conscious and politicized democratic production policies into the factory, basing themselves in the projects mentioned earlier. Together, they would lead to a broadening of the social functions of the state, and the public (that is, noncapitalist) sector would grow as noncommodity cells within capitalism. Clearly, "the state" for Hilferding, Naphtali, Tarnow, and the others was not a capitalist state but, rather, a state in a capitalist society; a state that as a democracy could be employed not only against capitalists but against capitalism itself. Unfortunately, the correctness of their position is a moot question, albeit a very important one. German capitalists and other nonproletarians stopped playing by the rules of the democratic state's game. Whether they stopped because the socialists were too successful or for other reasons is too much to broach here. In any case, in this confrontation, capitalism ultimately proved stronger than democracy.

The conceptualization of the state as a neutral instrumentality becoming, at the same time, an independent subject was a troublesome one, even for Germans. For trade unions' chief Theodor Leipart, for example, the formally democratic state was supposed to become a real people's state by progressive intervention in the economy. Yet, if the state was not yet democratic, why would it intervene in this fashion? And if a not-yet-fully democratic state can stand above civil society, then why should a fully democratic state simultaneously be an instrument of the working class or "the people" and be engaged in conflicts within society? One suspects that this confusion, if confusion is what it was, was grounded in the SPD's operative theory of pluralist democracy, which in turn was linked to the class cooperation, competition, and coalitions the SPD found necessary in the absence of an absolute working-class majority.[40] This would also account for the great eagerness to depict the interests of workers, indeed to reformulate them, as the interests of the nation, of the people, as the "general interest," something made easier by a protracted period of prosperity and a capitalism more amenable to planning. Cynically, one might simply label the program for economic democracy as a program to abolish capitalism within capitalism by taking part in its increasingly organized direction.

German advocates of economic democracy, no matter how radical their vision of future society, like other social democrats (and today's democratic socialists and Eurocommunists), abandoned the traditional sequence according to which the workers first captured political power, expropriated the capitalists, put the economy under social direction, and then organized and democratized it. Instead, as indicated above, German workers were to democratize and ultimately socialize an already-organized economic system by helping to direct it, of course on the basis of parity, as well as by encouraging the state to expand its economic role, and by establishing their own noncapitalist economic institutions.

Rather than passing judgment on any inherent virtues to abandoning both Leninism and the straightforward growth strategy, it is instructive to examine some of the possible consequences of several of the planks of the economic democracy program as enunciated in 1928.

In the case of entrepreneur-worker industrial self-administration bodies (Selbstverwaltungskörper), workers face the risk of becoming coresponsible for the failures of particular enterprises or branches; even if they obtain adequate representation, they remain vulnerable to a kind of vocational egotism or branch selfishness, overidentifying with the particular industry's needs and ultimately helping capitalists extend their control. This happened in the 1920s in the case of Taylorism, rationalization, and automation.[41] Representing the interests of the commonweal may also force workers at both the industry and factory levels into a kind of hyper-, self-exploitation taking the form of an obsessive promotion of production.[42]

In regard to state and trade union control of monopolies, the working class is faced here with a troublesome contradiction. On the one hand, monopolies appear to be the economic form most appropriate and amenable to social direction and eventual socialization; yet they are also a great source of private capitalist power and, through high prices and protectionism, place extra burdens on all consumers, particularly lower-income groups containing potential allies of labor.

In the case of democratically organized, state-owned production units and utilities, what is promised appears greater than what is possible, even if the state assumes control over more than just "sure losers." The promise here consists of profits for the people, movement away from commodity production standards, more equitable wage structures, and democratic management structures. The reality is likely to consist of adaptation to the capitalist environment—self-desocialization under the pressure for profitability. Business is business, and skill specialization, wage differentials, and productivity pressures are bound to appear, for no state can afford interminable subsidies.

As for the expansion and administration of social insurance and labor law, there is in the German case, as in other cases, an underestimation of how dependent these mechanisms are on the business cycle. In good times they certainly do limit the prerogatives of employers and provide a floor beneath which the workers' share of the social product will not fall. In bad times, however, even a democratic state may retreat from such measures, both because of the fiscal crunch and because only by permitting capitalists to make profits can production, consumption, and employment be guaranteed for the future. [43] Political democracy can do nothing to change this, and it is not even clear that an absolute socialist majority would be able to escape this dilemma; it is more likely to fall victim to the need for sacrifices and the dismantling of its own constructs or their reduction to empty shells. The dismal fate of compulsory binding arbitration after 1930 provided a good example of this. [44]

Space does not permit an evaluation here of the prefigurative or counterhegemonic aspects of the economic democracy program, most notably cooperatives, a Workers' Bank, and trade union-owned factories and construction companies. One obvious problem, however, and one that has surfaced often in the history of worker and union enterprises, is that to compete effectively with private capital, cooperatives and other union undertakings are compelled to treat their workers just as other employers do. Further, since private savings can never account for more than a very small percentage of investment funds, any Workers' Bank is faced with the impossible task, in Tarnow's own words, of "trying to buy out capitalism with the workers' pennies." [45] This is not to argue that all these undertakings are without merit, but it would be foolish and has been politically harmful to expect too much from them.

One final observation is in order on a signal moment of the German and most subsequent programs for economic democracy. Because of the emphasis they place on the role of the democratic state in redistribution of the social product, these programs generally tend to push into the future their concern with the actual ownership of the means of production. If class struggle is primarily over distribution, then all classes must be concerned with enlarging the aggregate social product—or what in U.S. parlance is called the pie. Once labor becomes party to the search for higher productivity and rationalization, it leaves itself open to the possibility that appropriate measures may have to come at its own expense. In this very important respect, the economic democracy strategy marks no advance over the growth strategy. In both instances, the state has to enter after the fact to compensate the victims through insurance, retraining, safety nets, and the like, all mechanisms vulnerable to a fiscal crisis likely to be explained as a result of a squeeze on profits. Concern with the pie and its distribution leads, in turn, to underconsumptionist (that is, insufficient purchasing power) theories of economic crisis; these then tend to move questions of ownership and control even farther out of the limelight.

All this renders economic democracy, as a strategy for the organized working class, much more suitable to periods of economic expansion and prosperity than to periods of unemployment and stagnation. It should, therefore, not be surprising that Wirtschaftsdemokratie emerged in Germany as an alternative to the growth strategy during the politically most stable and economically most expansive years (1925-28), and that updated versions of transformation-oriented socialist strategies were developed and propounded in Western Europe during the 1960s and early 1970s, that is, during and near the end of a fairly long period of economic expansion, one that had itself taken place primarily under the aegis of a growth strategy. And just as the German labor movement's campaign for economic democracy came to a standstill after 1930, when the effects of the depression had become severe and the capitalist bourgeoisie had abandoned any commitment to parliamentary democracy, so current European campaigns for transformation in the direction of democratic socialism have waned in the shadow of contemporary stagflation. It would thus seem that the alternative model that Germany has had to offer, economic democracy, like its more widely accepted growth model, has not yet demonstrated the ability to fulfill its central goal of insulating the past achievements and future gains of workers from the vicissitudes of international capitalism and the prerogatives of capitalists. Whatever strategy labor's leaders might propose either to augment or to replace it had better be forthcoming soon, for there are hard times ahead.

NOTES

1. Although this school of analysis reaches at least as far back as Thorstein Veblen's work on Imperial Germany, probably the two most influential works to appear in English stressing Germany's divergence have been Leonard Krieger, The German Idea of Freedom (Boston: Beacon Press, 1957); and Ralf Dahrendorf, Society and Democracy in Germany (Garden City, N. Y.: Doubleday, 1967).

2. "Corporatism" has become a diversified growth industry in the social sciences. For a sampling of the literature, especially as it pertains to West Germany and its utility for other countries, see Ulrich V. Aleman, ed., Neokorporatismus (Frankfurt: Campus Verlag, 1981); Prokla, vol. 38 (1980); Phillipe Schmitter and Gerhard Lehmbruch, eds., Trends toward Corporatist Intermediation (London: Sage, 1979); and Leo Panitch, "The Development of Corporatism in

Liberal Democracies," Comparative Political Studies 10 (1977): 61-90.
For Weimar Germany in particular, see Charles Maier, Recasting
Bourgeois Europe (Princeton, N.J.: Princeton University Press,
1975); and Friedrich Zunkel, Industrie und Staatssozialismus (Düsseldorf: Droste Verlag, 1974).

3. On the basic outlines and consequences of German labor's
policies from 1925 to 1933, see David Abraham, The Collapse of the
Weimar Republic: Political Economy and Crisis (Princeton, N.J.:
Princeton University Press, 1981), especially chap. 5; and Adolf
Sturmthal, The Tragedy of European Labor (New York: Columbia
University Press, 1943).

4. The literature for each of these countries has become quite
substantial. For a current overview, see the various numbers of the
new journal Economic and Industrial Democracy. On Scandinavia,
see Gösta Esping-Anderson, "From the Welfare State to Democratic
Socialism," Political Power and Social Theory 2 (1981): 111-40; and
Rudolf Meidner, Employee Investment Funds (London: Allen & Unwin,
1978). On German-speaking Europe, see the essays in Detlev Albers,
ed., Otto Bauer und der "dritte" Weg (Frankfurt: Campus Verlag,
1978); and Hans-Willi Weinzen, Wirtschaftsdemokratie Heute? (Berlin: DVK Verlag, 1980). On Mediterranean Europe, see Giorgio
Napolitano, The Italian Road to Socialism (Westport, Conn.: Law-
rence Hill, 1978); and somewhat indirectly, Nicos Poulantzas, State,
Power, Socialism (London: New Left Books, 1978). On the United
States, see Martin Carnoy and Derek Shearer, Economic Democracy
(White Plains, N.Y.: M. E. Sharpe, 1980).

5. The now-classic discussion of the fiscal crisis mechanism
is James O'Connor, The Fiscal Crisis of the State (New York: St.
Martin's Press, 1973); see also Adam Przeworski, "Material Bases
of Consent," Political Power and Social Theory 1 (1980): 21-66. For
a detailed analysis of how German capitalists withdrew from tacit co-
coperation with labor after 1929 and how the end of that cooperation
reverberated through the political system, see Abraham, Collapse,
pp. 261-91. On the asymmetrics involved in these kinds of compacts
and this kind of participation, see Claus Offe and Helmut Wiesenthal,
"Two Logics of Collective Action: On Social Class and Organizational
Form," Political Power and Social Theory 1 (1980): 67-115.

6. These are matters that cannot be accorded due attention
here; for a fuller discussion, see Abraham, Collapse, pp. 229-61;
and the figures reported by Gerhard Bry, Wages in Germany, 1871-
1945 (Princeton, N.J.: Princeton University Press, 1960), pp. 32,
75, 331, 362, 398-400, 473. Suffice it here to note that after 1924,
real wages, real earnings, social expenditures, and labor's share of
the national income all continued to rise through 1931, all to the dis-
pleasure of most of Germany's entrepreneurs and some of its neigh-

bors. As late as 1931, Fritz Tarnow could caution his fellow ADGB leaders that "especially as seen from abroad, the standard of living of German workers is rather respectable and, beyond that, we have the best Sozialpolitik [social welfare system]."

7. The agrarian sector was crucial to German politics and economics for two reasons: (1) members of the rural elite occupied central positions in the army and state bureaucracy and (2) one-fourth of the population was still rural, and it often provided Germany's economic elite with vital electoral support. Rural Germany will not be considered further here. On relations between industry and agriculture, see Abraham, Collapse, pp. 180-228; on relations between peasants and the agrarian elite, see ibid., pp. 53-115.

8. For an elaboration of these economic and policy cleavages and how they reverberated politically from 1925 to 1932, see ibid., pp. 116-79.

9. On the problem of the Mittelstand in Weimar Germany, see the work of H. A. Winkler, "From Social Protectionism to National Socialism," Journal of Modern History 48 (1976): 1-18; and idem, Mittelstand, Demokratie und Nationalsozialismus (Cologne: Kiepenheuer & Witsch, 1972). On the weakness of the "popular" middle-class parties, see Larry Jones, "The Dying Middle: The Fragmentation of Weimar Bourgeois Parties," Central European History 5 (1972): 23-54. Electoral figures for the Weimar years, especially after 1924, pointedly indicate how weak the draw was of the various bourgeois-popular parties: excluding the Catholic Center party and the conservative, largely rural German Nationals, these parties fell from a total of 16 percent of the vote in 1924 to a mere 3 percent in 1932. By contrast, the SPD and Communists (KPD) together regularly obtained from 34 percent to 42 percent of the vote.

10. By now the literature on organized capitalism has gotten somewhat out of hand; for some illuminating discussions, see H. A. Winkler, ed., Organisierter Kapitalismus: Voraussetzungen und Anfänge (Göttingen: Vandenhoeck & Ruprecht, 1974), especially the essays by Kocka, Winkler, and Wehler.

11. For two different interpretations of this olive branch, see Dirk Stegmann, "Die Silverberg-Kontroverse 1926," in Sozialgeschichte Heute, ed. H. U. Wehler (Göttingen: Vandenhoeck & Ruprecht, 1974), pp. 594-610; and Abraham, Collapse, pp. 138-41.

12. Jürgen Habermas, Legitimation Crisis (Boston: Beacon Press, 1975), p. 57. The more detailed analysis is provided by Claus Offe, Strukturprobleme des kapitalistischen Staates (Frankfurt: Suhrkamp Verlag, 1972).

13. Perhaps the most telling example of this tension within the SPD emerged in the conflict between Labor Minister Rudolf Wissell, who from 1928 to 1930 used the means and institutions at his disposal

(especially binding arbitration) to support worker demands, while
Finance Minister Rudolf Hilferding, who has always been associated
with the left wing of the party, begged and borrowed internationally
to keep the exchequer afloat while urging complete self-restraint on
Wissell and the rank and file. Finally, its bourgeois partners abandoned the SPD, and the unemployment insurance fund went bankrupt;
for details, see Helga Timm, Die Deutsche Sozialpolitik und der Bruch
der Grossen Koalition im März 1930 (Düsseldorf: Droste Verlag,
1952). On the SPD's dilemma, see Sturmthal, p. 35; and Ernesto
Laclau, Politics and Ideology in Marxist Theory (London: New Left
Books, 1977), pp. 124-42.

14. See the literature cited in note 5. On the effects of the reserve army, see the closing chapter of Ludwig Preller, Sozialpolitik
in der Weimarer Republik (Stuttgart: Mittelbach Verlag, 1949); on
the breakdown of the arbitration machinery, see H. -H. Hartwich,
Arbeitsmarkt, Verbände und Staat (Berlin: Walter de Gruyter, 1967).

15. On the details of the WTB program and the party and trade
union responses to it, see Michael Schneider, Das Arbeitsbeschaf-
fungsprogramm des ADGB (Bonn-Bad Godesberg: Verlag Neue Gesellschaft, 1975). On changes in the economic thinking of German capitalists and their relationship to various emergency Keynesian programs, see Abraham, Collapse, pp. 173-79, 274.

16. After all, from Babeuf through the ten-point plan of the Communist Manifesto and the struggles of 1918-19, social democracy
meant completing and transcending the accomplishments of 1789-91
with social gains, not in narrow economistic terms but, rather, in
terms of transforming the entire sphere of civil society as the political sphere had been transformed from one of subjects to one of citizens. The most forceful statement of this position remains that of
Arthur Rosenberg, Democracy and Socialism (Boston: Beacon Press,
1965).

17. This term was initially applied to Austro-Marxism, especially that of the interwar period, but it emerges in the analyses and
proposals put forward in most of the literature, including that cited in
note 4, above. See also, Klaus Novy, Strategien der Sozialisierung:
Die Diskussion der Wirtschaftsreform in der Weimarer Republik
(Frankfurt: Campus Verlag, 1978), pp. 35-63.

18. It is ironic that, in this country, Milton Friedman and numerous others are in the business of publishing books demonstrating
that democracy is possible only in/under capitalism, an analysis that
conveniently skips over the strange gap between the praxis of organized
capitalist interests in the history of Europe (and the United States) and
their subsequent ideological reflections on their role in the evolution
of democracy. At least de Tocqueville and Macaulay were more hon-
est.

19. On Hilferding's view of the content and possibilities of pluralist democracy, see Wilfried Gottschalch, Strukturveränderungen der Gesellschaft und politisches Handeln in der Lehre von Rudolf Hilferding (Berlin: Dunker & Humblot, 1962), pp. 189-218, 242-61. Hilferding repeated this theme in nearly everything he wrote during the 1920s, particularly in Die Gesellschaft, which he edited.

20. The ADGB program for economic democracy was published under the lead authorship of Fritz Naphtali, Wirtschaftsdemokratie: Ihr Wesen, Weg und Ziel (Berlin: Verlagsgesellschaft des ADGB, 1928). Naphtali was a lawyer-economist and, like those who assisted him in drafting the program, a full-time trade union intellectual. Naphtali also headed the Social Democratic Economic Research Unit. Unfortunately, all of the unit's archives were destroyed, some in anticipation of seizure by the Nazis and others in various fires. In one of those numerous ironies of realization/transformation characteristic of the period, Naphtali wisely fled to Palestine after 1933, where he became head of the Workers' Bank in Haifa, a member of the Left (but anti-Soviet) wing of the Labor party and Trade Union Federation and, later, an Israeli minister of economics.

21. For a representative, though far from complete, sampling of the debates that led to Naphtali's definitive program, see Protokoll des Kongresses des ADGB in Breslau 1925 (Berlin: Verlagsgesellschaft des ADGB, 1926), pp. 186-265; Theodor Leipart, Auf dem Wege zur Wirtschaftsdemokratie (Berlin: Verlagsgesellschaft des ADGB, 1928), pp. 3-19; virtually every issue of Die Gesellschaft and Die Arbeit during these years; the Protokoll des Kongresses des ADGB in Hamburg 1928 (Berlin: Verlagsgesellschaft des ADGB, 1929), pp. 170-224; the Jahrbuch des ADGB 1928 (Berlin: Verlagsgesellschaft des ADGB, 1929), pp. 54-58; and the very useful volume by Saloman Schwarz, Handbuch der Gewerkschaftskongresse (Berlin: Verlagsgesellschaft des ADGB, 1930), pp. 120-32, 183-96, 406-32. For more recent views, see Rudolf Kuda, "Das Konzept der Wirtschaftsdemokratie," in Vom Sozialistengesetz zur Mitbestimmung, ed. H. O. Vetter (Cologne: Bund-Verlag, 1975), pp. 253-74, where all this is unproblematic; and Hans Ulrich, "Die Einschätzung von kapitalistischer Entwicklung und Rolle des Staates durch den ADGB," Prokla 6 (1973): 1-70, where it, along with Hilferding's concept of organized capitalism, is only problematic. On how economic democracy was perceived by German entrepreneurs, see H.-A. Winkler, "Unternehmer und Wirtschaftsdemokratie," Politische Vierteljahresschrift 11 (1971): 308-22.

22. Naphtali, Wirtschaftsdemokratie, pp. 115-26.

23. Ibid., pp. 21-34.

24. Ibid., pp. 127-44.

25. Ibid., pp. 53-113. For some of the most interesting attempts during Weimar, see Novy, Strategien der Sozialisierung, pp. 221-66; and the Protocols of the 1928 ADGB Congress. By the mid-1920s already, Vienna had become something of an exemplar of this, particularly at the level of neighborhood organization, cooperative housing, and youth and sports organizations. Austria was, in fact, the home not only of Otto Bauer, who became a central figure for Left-social democracy, but also of several prominent German socialists, including Hilferding. See Anson Rabinbach, "Politics and Pedagogy: The Austrian Social Democratic Youth Movement," Journal of Contemporary History 13 (1978): 337-56; and Manfredo Tafuri, Vienna Rosa: La Politica Residenzilla nella Vienna Socialistica (Milan: Editrice, 1980).

26. Naphtali, Wirtschaftsdemokratie, pp. 129-43.
27. Ibid., pp. 144-50.
28. Ibid., pp. 144-55.
29. Ibid., pp. 151-55.
30. Ibid., pp. 35-52.
31. Ibid., pp. 53-72.
32. Ibid., pp. 97-113.
33. Ibid., pp. 73-86.
34. Ibid., pp. 83-96.
35. Ibid., pp. 157-72. The tasks were summarized under the heading "Current Demands for the Democratization of the Economy on the Way to Socialism" (Die Gegenwartsforderungen zur Demokratisierung der Wirtschaft auf dem Wege zum Sozialismus), ibid., pp. 175-82. All the items cataloged were discussed in the literature cited in note 21.

36. In this regard there is a good bit of corporatism in the economic democracy strategy, even if of a different sort from that involved in the growth strategy. See Leo Panitch, "Trade Unions and the Capitalist State," New Left Review 125 (January 1981): 21-46; and Adam Przeworski, "Social Democracy as an Historical Phenomenon," New Left Review 122 (July 1980): 27-58.

37. This perspective is one of the Marxist residues in the work of S. M. Lipset, Political Man (Garden City, N.Y.: Doubleday Anchor, 1963), pp. 230-79. This analysis almost appears to be derived from Hilferding and Kautsky; see Gottschalch and Massimo Salvadori, Karl Kautsky and the Socialist Revolution (London: New Left Books, 1979), pp. 115-80, 319-39.

38. Hilferding, for example, took pride in pleading guilty to the accusation, leveled at the SPD and ADGB by employers' organizations, that wages were being set politically rather than by market forces.

39. It is surprising how little the depth of economic crisis altered the socialist plans for economic democracy; German socialists were

rather orthodox in their evaluation of capitalism's cyclical and epi-
sodic crises. To the 12-point program discussed above, they added
primarily glosses: stringent control of monopolies; lowered tariffs;
regulation of the flow of capital, especially through greater influence
on the banks; and reluctantly some precocious Keynesianism through
the stimulation of mass purchasing power and demand by means of
maintained wages, public works and pump priming, work creation,
and institution of the 40-hour week. From the socialist perspective,
a collapse of capitalism would mean the collapse of the economy and
would not lead to the inauguration of socialism but, rather, to incal-
culable difficulties. Hence, socialists were not only certain to be the
"inheritors of capitalism" but might also be forced to be "doctors at
its sickbed."

40. Unwilling and unable to cooperate with the KPD, the SPD
in Weimar Germany was always compelled to form coalitions with
non-working-class parties to its Right. Even when its vote was twice
as large as that of the second-place finisher (30 percent in 1928 compared with 15 percent for the Catholic Center), the SPD was unable to
form a government by itself. The current coalition of SPD and FDP
is more clearly a matter of choice on the part of the SPD leadership.

41. The dangers of "buying into" such measures was already
noted at the time by both foreign observers and Germans. See Robert
Brady, The Rationalization Movement in Germany (Berkeley and Los
Angeles: University of California Press, 1933), for an extremely
keen appreciation of how these measures were made to redound to the
benefit of capitalists; and for a more agnostic view, see Elisabeth
Schalldach, Rationalisierungsmassnahmen der Nachinflationszeit im
Urteil der freien Gewerkschaften (Jena: Verlag Gustav Fischer, 1930),
pp. 94 ff., 164 ff. By and large, the European Left in the 1920s, including Lenin, Gramsci, Bauer, and nearly all social democrats,
displayed a near-reverence for technological advance, factory reorganization, efficiency, and the like. Today we have come full circle,
with most of the Left in Western Europe and North America champion-
ing "small is beautiful," artisanal craftsmanship, and the William
Morris mentality. The cachet for this regrettable development appears to be derived from Harry Braverman, Labor and Monopoly
Capital (New York: Monthly Review Press, 1971), and the work of
E. P. Thompson, though rank-and-file unionists seem less vulnerable
than intellectuals.

42. Gramsci already observed behavior of this sort during the
Turin council movement and factory occupations of 1918-19, and one
senses the same kinds of things in the current worker-run steel mills
of Youngstown, Ohio.

43. The closing pages of Preller are very poignant on this question, and it is not at all clear how Rudolf Hilferding and Rudolf Wissell

could have escaped their fiscal crisis dilemma any more effectively under an economic democracy strategy than under the growth strategy.

44. The mechanism of compulsory binding arbitration by the Labor Ministry, which had consistently worked to labor's advantage, under the pressure of a deteriorating economy suddenly turned against labor in 1930; see Abraham, Collapse, pp. 240–46, 255–57. This larger dilemma may also explain why the PCI has lately been less eager to join the Italian government.

45. Tarnow's comments appeared in Die Stellungnahme der freien Gewerkschaften zur Wirtschaftsdemokratie (Jena: Verlag Gustav Fischer, 1929), p. 18. On this question of capital formation the Meidner Plan marks a real qualitative advance over other economic democracy programs precisely because it plans to take over control of capital rather than simply raising its own. It is also interesting to note that the Israeli Workers' Bank, of which Naphtali became chairman, prospered and became one of Israel's big three only after the Israeli state, at the time a virtual one-party, Labor party state, made it the exclusive repository of all government, pension, and foreign loan funds.

7

THE LEGACY OF LIBERALISM AND COLLECTIVISM IN THE LABOR MOVEMENT: A TENSE BUT FRUITFUL COMPROMISE FOR MODEL GERMANY

ANDREI S. MARKOVITS

INTRODUCTION

Most of the popular and scholarly literature dealing with the West German success story has emphasized worker discipline and union moderation as being among the major components in what has often been referred to as "Model Germany." Indeed, this view is replicated in the common discourse of popular opinion, where it is not unusual to hear that attributes of a particularly "Germanic" kind, such as punctuality, discipline, a near blind faith in authority, and a certain sense of frugality, all characterize the attitudes of West German workers toward their jobs. These arguments lead often to one of two implicit views: the first, perhaps best labeled "optimistic," seems to wish that if only our workers could assume similar traits, we would be well on the way to alleviating one of the most serious impediments to our own economic well-being. The second view, more "pessimistic" in nature but perhaps more accurate analytically, recognizes the uniqueness of the West German constellation and thus concedes its inherent inapplicability to other milieus. With admiration bordering on envy, it writes off the West German advantage by attributing it to such ephemeral, yet powerful, notions as the "German character," the "German political culture," or some mixture of the two.

This chapter[1] argues that, in fact, the pessimists are closer to the truth than their optimistic colleagues. Indeed, the situation of the West German worker is unique and probably inimitable in any other social context. Although this study does hold that the character of the contemporary West German worker has been determined by the particular development of the German labor movement within German society and state, it will part ways from the pessimists' cultural explanation of the West German workers' contributions to their country's success story. Briefly put, the main feature of the argument consists in highlighting the German labor movement's sometimes noble, at other times more calculating, yet always difficult, balancing act between two identities. On the one hand, German unions have been perhaps the most consistently dominant liberal force in an environment with a notoriously antiliberal tradition, while at the same time, on the other hand, they also embody the most viable collectivist alternative in the country's history. This precarious and often mutually exclusive synthesis was forged during the Bismarck era of the German Reich and has continued as organized labor's major predicament to this day. In short, because of its liberal legacy, the German labor movement not only found itself advocating certain reforms by the state, but also assumed the de facto position of being the prime defender of the only two experiments with liberal democracy in German history: the completely unsuccessful Weimar experience and the hitherto almost model-like Bonn Republic.

Organized Labor's crucial role as the major exponent and defender of Germany's liberal democracies made the union movement repeatedly staatstragend (state-supporting or state-carrying), even despite itself, in the two liberal episodes in German history. Despite the tremendous costs exacted by these periodic staatstragend compromises, the labor movement nevertheless still managed to maintain more than a mere semblance of its collectivist traditions. To this day, it has seen its raison d'être in its all-encompassing, universalistic class orientations as distinguished from the particularistic, interest-group approach of most Anglo-American unions. Furthermore, again in notable contrast to their foreign counterparts, the German labor unions have always seen themselves as fulfilling the role of a larger political movement as much as providing immediate economic protection for their members. If any common denominator in these disparate, indeed often contradictory, strains can be found, it would certainly have to be the resilience, eclecticism, and compromise-prone nature of social democracy.

The following pages will highlight these tensions and their manifestations in the context of the development of the German labor movement. After a brief historic section, which will anchor the fundamental dichotomy between the unions' support for liberal democracy and intraclass collectivism, the study will focus on its legacy in the Federal Republic of Germany (FRG). Concretely, this part of the chapter will feature an analysis of certain structures of the post-World War II West German labor movement that not only has contributed to the creation and successful maintenance of Model Germany but in fact could only do so precisely because of the close continuity from its antecedents in earlier epochs of German history. The concluding part will venture some possible scenarios for the future development of the West German labor movement and offer some hypotheses on its consequences for the continuation of Model Germany under changing structural conditions.

A BRIEF HISTORICAL SKETCH: THE SPECIFIC
NATURE OF GERMAN UNIONS AS A CONSEQUENCE
OF CERTAIN UNIQUE CONDITIONS IN
PRE-WORLD WAR II GERMANY

The Initial Development of Union Ideologies

German unions developed under very unique conditions in the latter half of the nineteenth century. They formed the organizational core, on a grass-roots level, of a strong and rapidly growing working class, which nonetheless remained excluded almost completely from all legitimate forms of participation in the country's political, social, and economic life. Both the agent and the arena of labor's exclusion was a strong and authoritarian state (Obrigkeitsstaat), which not only opposed such liberal reforms as parliamentarism, a multiparty system, free elections with "one man-one vote," an independent judiciary and civil liberties, but also tried to stymie all collectivist challenges to its hegemony "from below." This state and the dominant classes contributing to and benefiting from its existence would have most probably preferred using only repressive mechanisms in trying to keep the working class under control. That they also had to resort to concessions only attests to the relatively impressive power of the working class, most notably via its trade unions. This well-known "carrot-and-stick" combination of the Bismarckian state's policy of repression (the notorious Socialist Laws) and of reform (the famous introduction of the world's most comprehensive social welfare package) had profound effects on the German labor movement's subsequent developments.

The repressive aspect of this response by the Obrigkeitsstaat was largely the source of the German trade unions' dual allegiance to both liberalism and collectivism. It would be wrong to see liberalism as representing the unions' political reality and collectivism merely as window dressing or lip service to an illusory "true" radicalism. If anything, a "short-term versus long-term" characterization of these two political strains informing the unions' activities would be closer to the truth as a reflection of their respective roles in the development of the unions' position in German society. Excluded from participating in most aspects of German political life as individual citizens and as a collective class, German workers grew to appreciate both forms of political participation. Indeed, from the very beginning of working-class political organization, the two forms of progress (that is, liberal democratic and intraclass collectivist) often became intertwined in the concrete experience of daily union politics.

Repression clearly fostered the structures and values of intra-class collectivism,[2] an ideology that called for a strong collectivity based on the conscious perception of class solidarity. Furthermore, since all workers suffered more or less equally from the repression, the union movement developed an intraclass universalism from the very beginning, which countered various tendencies toward fragmentation along particularistic lines, such as different skills and occupations. This universalism transcended the sociology of the early labor movement and dominated its entire outlook and agenda. Owing to their complete exclusion from the country's dominant political, social, and cultural life, the German unions always perceived themselves to be first and foremost a political movement, addressed to all aspects of human emancipation and not simply the pecuniary issues specific to each employment. All these factors catapulted the German unions beyond what is the common notion of an interest group. Indeed, they became the organizational and existential centerpiece of an entire sub-society with its own culture, habits, language, means of communication, and politics. Thus, as a consequence of their political response to the repression of the Bismarckian Obrigkeitsstaat, a strong and universal sense of class, an all-encompassing mission of purpose well beyond pure job-related demands, and the notion of the need to be self-sufficient and unified in an ultimately successful struggle, could be viewed as the unions' major Marxist-collectivist legacy.

The authoritarian and feudal character of the Obrigkeitsstaat denied any citizenship rights, in the bourgeois sense, to most of Germany's workers. Thus, the struggle for universal suffrage, secret ballot, and a parliamentary system also assumed centrality for the German labor unions at the time. This provided the stimulus for the development of a liberal character in the unions' programs within the Bismarckian state. While liberalism most certainly fell short of offering the workers a collective human emancipation in the sense that I have termed Marxist-collectivist, it nevertheless provided a certain degree of freedom, dignity, and political emancipation, all of which were woefully absent in the German Reich. Given the unions' objective situation, it made perfect sense from their point of view to embrace the cause of liberal reforms, at least for "the short run."

It is in this context that one has to search for the strong roots of the political reformism that has been so prevalent throughout the history of the German labor movement. Short-run improvements,

especially if at least partially realized, do undoubtedly assume a dynamic of their own, whereby they are easily transformed from a means
to an end. This "corrupting" dimension of reformism clearly originated, in the case of the German labor movement, with its endeavors
to gain, via liberalism, certain political and civil rights in an authoritarian society.

The movement, however, received some added stimuli from the
"patronizing" and "caring" aspects of the Obrigkeitsstaat, which, of
course, represented merely the other face of its feudal-authoritarian
character. The "stick" of repression and labor exclusion could only
be wielded with efficiency when accompanied by powerful agents of
legitimation, notably social welfare reforms. Thus, peculiar as it
may sound, the German organized working class enjoyed the benefits
of some substantial "carrots," which it received relatively early in
comparison to the working classes of other countries, paradoxically
from its major tormentor, the authoritarian state.

Two crucial consequences for the German unions emanated from
this active reformism by the Bismarckian state. Both have continued
to inform much of the unions' structural characteristics and political
outlook to this day. The first could be summarized by the term
state fixation (Staatsfixierung). This factor comprised both attitudi-
nal and behavioral components, which have largely remained intact
for nearly a century. Briefly put, the unions developed certain hopes
and expectations vis-à-vis the state. They started to look to it for
concrete reforms and indeed began to rely on it to provide them with
certain benefits that otherwise they themselves would have had to
obtain via "their own strength." Hence, this union attitude regarding
the state has been characterized by some as a "fixation."[3]

Clearly, this outlook and value system exacted certain structural adaptations on the part of the organized labor movement, which
forms the second consequence for the unions concerning their relationship with an interventionist state. German scholars have used
the concept of "juridification" (Verrechtlichung) to describe and analyze this particularly crucial aspect of their organized labor movement.[4] Basically, this term denotes the fact that, partly as a consequence of the unions' state fixation, German industrial relations
and the unions' role therein have been heavily influenced by laws, le-
galisms, and a "primacy of legislation." By using the state as their
reference point—both negative and positive—the unions inadvertantly
entered the political arena on the state's terms, which meant, of
course, that they had to adopt the state's discourse or "rules of the
game." One of the main consequences was a state-fixated outlook,
which in turn entailed a juridified structure.

Yet another related dimension conveys the state's crucial
structural influence on Germany's organized labor movement. De-

spite the obvious antagonism between the two and the antinomian character of the labor movement in Imperial German society as a whole, it is noteworthy that the internal organization of the unions assumed key characteristics of its largely hostile environment. Thus, the unions internalized typical traits of the German state, such as a relatively early and thorough centralization, the discouragement of local autonomy, systematic hierarchization, strict division of labor, written rules, regularized reporting, and a clear sense of the primacy of the office as opposed to that of the office holder. In short, by the beginning of the twentieth century, German union life had undergone a thorough bureaucratization in terms of its rational organization. This is not to say that the German labor movement had become fully integrated into the Wilhelminian Reich. It merely meant that in its clear posture as the main opposing force to the authoritarianism of this empire it had simultaneously—perhaps even inadvertently—assumed some of the very characteristics that it found rather objectionable in its major opponents.

Thus, it would not only be simplistic but indeed false to see the German labor movement either as a Gegenmacht (oppositional force) or as an Ordnungsfaktor (integrating and co-opted force of the established order) at any period of its existence. The difficulty in analyzing its actions and thoughts lies precisely in the fact that it simultaneously fulfilled both contradictory functions as early as the late nineteenth century; it has continued to do so to this day. It placed a heavy emphasis on its self-sufficiency and autonomy as a political movement while at the same time increasing its orientation and expectations vis-à-vis the state. The first attribute made the unions fight hard for their recognition in the market by achieving the right to bargain collectively and sign contracts; the second aimed for a legitimation of this gain by the state via appropriate legislation.[5] Thus, it was never a question of "either-or" but, rather, of "both." It was the "both" that all along made the German unions unique, especially in terms of their structural contribution to what later became Model Germany.

The same pertains to the unions' liberalism versus their Marxist ideologies. Again, it was never a question of "either-or" but, in fact, a constant coexistence of "both." This was in part facilitated by the numerous commonalities in values that both of these political philosophies and movements shared, above all in their German expression in the pre-World War I period. Thus, for example, both attached absolute centrality to economic growth as a necessary prerequisite for progress, which, in turn, was the only vehicle toward the improvement of human life and thus the only true road to full emancipation. Liberalism and Marxism shared, in addition to this positive teleology of growth, an admiration of technology and its potential for improving all aspects of the social condition. Moreover, they were both profoundly universalistic, with liberalism emphasizing the universe of humanity via the individual and Marxism equally upholding ideals of universal humanitarianism to be achieved via the particular mission of the collectivity of the working class. Lastly, both believed in the necessity of reforms, with liberalism viewing them as ends in and of themselves and Marxism still attaching greater importance to their character as means.

The "both" of liberalism and Marxism achieved its structural synthesis in the form of German social democracy, especially as embodied in the Second International's showcase, the Social Democratic party (SPD). While the party never became coterminous with the German labor movement and never achieved the structural and organizational overlap experienced by party and union in, for example, Great Britain, Sweden, and Austria, there can be little doubt that the fate of the German union movement and that of the SPD have remained closely intertwined to this day. Although the unions never abdicated their role as a political movement in terms of being more than simple "wage machines" and always stressed the universal nature of their interests, there was also a strong tendency to view the SPD as the political arm of the labor movement. Political, in this case, remained always narrowly defined in terms of gaining particular reforms via the state. As such, this represented yet an additional framework for the unions' state fixation. It met its perfect match in the SPD's own state fixation, which, of course, was common not only to the parties of the Second International but also to those of the Third International.

Lastly, the SPD bore the same burdens of ambivalence in Imperial Germany as did the unions. Both were "in" the system without being "of" it. They had to fight for both liberalism and Marxism simultaneously, which, no matter how similar in many ways, were also fundamentally incompatible. This inherent tension created severe organizational problems for both the party and the unions, which were further exacerbated during the Weimar Republic and after World War II. By trying to achieve liberal reforms and attain the collective representation of an entire class under adverse conditions, both the SPD's and the unions' immediate results on the eve of World War I would have to be judged mixed at best. Whatever the actual achievements at the time may have been, the day-to-day struggle of the unions and the SPD to reconcile their political existence in the unique context of the authoritarian Obrigkeitsstaat created not only nearly insurmountable contradictions for the entire German labor movement, but in the very same process also laid the foundations for certain institutional arrangements. Although these contradictions could never be resolved, they could, in fact, under different socioeconomic and geopolitical

conditions, such as the post-World War II Bundesrepublik, contribute
to a new entity's stability and prosperity. But only after suffering
the consequences of having tried to resolve their inner contradictions
in a Manichean way, emphasizing one component to the exclusion of
the other, could the unions be ready to contribute actively to the construction of these new institutional arrangements.

Test and Failure of the Labor Movement's Cohesion: World War I and Weimar

The German Reich's Obrigkeitsstaat may have delivered substantial social reforms to the labor movement; it, however, never
failed to show its animosity vis-à-vis the unions and the SPD. Both
were "in" the system without ever being "of" it. It was not until
World War I, with the tremendous sacrifices it exacted from Germany,
that the unions and the SPD gained the so-called recognition (Anerken-
nung) from both the state and capital. This recognition was concre-
tized in the form of a genuine increase in union power during the war
years. Specifically, this era witnessed the earliest precursors to
what later became the much-celebrated structure of codetermination.
The unions gained various schemes of institutionalized participation
at the shop floor, at the plant level, in regional frameworks, even
within the state itself. Paradoxically, it was the Great War and its
most consequential development for Germany, namely the demise of
the imperial Obrigkeitsstaat, which catapulted the unions, the SPD,
and social democracy onto the center stage of German politics.
    What is so crucial to understand in this context is the fact that,
despite this monumental systemic transformation, little, if anything,
changed in the quality of the union movement's overall strategies,
policies, and daily activities. Rather, they developed by means of
the substantial shifts in the stakes at hand and the arenas of formulation and implementation. The unions' ambivalence—their theoretical contradictions and strategic vacillations—suddenly assumed implications that decided more than the immediate well-being of their
members. No longer were they a politically powerless subsociety
"in" the German state. They had, perhaps despite themselves,
become a fundamental pillar "of" the new republic. The meanings
of the reforms extended a good deal further than the particular terms
of their content. They determined revolution or counterrevolution;
they undermined more and perhaps better progress while defending
an already weakened liberal democracy from the onslaught of reaction.
In short, the change was not so much in the unions' thought and action,
but rather in the fact that both counted in the daily existence of German politics, perhaps more than those of any other political group
in the Weimar Republic.

World War I and the fall of the Bismarckian Obrigkeitsstaat made the unions come of political age. They became fully integrated into Germany's political life. This does not mean that they simply became "lackeys of capitalism" or uncritical sentries of the status quo. Far from it. It only conveys the fact that the German labor movement henceforth had to reconcile its contradictions, come to terms with its ambivalences, and account for its successes and failures outside the shell of a protective, albeit unequal, subsociety. The German unions had reached the emancipated stage of "high politics" in the Weimar Republic; for the first time, their words and deeds mattered.

Nowhere was this to become clearer in the course of the Weimar Republic than in the unions' old ambiguous position of being the major pillars of liberal democracy at the same time as they were assuming the role of the most important advocates of social redistribution in German society. The predicament of the unions in Weimar consisted of an inherently impossible situation: They at once became the defenders of the young republic and of the working class. The unions' and social democracy's liberalism and collectivism assumed staatstragend dimensions from the very beginning of the Weimar Republic. This already difficult task was further aggravated by the fact that much of the bourgeoisie and almost all institutional and sociological structures of the ancien régime wanted nothing more than the destruction of liberal democracy and the reestablishment of the Obrigkeitsstaat. Thus, faute de mieux, the German labor movement stepped into this power vacuum. It would be simplifying matters to see the unions and the SPD as martyrs in an hour of despair. Their past history and structural development in which reformism, gradualism, and other liberal values had assumed dominant proportions clearly provided the right preparation for organized labor's key role in participating in the conduct of Germany's first liberal democracy. Furthermore, the unions' long-held state orientation, which had become stronger with their gradual integration into mainstream politics during the Great War, was finally "consummated" in the Weimar Republic in that the unions and the SPD had suddenly become part of the state themselves.

But the unions were in a real bind. While, on the one hand, they clearly believed in the political and, above all, moral superiority of the Weimar Republic, as compared to its imperial predecessor, they also had to heed to their mandate of being the foremost protectors of working-class interests. The labor movement's near-integration into "the system" during World War I may have mitigated its original collectivist fervor, but it could not obliterate the unions' truly felt obligation to defend their membership. The successful integration of the unions into the Weimar Republic heightened the tension within the labor movement between its liberal and collectivist strains.

The labor movement's irreconcilable position of being a staunch defender of a shaky political arrangement qua its liberalism, yet at the same time also an inadvertant contributor to this system's instability qua its Marxism, eventually led to the tragic, internecine battles within its ranks which, as is well known, achieved neither liberalism nor Marxism but, in weakening both, aided the eventual triumph of fascism. The liberal-statist faction—largely, though not exclusively, centered around organized labor's social democratic wing—became increasingly preoccupied with a mere defense of the Weimar Republic, which it still perceived as much more beneficial to the working class than any other realistic alternative within the given context of German political history. Its obsession with defending the status quo led to an immobilisme, which gradually not only contributed in and of itself to the ultimate failure of the Weimar Republic (precisely the outcome it was intended to prevent) but also to an open split within the organized labor movement. Thus, the collectivist-Marxist faction—largely, though again not exclusively, centered around organized labor's communist wing—exhausted much of its energies in battling its liberal-statist rival, since it perceived the latter's strategy as having betrayed the principles of its original mandate, thereby not only "selling out" the working class but, in fact, helping to bring about the triumph of the very reaction its moderation was intended to prevent.

This destructive, internecine struggle was carried out on all political levels, ranging from the state's central organs, such as the legislature and administration, all the way to the shop floor of Germany's industrial plants. The all-encompassing nature and intraclass universalism of the German labor movement had given way to political fragmentation and centrifugal particularisms that were, in fact, strong enough to make the German working class the most bitter loser in the failure of the Weimar experiment. This was all the more tragic since it was precisely this class more than any other that believed in the ultimate values of this ill-fated republic. But the combined traditions of its liberalism and Marxism made certain that the German working class remained by and large immune to the lures of fascism and its most pernicious manifestation in the German context, namely virulent anti-Semitism. The legacy of August Bebel's famous words (that anti-Semitism was the socialism of fools) provided the German labor movement with the dignity of surrendering to fascism with its democratic ideals largely intact. The movement failed to create, however, the necessary structure that would have made it perhaps more possible for German labor to resist, maybe even defeat, fascism. The creation of such a structure was left to be one of the first and most crucial tasks of the immediate post-World War II period.

THE LABOR MOVEMENT IN THE FEDERAL
REPUBLIC OF GERMANY: THE CONTINUATION
OF UNIQUENESS UNDER DIFFERENT
CONDITIONS

A New Beginning: Intraclass Unity as
a Paramount Goal

The question originally posed in this chapter was, What exactly
was it about German labor that made it dependable, hard-working,
punctual, conscientious, frugal, and disciplined? In other words, how
and why did German workers acquire these much-admired "Teutonic"
qualities, which have made them the envy of the advanced industrial
world and which have provided more than their share in labor's substantial overall contribution to the success of Model Germany? The
first part tried to show some of the structural antecedents that were
among the important precursors to this development. Among them
were organized labor's early state orientation, which fostered a belief in the values of gradualism and reformism; moreover, this state
orientation also had significant organizational implications for the
unions, in that they developed a rather centralized, bureaucratized,
and "expert-like" or "technocratic" form of representation. The
spirit of reformism was also anchored in the strong tradition of liberal democracy that the German labor movement developed as an important progressive tradition, in opposition to the authoritarianism
of the dominant classes and the Obrigkeitsstaat. Moreover, the unions'
Marxism emphasized the instrumental necessity and moral superiority of collectivist politics; the unions perceived their mission as an
intraclass, universalistic endeavor that encompassed the entire
working class regardless of specific skills and particular occupations.

The second part of this chapter will show in what form and in
which context these traditions persisted in the Bonn Republic. Moreover, it will try to assess how they changed and why. It will discuss
some key elements in the labor movement's post-World War II development that have played a major role in the shaping of the Federal
Republic of Germany (FRG) as we know it today. Some of these developments have barely changed from their pre-World War II predecessors; others, however, are completely new creations in the context of this new entity called Bundesrepublik. It is important to understand that the unions' post-World War II world represents a synthesis of some of the major pre-World War II characteristics discussed
above and a clear reaction against others. In other words, the unions
in the FRG have confronted very similar yet also very different problems than before. They have had to fulfill almost identical tasks in
their pre- and post-World War II existence, but often in completely

different structural situations. In short, although the FRG clearly
adopted many characteristics from its predecessors, it also created
a new political reality for the unions. Thus, some of the major elements discussed in the previous section occurred once again. The
liberalism-Marxism tandem assumed a place of importance as did
such issues as state orientation, juridification, reformism, intraclass
universalism, organization centralization, the quest for the democratization of all aspects of human life, and the special relationship of
the unions to the Social Democratic party. But their existence had
substantially altered weightings and qualities in terms of their individual and collective presence in the unions' post-World War II world.
All remain, but in a different context and atmosphere.

The most notable change vis-à-vis Weimar was the much les-
sened polarization permeating most aspects of public life in the FRG.
The key word here is moderation. Moderation has characterized
capital-labor relations in the FRG, as it has intraunion politics and
union-party interactions. It was largely this all-encompassing framework of moderation that created a sense of dependability, predictability, calculability, and accountability on the part of the state and the
two major social forces, capital and labor, vis-à-vis one another.
Herein resided the secret of Model Germany. Cleavages and conflicts, albeit still dominating all aspects of West German political
and industrial life, assumed a more muted form in the Bonn Republic
than in its Weimar predecessor. The organized labor movement
contributed its share to this new and all-important development.

Perhaps the unions' most fundamental contribution to the political moderation in West Germany and certainly their most cherished
innovation in the immediate post-World War II period consisted in the
introduction of the so called Einheitsgewerkschaft (unitary trade union
movement) and Industriegewerkschaft (industrial union organization).
Both constructs were immediate reactions to the labor movement's
divisive and internecine experience in the waning days of the Weimar
Republic—a repetition that many labor leaders wanted to avoid at all
costs. Interpreting their shortsightedness and internal disunity to
be a result of the unfettered nature of their differing political ideologies, West Germany's labor leaders developed the strong desire to
form a powerful, all-encompassing, intraclass union movement in
which political factionalism and organizational centrifugality would
be kept to a minimum. Although the precise formulations of Einheitsgewerkschaft and Industriegewerkschaft had to await their formal
codification at the Deutscher Gewerkschaftsbund's (DGB)—German
Trade Union Federation's—official founding congress in Munich in
October 1949, the notions themselves had numerous antecedents
throughout the history of the German labor movement, as outlined
above. [6] Briefly put, they both aimed at a comprehensive, univer-

salistic, and centralized class organization as the best form of labor
representation at the shop floor and in society at large. In other
words, they hoped to institutionalize the collectivist component in
their tradition to safeguard against a Weimar-like backlash in this
new democratic beginning.

The Einheitsgewerkschaft established the post-World War II
organized labor movement as a politically inclusive, yet also structurally independent, force. Indeed, inclusiveness and independence
were the two sides of the same coin. By welcoming the membership
of every working man and woman regardless of their particular political beliefs and party affiliations, this newly created structure
could legitimately claim to be the universal and all-encompassing
representative of all West German workers. To enhance the legitimacy of its representational monopoly and in full agreement with its
legacy of speaking for an entire class, the DGB made it very clear
from the beginning that its struggles were always to be conducted on
behalf of the entire West German working class and not only its
unionized third. Concomitant to this inclusiveness, the DGB abdicated any possible affiliations with any of the FRG's political parties,
thus explicitly establishing itself as a major societal force outside the
country's official political institutions. Fully aware of the divisive
nature of party-affiliated unions for the working class as a whole,
the Einheitsgewerkschaft has to this day remained independent of
party politics in the FRG. Independence from party affiliation should,
however, in no way be misconstrued as political abstinence. The
frequently repeated DGB slogan well summarizes the West German
labor movement's consistent position on this matter since the inception of the Federal Republic of Germany: "We are politically independent but not neutral."

Yet another important corollary of the Einheitsgewerkschaft's
suprapolitical position developed in the form of its pragmatism. Its
autonomy from particular political parties and its legitimation in
terms of being an all-inclusive worker organization necessitated an
early orientation toward realistic alternatives and discouraged radical thinking in quest of a narrow Weltanschauung. The integrative
dimensions of the Einheitsgewerkschaft fostered a pragmatic approach
to problem solving without, however, thereby becoming agents of
political emasculation.

The political all-inclusiveness of the Einheitsgewerkschaft fulfilled the legacy of the unions' collectivity-oriented "class" tradition.
At the same time, it also addressed West German labor's long-held
values concerning the positive contributions of a liberal democracy
to the dignity of human existence. Thus, every worker who shared
this position was included in the movement. Those who did not were
explicitly excluded, however. Until the early 1950s, this notion of

incompatibility (Unvereinbarkeit) pertained only to National Socialists
and members of various neo-Nazi or right-wing organizations. Thus,
from the very beginning, the unions again became staatstragend of a
liberal democratic Rechtstaat (state based on the rule of law and due
process), not only qua their tradition of upholding liberal democratic
values but also as the major and most vociferous opponents to National Socialism before its onslaught in the early 1930s and after its
fall in the mid-1940s. The unions' consistently uncompromising positions against any neo-Nazi or right-wing activities and issues in
the course of the FRG's political development found their early expression in the conviction that being a Nazi or neo-Nazi was incompatible with being a unionist, since the latter implied the full support
of a liberal democratic social and political order, whereas the former
stood for its very destruction.

With the unions' systemic integration by the early 1950s as a
consequence of the cold war, important political setbacks, weak position in the labor market, and many of their members' diminished
interest in the collectivist-class aspect of politics, "incompatibility"
was extended to include Communists as well. To this day, many of
the DGB's 17 constituent unions, as well as the DGB federation itself,
maintain "clauses of incompatibility" (Unvereinbarkeitsbeschlüsse)
explicitly directed at Communists and other leftists on the one hand
and neo-Nazis and rightists on the other. The structure of the Einheitsgewerkschaft and the unions' liberal democratic legacy assured
the labor movement's early staatstragend identification with the FRG.
Yet, once again the unions assumed this staatstragend role in a sense
faute de mieux because many other segments of the West German
population (notably the industrialists) remained too compromised by
their record of active support of National Socialism to participate
fully in the new republic's development. Thus, with political extremism of both the Right and the Left discredited, the post-World
War II labor movement experienced an early structural integration
into the liberal democratic Rechtstaat of the FRG.

In addition to the political dimensions of inclusion that have
characterized the organized labor movement in the FRG, some economic ones have attained at least similar structural importance over
the years. It is in this context that the notion of Industriegewerkschaft
has played such a crucially cyrstallizing role. Based on the concept
of "one plant-one union," this structure aimed at organizing every
employee in a particular plant in only one union. Thus, be they
white-collar or blue-collar workers; skilled, semiskilled, or un-
skilled; male or female; German or foreign, they all belong to only
one union in a plant. In addition to alleviating interunion rivalries
on the shop floor and at the plant level, the principle of Industriegewerkschaft further reduces interunion hostilities by placing entire

industries within the organizational purview of only one union. Thus, be they huge multinationals or small enterprises, profitable firms or companies in poor financial condition, they all fall under the organizational purview of one union, which is their only official and common bargaining partner.

The implementation of this concept has created an important equalizer among all the workers employed in a particular industry. Although falling short of a Swedish-style solidaristic wage policy, the contract signed by one union for an entire industry clearly represents at least one initial common denominator for all the workers' benefits in that industry. Moreover, by having only 17 of these structures constitute the entire DGB and thus comprise all activities— private and public—in the West German economy, the FRG's industrial relations system is more centralized than those of most of its competitors in the advanced industrialized world.[7] With only 17 units doing all the negotiating for most of West Germany's organized labor and with a relatively great similarity in demands and attainments among these 17 nominally autonomous structures, the principle of Industriegewerkschaft has lent a high degree of predictability and clarity to the FRG's overall system of collective bargaining. Enhancing the calculability and centralization of this system is the fact that slightly over one-third of the DGB's membership belong to one union alone; with its nearly three million members, IG Metall (the capitalist world's largest single union) concludes contracts in its organizational purview comprising such key sectors as the FRG's steel and automobile industries, machine tools, electronics, and most everything else belonging to metal processing.

All in all, the structure of Industriegewerkschaft has represented a very decisive stabilizing factor in the FRG's industrial relations system. With its "one plant-one union" principle it alleviated multiunionism on the shop floor of West German factories, which not only plagued the German labor movement throughout the Weimar Republic, but has consistently been one of the most divisive and destructive mechanisms in the industrial relations of many countries, notably, of course, in the United States and the United Kingdom. Moreover, interunion rivalry has been kept to a minimum by the structure of Industriegewerkschaft even outside West Germany's factory gates. By extending the "one plant-one union" principle to one that could read "one industry-one union," very little territorial "raiding" among West German unions has plagued capital-labor and intralabor relations in the FRG, a notable distinction from the Anglo-American situation.

The Industriegewerkschaft, just like the Einheitsgewerkschaft, represented a profoundly unifying, regularizing, centralizing, and stabilizing factor in post-World War II West Germany's industrial relations. Both components embodied the major structural pillars upon which the union movement of the FRG was to be erected. As such, they were completely new phenomena anchored, however, in the labor movement's legacies from its turbulent past.

The immediate post-World War II period saw the West German labor movement thrust into a state-carrying position quite similar to parallel developments following the end of World War I. In both cases, the labor movement assumed quasi-governing roles in a power vacuum created by the structural changes accompanying the respective transitions from the old to the new orders. Again, not unlike the transfer from Imperial Germany to Weimar, many elites of the previous regime (national socialism) remained too discredited, for a short time, to assume their regular duties as major participants in the governing of this new order. This was especially the case with Germany's "steel barons" of the country's Rhine-Ruhr region, whose enthusiasm for Hitler's war provided the basis for the necessary hardware with which to fight it. In this area numerous grass-roots workers' committees assumed steel production on their own immediately following the end of World War II and stopped the British occupying forces from dismantling the mills.

This act on the part of the steel workers had a staatstragend function in that it maintained the essential infrastructure for the future of the West German industrial economy. Yet, at the same time this takeover had strong anticapitalist and antinomian overtones, because it challenged capital's control over the means of production in a concrete setting. Thus, in this move on the part of the workers, the traditional tension in the German trade union movement became once again manifest. While consciously attempting to transform the system via workers' control, the eventual institutionalized arrangement growing out of this act proved to be yet another staatstragend contribution by the unions to liberal democracy in the FRG. Ultimately, most control passed back to capital. Yet, what the West German labor movement retained from this crucial episode was the most far-reaching scheme of union involvement in industrial decision making to this day. This new arrangement was of course the system of Mitbestimmung or codetermination.

Mitbestimmung: Confrontation and Integration

Again, the idea behind this structure harkens back to Weimar days and has important precursors in working-class politics of the German Reich as well. The basic issue underlying the notion of codetermination has been that of political and economic control on behalf of the working class as implemented by its institutions, either a party, the union movement, or both. Working-class control has been at the heart of almost every labor movement in the capitalist world; thus, the German preoccupation with this phenomenon represents nothing unusual.

In terms of content and eventual aim of this control, few differences separated the visions of the various labor movements in capitalist countries. All hoped to achieve societal transformation by controlling the means of production in some fashion. It was the form of this process and its timing that clearly distinguished the numerous intralabor factions to the point of open hostility among them regarding this issue of control. Whereas the Communist model envisioned the party as the major agent of control to whom unions would have to play the subordinate role of "transmission belt" in the transformation of society's ownership of the means of production, the syndicalist model placed its hopes entirely in the unions regarding this endeavor. Common to both models was a willingness to apply force if necessary to achieve working-class control over the means of production.

The Social Democratic model differed from both of these, especially concerning its reluctance to deploy force in its quest for working-class control. It was this clear difference in means that contributed substantially to social democracy's overall gradualism and reformism, both of which assumed a content of their own in due course beyond their original purpose as a form of short-run tactics. In one expression of social democracy, perhaps best represented in its Bernsteinian version, gradualism and reformism assumed such paramount importance that the "here and now" dominated all political activities and horizons, thereby relegating any concrete realization of workers' control to a distant and very hazy future. Yet, another view also played an important role in the traditions of German and Austrian social democracy. Known as the "third way," it basically attempted to reconcile liberal democracy with Marxism. Thus, while accepting the validity and legitimacy of liberal democratic institutions for short-run improvements in working-class life, this version of social democracy never surrendered its fundamentally Marxist tenet, which held that only via some form of collective control over a country's economic activities were the workers to achieve a qualitatively better life for themselves and thus for society as a whole. True to Marx's spirit and letter, this interpretation envisioned genuine human emancipation and its commensurate political expression—genuine democracy—only as a result of collective action on the part of the working class. Concretely, the center of this collective action was to rest in various control mechanisms exercised by the working class via its full participation in the decision-making process at all levels of a country's productive life.

This vision dominated the famous Wirtschaftsdemokratie debate in the social democratic institutions of the Weimar Republic. With the unions playing a central role in this process, the emphasis was always on various collective schemes of worker participation at the shop-floor, plant, company, regional, and countrywide level for purposes of democratic control, rather than on worker ownership of the means of production. Following the 12-year hiatus created by national socialism, the German labor movement resumed its interrupted ideas immediately after 1945 with the full intention of implementing them in post-World War II West German society. The "third way" was finally to become reality in a new West Germany. This was the unions' fervent hope for the democratization of West German society. Thus, it is important to point out that, despite the unions' staatstragend position and early identification with the FRG's liberal democracy, they were far from satisfied with that system. Indeed, they hoped to transform it, using the whole complex of Mitbestimmung as their most important vehicle toward a collective democratization.

It is crucial to delineate the German unions' comprehensive view of Mitbestimmung, since it is only in its skeletal nature that this concept has become a "household word" in the international literature on West Germany. One of the four fundamental demands of the DGB at its founding congress in October 1949 asked for "the codetermination (Mitbestimmung) on the part of organized workers in all economic and social questions concerning the overall guidance and daily management of the economy."[8] Rather tellingly the demand following the one on Mitbestimmung stated the unions' desire for "the gradual socialization of key industries, especially in mining, iron and steel, large chemical firms, the energy sector, important transportation networks and key banks."[9] Thus, following the tradition that emphasized control over the means of production rather than ownership, the West German labor movement placed much greater weight on its participation in economic decision making via Mitbestimmung than on the nationalization of the economy as commonly demanded by many European labor movements following the conclusion of World War II. This clear hierarchy of priorities has been practically and programmatically maintained to this day. Whereas the 1963 and 1981 revisions of the DGB's Basic Program (Grundsatzprogramm) of 1949 provide little more than perfunctory lip service in rather obscure passages to the unions' desire for the socialization of some key industries, both documents feature further elaborations on the positive contributions of Mitbestimmung to the quality of life and the state of democracy in the Federal Republic of Germany.

The fact that the unions continue to demand its improvement and expansion is, of course, prima facie evidence that Mitbestimmung, the way the unions had envisioned it in its totality in 1949, still awaits its implementation in today's FRG. The unions took the literal meaning of the word very seriously. They wanted to codetermine all economic activities in the country as totally equal participants. This meant concretely that labor hoped to be present in all bodies that made consequential economic decisions ranging all the way from the shop floor of a small plant to the highest "command posts" of the state. Labor's representation would be on a parity basis where only its own participation and that of capital was required. It would assume a tripartite fashion where representatives of the public were to join the two "social partners," as capital and labor have been characteristically referred to in the structure of West German industrial relations.

The unions, however, were to be denied their dream. By the time they were ready to begin with the serious implementation of this comprehensive scheme of participatory democracy, the political climate in the world, in Europe, and especially in what was to become West Germany, had drastically changed. It could be argued that the Federal Republic of Germany in and of itself was a conservative creation to oppose the increasing Soviet threat in Europe. Whatever the merits of this particular point, there seems far less doubt that conservative forces dominated the newly established political entity of West Germany. The cold war quickly ended any realistic hopes on the part of the unions for far-reaching, system-transforming reforms. Indeed, an opposite trend engulfed the political climate of this young country in which many hitherto discredited people—quite a few industrialists among them—suddenly became salonfähig ("system proper") despite their rather supportive position of national socialism. Communism became the number one enemy and past political "mistakes" lost their significance in this new struggle, as long as loyalty was assured against the new opponent.

This atmosphere was hardly conducive to the implementation of the unions' comprehensive vision of Mitbestimmung. Indeed, it took the threat of a general strike in 1950 to defend the relatively modest results that the unions had eked out in the country's coal and steel industries largely before the establishment of the republic proper in 1949. Thus, the famous codetermination act of 1951—the so-called Montanmitbestimmung law—represented nothing else but the legal codification of a skeletal system of labor participation as exercised in the country's coal and steel sectors before 1949. Thus, Montanmitbestimmung "froze" an already existent system rather than create a new one. It was this "rump" codetermination embodied in Montanmitbestimmung that was to become world famous partly by being the only topic on West Germany usually discussed in introductory college courses on comparative industrial relations. Yet, the far-reaching and progressive nature of Montanmitbestimmung, as conceived by the unions, is clearly revealed by the vehement opposition on the part of West German industrialists to any further extension of the principle to other areas of the country's economy.

Although Montanmitbestimmung remained geographically, sec-
torally, and structurally confined (it only pertained to the upper
echelons of the country's steel and coal companies, most of which
are located in the Rhine-Ruhr area), it would be wrong to categorize
it as a defeat for West Germany's organized labor movement. To be
sure, it fell short of labor's ideal scheme of comprehensive participation; but its beneficial dimensions could be gauged by the mere fact
that the unions regarded its existence as an important victory, the
results of which they have continuously hoped to extend to the rest of
the West German economy. The hitherto unfulfilled nature of this
wish as a consequence of the massive resistance to its realization on
the part of West German capital, the two "bourgeois" parties—the
Christian Democratic Union/Christian Social Union (CDU/CSU) and
the Free Democratic party (FDP)—and the SPD's ineffective, albeit
vocal, support, further attest to its system-transforming potential
by giving labor at least some amount of real control over important
areas of decision making. Thus, for example, labor has access to
all of the information pertaining to a steel company and its environment. If properly used, this factor alone can yield important benefits to labor that it otherwise could hardly obtain. Furthermore,
through its parity on the policy-making supervisory board, labor has
the power of negation, or at least that of serious impediment. This,
in turn, can be traded for concrete gains in labor's favor, which
capital would hardly grant under "normal" circumstances. In short,
Montanmitbestimmung has provided IG Metall and IG Bergbau und
Energie, the two unions responsible for organizing workers in the
steel and coal industries, respectively, with concrete tools that have
not only made these two unions serious powers in the overall decision
making of their respective industries but have also yielded substantial gains to their members that otherwise would either not have been
possible at all or would have been exacted at much greater costs to
the unions. Thus, for example, many experts—in addition to the
unions—have credited the mechanism of Montanmitbestimmung with
devising the famous social plans (Sozialpläne) that have proved to be
remarkably effective "cushioning" devices for the country's crisis-
ridden coal and steel industries. By providing a combination of early
retirement schemes, generous severance payments, and opportunities
for retraining, the severe problems of unemployment during the early
1960s in coal and throughout the latter part of the 1970s in steel would
have undoubtedly caused a much greater disruption in the West German political economy than they actually did.

Critics of the social plans—usually situated on the left of the
FRG's political spectrum—always deride their "phony" qualities in
that they simply "soften the blow" without ever getting at the root of
the "true" problem. Indeed, this notion of a "cover up" and of quick

pacification has also been used (hardly by chance one might add) to "expose" the "real" elements of the entire complex of Mitbestimmung, probably the prime vehicle behind the social plans. Mitbestimmung, the argument goes, can only provide a superficial palliative at best that, however, even accentuates its inherently cooperative tendencies, since it provides the semblance of helpful action for labor without in actual fact being that. Mitbestimmung to its many critics among the West German Left and in the view of most labor movements of the advanced industrial world, has emasculated the West German unions without giving them much in return. "Co-optation" is the concept most frequently associated with Mitbestimmung.

To this writer, these criticisms seem somewhat unfair, perhaps even misleading. First of all, Mitbestimmung as a whole cannot be judged based on its present existence in West Germany, since only a small portion of the unions' overall scheme has so far been implemented and this in declining industries and depressed geographic regions. Thus, from its very setup, we have mainly witnessed Mitbestimmung's defensive capabilities. Second, if the whole framework is so conducive to labor's co-optation, then why can we observe one of the most determined and concerted efforts on the part of West German capital and a coalition of all conservative forces in the country to resist any further extension of Mitbestimmung—be it geographic, sectoral, or structural—over the course of 30 years? This fierce opposition has been clearly more than just an ideology. Indeed, it is based on the correct assumption that if ever properly implemented, the unions' equal participation in controlling the country's major economic decisions would in fact slowly but surely transform the present West German system. Third, if co-optation and cooperation mean to delineate a nonrevolutionary posture on the part of the unions and an acceptance of their role in a capitalist order, then indeed the West German unions have long been co-opted with or without Mitbestimmung. So, of course, have most labor movements in all advanced capitalist societies. If, however, co-optation and cooperation try to convey the notion that West German unions have approvingly embraced all of capitalism lock, stock, and barrel and are simply out to "satisfice" their position and that of their members by pursuing a narrow "bread-and-butter" policy as best they can, then there seems ample evidence over the course of the last 30 years that these characterizations are simply fallacious.

Mitbestimmung provides an excellent case in point. While clearly operating within the confines of capitalism, its very existence— most certainly in its extended form— is contrary to Kapitallogik (the "logic of capitalism"). Its entire premise rests on the collective participation of workers as a class in order to enhance their collective control in economic decision making. Never purporting to be a revolutionary tool, this mechanism was designed to strike compromises. In so doing, it has helped "the system" without, however, automatically reneging on its original mandate of furthering the collective participation of West German workers in the shaping of their lives. Thus, Mitbestimmung has remained a double-edged sword from its very inception. It clearly aided the construction of Model Germany by providing a centralized, well-structured, and routinized framework for labor's restricted participation as a junior partner. This, however, in no way implied labor's full-scale and uncritical integration into the system nor its acceptance by it.

Successful Liberalism: The Unions' Experience

Indeed, the 1950s brought to a focus some of this dilemma and ambivalence. Roughly speaking, the beginning of this decade set an overall arrangement among state, capital, and labor that was to last until the FRG's first major economic recession in 1966 and 1967. Its main features included elements of both exclusion and integration: an exclusion of union participation from the shop floor and the state, yet at the same time the development of union integration via the common political culture of anticommunism and the establishment of a highly juridified, detailed, and routinized bargaining system.

The unions' overall reform endeavors—including, of course, the extension of the Montanmitbestimmung model to the rest of the West German economy—came to a rather abrupt, decisive halt by the early 1950s. A period of general consolidation was established, which, in fact, exhibited clear qualities of a "rollback," again not unlike some trends during the 1920s in the Weimar Republic. Yet, the differences seem perhaps even more important than the similarities. Whereas the "rollback" in Weimar was based largely on reactionary developments endogenous to the German political atmosphere at the time, its counterpart in the Bonn Republic had its major source in the exogenous events related to the cold war and the role of the two Germanies therein. This crucial difference, in and of itself, implied some further distinctions between Weimar and Bonn that help to explain the varied results yielded by these two experiments in liberal democratic rule on German soil. The largely exogenous nature of the conflict and the close proximity of the major enemy, a rival yet also a negative example, created a sense of internal unity of purpose hardly present in the days of Weimar. Strong sentiments of anticommunism and a general hostility toward the USSR and its East European allies engulfed most of West German society, including the unions. Organized labor's anticommunist attitudes received perhaps yet an added structural and sociological dimension by having to accommodate and compete against millions of refugees and expellees from the East. In addition to weakening the unions' position in the labor market (a structural component of deradicalization), most of these people were, to say the least, hardly enamored with socialist—let alone communist—ideas (a sociological component for moderation). As already mentioned, it was this atmosphere and general conviction that led most unions to expel many of their trusted members simply because they belonged to or sympathized with the Communist party, hence deemed incompatible with the liberal democratic order upheld by the unions. That the unions' attitude and behavior vis-à-vis communism conformed with the state's position and thus enhanced labor's legitimacy and staatstragend posture was borne out by the Constitutional Court's declaring the West German Communist party unconstitutional in 1956.

Anticommunism provided a common denominator between the unions and the employers. As such, it was an integrating factor. Yet, at the same time the employers used anticommunism with all its ancillary and accompanying forms of reaction to exclude the unions from particular loci of decision making, notably the shop floor. In so doing, they availed themselves of their own power, as well as the state's, where labor already suffered from exclusion not only by failing to have the party closest to its cause, the SPD, in government but also by witnessing an increasing hostility on the part of the CDU vis-à-vis most of its beliefs.

Despite the employers' unmistakable antagonism toward organized labor in the FRG, a very important contrast to the Weimar Republic may explain much in the nature of the crucial difference between the two eras in German history. Capital in the FRG wanted labor excluded from certain areas from the very beginning. It did not want union interference on the shop floor, and it vehemently opposed any form of labor's collective participation on a basis of true parity at any level of the firm or society. Capital wanted the unions to be predictable and confined, perhaps even emasculated at times. Unlike in the Weimar Republic, there seems no evidence that capital ever wanted organized labor destroyed. This is a big difference indeed!

Perhaps the most drastic defeat for the unions in this "rollback" occurred in the form of the Works Constitution Act (Betriebsverfassungsgesetz) of 1952. The act basically banned the unions' official presence on the shop floor. It made the works councils—nominally independent of the unions—the sole legally recognized representatives of the workers in the plant. Every West German unit of production employing 20 or more workers was henceforth entitled to hold works council elections in an interval of three or four years. In addition to removing the unions' legal presence at the point of production, the

act also severely limited the works councils' range of activities on
the shop floor.

Essentially, it forbade them to initiate or participate in any
mobilizing activities. Thus, for example, members of works councils were explicitly forbidden to participate in any phase of a strike;
were bound by Friedenspflicht ("duty to maintain labor peace"); were
prohibited by Schweigepflicht ("duty to maintain silence") to divulge
any information regarding the company to anyone, including the workers who elected them and, of course, the unions; and were obliged to
help maintain a harmonious relationship between employees and management. Their tasks, according to the act, remained largely confined to the supervision of grievance procedures and certain forms
of workplace safety. Thus, the unions' original vision of an ideal
works council consisting of their active shop-floor representatives
participating in all economic, political, and social decisions that have
a direct effect on the daily lives of the workers in the plant was
shattered on most counts by this act. First, the works councils were
legally not the unions' shop-floor representatives; second, they had
little, if any, voice in political and economic matters; and third,
even in the social area, their tasks remained largely passive and defensive according to the letter of the law.

Yet another example of the fundamental commitment on the part
of the unions to support the basic functioning of liberal democracy in
the FRG could be gauged by the fact that despite this severe setback,
they did not assume a completely "antisystemic" posture. Clearly,
their own sense of vehement anticommunism helped to stymie the
development of any serious challenges that potentially could have
arisen within the labor movement in response to the "rollback."
Having suffered such painful disappointments at the hands of the state,
whose actions not only prevented the unions from seeing their much-
desired participation scheme come to fruition but also stripped the
unions of their legal rights of representation on the shop floor, there
seemed little left for the labor movement but to seek some recourse
by "relying on its own strength." Far from being a quasi-syndacalist
approach to politics, which would not have corresponded to the tradition of the West German labor movement, this strategy simply entailed a deemphasis of the state's potential for reform and a concomitant shift toward the unions' collective bargaining mechanism. The
immediate results may not have furthered the unions' larger cause
of societal democratization, but they certainly yielded such tangible
improvements as reduced weekly working hours, continued payment
during prolonged periods of illness, and respectable wage increases.

The framework of West German collective bargaining is yet
another major structure whose main features possess precisely those
characteristics that have turned out to be the West German indus-

trial relations system's most important contributions to Model Germany: high predictability, clear delineation of boundaries, accountability of action, centralization of decision making, and a prominent state presence via the law (that is, juridification). Although the state fully respects the bargaining autonomy (Tarifautonomie) of the two "social partners," the system itself derives its legitimacy from a law passed in April 1949, the so-called Collective Bargaining Contract Act (Tarifvertragsgesetz). Thus, albeit free from direct state intervention, the process of collective bargaining occurs in a state-sanctioned and state-defined arena. The legal origin of this system is constantly verified by the existence of contracts in the FRG, all of which are legal documents. Thus, the terms of a collective bargaining contract are binding for its designated duration not only qua agreement between capital and labor but qua law. This allows for important stability, continuity, and predictability in the West German framework of industrial relations.

All three have been reinforced by other features of the West German collective bargaining system that have legal or quasi-legal standing by virtue of a legislative act or a court ruling. Take the issue of Friedenspflicht (obligation to maintain peace) for example. The state and West German political culture view labor and capital as "social partners." But at the same time, they also see them as antagonistic enemies whose behavior and interaction have to be guided by strict rules, not unlike those regulating the conduct of war. Thus, during the course of a contract, both parties are to refrain from hostile activities vis-à-vis each other; the unions are not to strike, and the employers have no right to resort to their major weapon, the lockout. Infractions by either party are punishable by law. Friedenspflicht obviously accounts in part for the relatively low strike rate in the FRG, especially when compared with that in other advanced capitalist countries.

Indeed, the notion of highly routinized conflict and regulated warfare permeates many other aspects of the West German collective bargaining framework. Thus, for example, the terms of the "spoils" are typically separated into three categories of contracts with differing duration periods. Moreover, each of these only covers the exact issues pertinent to its area. All issues related to pecuniary forms of remuneration are covered by so-called wage and salary contracts (Lohn-und Gehaltstarifverträge) with the usual duration of one calendar year. The frameworks of remuneration, such as wage categories, are covered by so-called wage framework contracts (Lohnrahmentarifverträge) lasting between three and five years. Finally, all other issues pertaining to general work conditions and the "qualitative" aspects of jobs, are concluded in so-called general framework contracts (Manteltarifverträge), again with a typical three-to-five-year duration. This system not only makes the potential timing of "battles" predictable; it also puts strict limits on the content of their objectives. Thus, industrial conflicts in West Germany do not occur over vague, diffuse issues of general discontent or disagreement. They can be waged only over particular "spoils" delineated in the contract at hand. It is hardly surprising that few, if any, strikes over ideological issues were conducted in post-World War II Germany, especially in light of some court decisions that have ruled such activities illegal by calling them political strikes. By making the strike a highly confined expression of grievance pertaining only to particular terms of a contract, strikes supporting other issues or "third parties" are illegal. Solidarity strikes, for example, are disallowed in the Federal Republic of Germany.

The ritualization and rules-orientation of West German collective bargaining also extends to other areas, including the unions' internal decision-making process. Thus, for instance, no steps toward any strike activities can be taken until certain prerequisites have been met: appropriate formal cancellation of the existing contract; proper awaiting of its actual expiration date; a genuine attempt "in good faith" to reach a settlement via negotiations. Only after a complete deadlock is declared by both parties does the initiation of arbitration procedures begin. Following their failure to reach a settlement, the union leadership is then allowed to conduct a strike vote only involving its membership in the bargaining region of the disputed contract negotiations. Once 75 percent of this eligible group approves the strike, the union leadership is then free to commence with it. [10] There seems little doubt that striking is made rather difficult in the FRG, since the skipping of any of these steps would violate the rules and thus expose the union to adverse consequences via legal action. Strikes in the FRG are therefore major expressions of discontent. They have, up to now, occurred with lesser frequency than in most other advanced capitalist countries, but have hence been of weightier consequence in their respective social setting.

The establishment of the Federal Labor Court in 1954 added yet another dimension to the already prominent existence of juridification in the tradition of West German industrial relations. In a series of rulings very much in line with the court's notion of liberal democracy and the role of interest groups in such a political system, the court basically set out to establish even more stringent guidelines as to the appropriate conflict behavior of West German society's two most prominent interest groups, the employers and the unions. Following liberal theory, in which all interest groups are assumed to possess equal resources and power to conduct their political activities in society, the court introduced further concepts in its decisions that aimed at regulating and routinizing the conflict between two supposedly equal combatants, in consideration of the greater "general good." It was by acts of this court's jurisdiction that the lockout was declared the employers' equivalent "weapon" to labor's strike. Both, however, had to be used sparingly and with prudence; moreover, an "overkill" on the part of either party was declared illegal, since it would not only unduly hurt its opponent but also thereby harm "the general good." In other words, deployments of either party's "weapons" had to occur in a measured way. They had to be proportional to the battle at hand, could not be geared toward the destruction of the other party, and always had to keep society's overall welfare in mind. In few other advanced capitalist countries has the industrial relations system been influenced to such an explicit degree by notions like the "obligation to maintain industrial peace" (Friedenspflicht), "proportionality" (Verhältnismässigkeit) of measures in industrial conflict, and the "necessity to keep the commonweal in mind" (Allgemeinwohlbindung).

The unions' reaction to the entire complex of juridification was mixed. This, in many ways, represented a rather accurate reflection of some of the contradictory strains that informed their tradition well before the existence of the FRG. Thus, in a sense, they were rather upset, and remain so to this day. The Federal Labor Court's jurisdiction especially has consistently evoked the unions' ire and disappointment, since—although they are supporters of liberal democracy—they do not buy one of its major tenets: namely, the equality of power available to labor and capital. Here, one can still see a vivid example of their Marxist heritage, in that the unions maintain that the very fact that capital owns the means of production and labor does not, makes any claim as to an equality of power for each of the two "social partners" quite fallacious and rather unjust. Juridification also has impeded much of the unions' offensive capabilities by placing them in a legal straitjacket. Thus, there is ample evidence that the unions were not particularly happy with many aspects of juridification and regarded its most pronounced articulation, namely the rulings of the Federal Labor Court, as yet another vivid example of the general "rollback" besetting labor in the conservative period of the 1950s.

On the other hand, however, there were aspects of juridification the unions did not seem to mind at all. Again, parts of their heritage provide some of the explanation. If it was their Marxist legacy that disapproved of juridification, then elements of their liberal tradition seemed quite comfortable with it. "Rule of law," "due process," and "rules of the game" are integral dimensions of liberalism that always found ardent admirers in West German trade unions. The unions' liberal tradition basically made them believe in, hence follow, the maxims of law and order. In addition to their liberal propensity

for juridification, one should also mention the unions' social democratic values, which developed tendencies in a similar direction, although emanating from different intellectual and political origins.
Social democracy's reformism and gradualism created a "state fixation" that depended rather heavily on legal output for its rewards.
After all, it was via the state's legal actions that the West German
labor movement came to enjoy some of the most substantial rewards
in its history. Moreover, juridification increased predictability and
governability of the entire industrial relations system, which could
only benefit the unions, especially in their post-World War II structural form of the Einheits- and Industriegewerkschaft. Rules and
regulations clearly curtailed the unions' realm of activity, especially
vis-à-vis the working class, by establishing them as a legal presence
in the West German political economy. Moreover, juridification provided the unions with a welcome justification for their own centralized
and highly regulated internal organizational framework—for what better way was there to exist effectively in a highly regulated and juridified world than to incorporate these characteristics into one's own
structures for the purposes of both efficacy and control.

In a way, it was via the highly regularized collective bargaining
system and the unions' centralized organizational framework (partly
as a consequence of juridification) that the unions succeeded in regaining some of their lost shop-floor control "through the back door,"
so to speak. The centralized and juridified nature of the West German collective bargaining system has been partly responsible for
making the unions into an effective "countervailing power" to the
works councils in the FRG's industrial plants. With the passage of
the 1952 Works Constitution Act, a dual system of labor representation was introduced in the FRG, which potentially could have led to
an irreparable schism in the West German labor movement. The
built-in centrifugality of this dualism could have endangered the very
existence of the organized labor movement's new structures, the
Einheitsgewerkschaft and the Industriegewerkschaft, or severely
weakened their whole purpose of unity. By creating, in effect, two
bodies of labor representation—one inside the plant in the form of the
works councils and one outside the factory gates in the form of the
unions—a horizontal split of the organized labor movement was at
least theoretically conceivable. Although mainly traumatized by the
vertical divisions along party-political lines in the Weimar Republic,
the post-World War II West German labor movement clearly wanted
to prevent any forms of similar developments in the Bonn experiment.
Structural and political unity were paramount. After all, those were
the two main reasons for the creation of the Einheitsgewerkschaft and
the Industriegewerkschaft. While it would be somewhat exaggerated
to argue that it was mainly due to the formalism and juridified na-

ture of the West German collective bargaining system that a schism
between the unions and the works councils never occurred, there
seems little doubt that the unions used these mechanisms to gain
some shop-floor control, which in turn meant that a symbiotic relationship could develop between these two organizational entities.

Symbiosis, however, does not imply harmony. Indeed, in this
case it meant an often uneasy and always complicated relationship
between labor's "inside" and "outside" representatives. There developed a division of labor, of sorts, in which the "insiders" took
charge of shop-floor issues and the "outsiders" provided the necessary setting for these issues via their control of the collective-bar-
gaining mechanism. One could not exist without the other. Thus,
all microlevel matters pertaining to plant-related issues, such as
hiring, firing, job content, and grievance procedures, remained the
prerogatives of the works councils, which, after all, remained the
sole legitimate and legally mandated representatives of the West
German working class in the factories. Yet, the unions gained considerable influence over the existence of these microlevel matters
via the terms of their macrolevel contracts, which often provided the
bases for the works councils' concrete activities. The elaborate nature of the unions' general framework contracts (Manteltarifverträge),
with their minute details concerning issues of work procedure, job
content, and most other aspects of factory life, clearly aimed for
regaining some of the unions' lost shop-floor presence by setting
macrolevel parameters for the works councils' microlevel existence.

It was mainly via the collective bargaining mechanism's yield
of relatively predictable and widely applicable results that the West
German unions have, up to now, succeeded in fending off any potentially damaging consequences to the unity of the labor movement as a
result of the built-in structural centrifugality of the works councils.
Peculiar as it may sound, certain characteristics, such as the unions'
centralization, thorough bureaucratization, and general legalism, all
developed in close conjunction with the industrial relations system's
juridification, have provided their respectable share in maintaining
the effective coherence of the Einheitsgewerkschaft as an overall integrative structure of the entire working class.

Works councils have certainly proved to be rather successful
representatives of West German workers on the shop floor, but precisely therein lay the danger. Since their entire frame of reference
in terms of legitimation and gratification derives from plant-level
activities, works councils on the whole would have few incentives to
maintain any forms of intraclass allegiance. Their latent "company
syndicalism" (Betriebssyndikalismus), if left unbridled by the absence
of a viable countervailing power in the industrial relations system,
could easily reach manifest proportions, which would bring the end

of the unitary trade union movement in all but name. Tendencies of "company particularism," or "firm-specific egoism," have not, of course, been absent in the history of the post-World War II labor movement. In fact, they are pervasive. However, as a consequence of a strong union movement benefiting in terms of its shop-floor influence from the juridified nature of the collective bargaining system, this firm-specific egoism could coexist side-by-side with a comprehensive, all-encompassing class strategy as pursued by the Einheitsgewerkschaft. Works councils in prosperous firms could thus still realize for their own workers better terms in excess of the overall contract agreements achieved on an industrywide basis by the union, without, however, thereby jeoparadizing the organizational unity of working-class representation. So-called second wage rounds permitted the works councils to express their due autonomy by gaining additional benefits for their own constituents above and beyond those reached by the union.

The overall basis, however, was provided by the unions' bargaining arrangement, which relied on a welcome support system in the form of the country's juridified industrial relations. Thus, the uniform nature of the collective bargaining arrangements protected all workers in a particular industry, even those in small or unprofitable firms, whose works councils would otherwise barely be in a position to eke out a proper standard of remuneration for their constituents, let alone attain additional plant-specific benefits. In the final analysis, juridification helped the West German labor movement maintain the organizational pillars of its post-World War II existence, the Einheits- and Industriegewerkschaft, both of which proved vital ingredients in the unions' successful pursuit of an all-encompassing class strategy.

The structural situation described above dominated the unions' existence with minimal changes between 1952 and the late 1960s. Disappointed by the curtailment of Mitbestimmung in the coal and steel areas, by their reduced leverage on the CDU-dominated state, and by the attempt to dislodge them from the shop floor via the Works Constitution Act of 1952, the unions nevertheless did rather well for themselves by "relying on their own strength," mainly in the form of collective bargaining. Clearly, the existence of a booming economy with a strong export orientation helped the labor movement to obtain some of its much-cherished gains, such as a shorter work week, more vacation, and continued payment during a prolonged period of illness. Politically, this was the era wherein the labor movement's liberalism definitely outweighed its collectivist traditions. Cowed by the initial shocks of the "rollback," as experienced in the late 1940s and early 1950s, the labor movement's radicalism further abated owing to the influx of millions of refugees and expellees from East Germany

who not only weakened the unions' position in the labor market but
also infused the already anti-Communist atmosphere shared by most
unions with additional anti-Marxist views. By the late 1950s and
early 1960s the West German economy's success certainly showed
some "spoiling" effects on the "purity" of the labor movement's political consciousness. After all, this was the era of the SPD's famous
(or notorious) Bad Godesberg reforms in which social democracy's
liberal dimensions emerged as the unambiguous victors over its
Marxist strains. The unions' programmatic parallel to the SPD's
deradicalization occurred a few years later in the DGB's 1963 Basic
Program, the first major written revision of its founding principles
enunciated in the Munich Program of 1949. Liberal reformism seemed
triumphant; the workers' sole concern appeared to be their preoccupation with cashing in on the country's "economic miracle" as quickly
and as effectively as possible; finally, the unions and the labor movement seemed completely integrated.

Yet, even during the peak of this liberal period in the history
of West German labor, one could detect important antinomian tendencies in the unions' Weltanschauung, especially in terms of their overall
political positions. Once again it became clear that few, if any, other
institutions in German history took liberalism, in its reformist-hu-
manist sense, as seriously as did the unions. In the post-Nazi world,
this included foremost an awareness of the FRG's special role and
mission to erase the legacy of the heinous events of the recent German past. The unions developed an almost unparalleled consistency
in demanding that West Germans do more to atone for the wrongs
they had committed in the past. They insisted, like few others, that
a combination of the cold war and the reconstruction period culmi-
nated in a social and political "rollback" whose morally most repre-
hensible ramification manifested itself in the de facto—and often
also de jure—rehabilitation of Nazi war criminals. Thus, the unions
never wanted to forget the past, as did so many other institutions in
the FRG. They consistently fought against the expiration of the
statute of limitations for war criminals as a pernicious cover up of
specific crimes and a general episode in German history that one
could only begin to "come to terms with" (bewältigen) following a full
disclosure.

The unions' humanitarian liberalism assumed many other dimensions in addition to those connected to a genuine appraisal of the
German past. In the 1950s, most unions vehemently opposed the
FRG's rearmament and complete military integration into the Western Alliance. Organized labor played a crucial role in the ban-the-
bomb and peace marches of the late 1950s and early 1960s. Although
vehemently anti-Communist, this hostility toward the East never
manifested itself in union publications in the militaristic jingoism not
uncommon in other segments of West German society at the time.

172 / THE POLITICAL ECONOMY OF WEST GERMANY

One can discern yet another dimension of the unions' humanitarian liberalism in their genuine internationalism. Partly as a consequence of the internationalist tradition of German social democracy but perhaps even more as an expression of the unions' genuine atonement for Germany's crimes during national socialist rule, the unions developed a pervasive sense of internationalism quite unparalleled elsewhere in the advanced capitalist world. Be it in the form of enthusiasm for European integration on all levels, or strong support and genuine concern for the workers' movements of the Third World, West German unions have from the very beginning of their post-World War II existence taken their internationalism very seriously. Indeed, they have always regarded this dimension of their politics as one of the most important mandates and missions in the world.

Lastly, the unions' liberalism during this period manifested itself in the unmitigated defense of perhaps the most fundamental of liberal principles: the sanctity of the individual's freedom from encroachments by the state. From the very beginning of their conception in the mid-to-late 1950s until their passage into law in the late 1960s, the so-called Emergency Laws (Notstandsgesetze) were most staunchly opposed by the unions. Although in favor of state intervention in the economy (precisely what the unions failed to obtain during this time in an amount they deemed satisfactory), they always feared the state's intervention in the realm of civil liberties and political freedom, especially given the context of Germany's national socialist past. State fixation, after all, also had its negative antecedents in the unions' political history. It was the same Bismarckian state that introduced the world's first comprehensive and compulsory social welfare system, which also suppressed unions via its infamous Socialist Laws. Thus, the unions' fear of the repressive dimensions of the West German state was not self-serving hysteria. Indeed, in their opposition to the Emergency Laws, most West German unions broke with the SPD on this particular issue, surely a sign of the deep-seated nature of their concern.

Thus, even in the complacent and strike-poor period of the late 1950s and throughout most of the 1960s, West German unions were more than mere wage machines. They were concerned with politics, as properly behooves their self-image of being political organizations. Liberalism to most of the unions never entailed the abdication of their role as a countervailing power in society. It never meant the uncritical acceptance of the system. Rather, it encouraged the unions to force the powers that be to live up to their liberal tenets in practice, thereby instituting important—albeit "system-maintaining"—reforms. By the end of the 1960s, the West German political economy and the unions as key actors in it had both reached a stage that required some adjustments in the hitherto pursued course of action. It was in this context that the Marxist tradition of the labor movement was once again revived to fit the particular needs of the times.

Crisis and Resurgence of Collectivism: Old Tensions Renewed

"Marxist tradition," of course, in no way implies anything revolutionary. West German unionists were not about to storm the barricades. However, they did develop a much more activist articulation of their political beliefs, in which once again the notions of collectivity and participation received places of prominence as central means, as well as ends, in the unions' daily existence. Suddenly, these terms received a political immediacy and concreteness that they had partly lost during the 1950s and most of the 1960s. As of 1969, West German workers became mobilized once again. It was this mobilization that reintroduced some of the West German labor movement's Marxist heritage in a more active way than had been manifest since the unions' political defeats in the early 1950s.

Unlike the case of similar developments in many European countries, the West German unions' mobilization never even pretended to represent a serious challenge to the existence of West German capitalism. Yet, the labor movement's mobilization did in part mean an intensified questioning of the hitherto almost irreproachable liberal paradigm. In assuming a much more politicized form of expression (in and of itself a rather telling fact) the challenge to the liberal paradigm mainly lay in the unions' insistence on the necessity and urgency of collectivity-oriented reforms that had been neglected, or at least minimized, during the conservative rule of the CDU-dominated state. The mobilization, in a sense, returned the unions to their original hopes and demands voiced immediately after World War II. Their vision, then, of an all-encompassing participatory democracy along the "third way" was rekindled in the late 1960s. It was thus that the unions' Marxist traditions found an expression in the general societal mobilization engulfing much of West German life in the late 1960s and early 1970s.

In many ways, the decade of the 1970s has thus far proved to be the most difficult in the unions' post-World War II history. If their existence until the late 1960s could be described as unencumbered by the absence of a directly staatstragend position on the part of the leadership and as a consequence of a rather unmobilized base, the subsequent period clearly represented a change. The unions' leaders often found themselves directly in the corridors of power, while at the same time the rank and file exhibited a degree of restiveness quite unprecedented in much of the FRG's existence. The combination of a much-improved access to the state, with a mobilized base, definitely improved life for the unions through the benefits extracted from the "system." This improvement, however, was accompanied by a commensurate growth in complications, difficulties, and contradictions besetting union life. Basically, these derived from the heightened tensions between organized labor's liberal and collectivist strains, which experienced added intensity as a consequence of the acute mobilization. Simply put, the main tension originated between the leadership's propensity to carry out a staatstragend policy more or less in full support of the SPD-dominated government (the liberal strain), on the one hand, and the rank-and-file's pursuit of far-reaching, radical, and grass-roots-oriented reforms, on the other (the collectivist strain). This cumulative cleavage in terms of the differences in political content (liberal-collectivist) and organizational position (leadership-base) was further exacerbated following the period after the crisis of 1973 and 1974. With the social-liberal coalition's pursuit of a relentless policy of severe austerity and a consistent pool of at least one million unemployed, the crisis experience placed additional burdens on this potentially serious cleavage. Yet, it also had a coagulating effect, which once again proved an impressive testimony to the unions' organizational resilience.

In the late 1960s and early 1970s, however, hardly any problems seemed to cloud the skies of the West German economy. Indeed, this was a rather unique period for West German society as a whole, in which sometimes quite substantial reforms hardly left any major segment of West German life untouched. Often referred to somewhat cynically and with the benefit of hindsight as the period of "reform euphoria," one could characterize this era in union politics as a rare confluence of one mobilization "from above" and one "from below." Both, in many ways, were direct outgrowths and definite legacies of the student movement of the mid-to-late 1960s. This movement had two major ripple effects on the unions: first and foremost, it reintroduced Marxism into the political discourse of the FRG on a wide basis. It made the open deployment of Marxist terms and thought acceptable once again, especially within the SPD and the labor movement. Thus, it would not be completely farfetched to credit the student Left with a rather thorough exorcism of the cold war mentality, which did not stop short of the SPD and the unions. Second, the reconstitution of Marxism per se—as opposed to aspects of its tradition, which had always, as argued in this essay, remained intact—in some union circles and parts of the SPD, occurred via a sociological "spillover" in which many of the student radicals continued their activism as union or party officials upon graduation from university.

The mobilization "from above" entailed crucial reforms for the unions via the SPD's governmental power. In addition to the introduction of a comprehensive manpower policy via the Works Promotion Act and an improvement in the unions' representational position on the shop floor via a revision of the Works Constitution Act, as well as numerous other substantial legislative packages closely in line with the unions' long-standing desires, the unions also gained "positional" power via the numerous personal ties between unionists and leading government officials. Although the Einheitsgewerkschaft was meticulous in maintaining its independence from any political parties, it was also—as will be remembered—never politically neutral or abstinent. In effect, this has meant, throughout the history of the FRG, that the unions have maintained, true to their tradition, a very close and special relationship with the SPD. Thus, it is hardly surprising that, once the SPD achieved its long-sought goal of governmental power, the unions tried to make the best of this. So, of course, did the SPD. Part of this mobilization "from above" also entailed the unions' cooperation with the SPD not only as the "party of the workers" but also as the "party of government." In other words, the benefits the unions undoubtedly derived from the SPD's legislative power exacted certain reciprocal "favors," most of which the unions had to render in the form of "reasonable" wage settlements (in other words, wage restraint). It is at this point that the structure of the mobilization "from above" also assumed a dimension of a disciplining "from above" as implemented by the mechanism of concerted action. Here, the simultaneous development of mobilization "from below" clashed directly with some of the unions' policies in support of the SPD-led government, thereby fully taxing the unions' organizational savvy.

The mobilization of the workers "from below," starting with the famous September strikes in 1969, exhibited great similarities to the student movement's actions, in terms of both form and content. The workers' massive demonstrations aimed not only at such immediate quantitative gains as pay increases, but also included more qualitative concerns, featuring greater shop-floor autonomy for the workers and, thus, a general expansion of participatory democracy on a collective basis throughout West German society as a whole. Just like the students, many workers in West Germany (as opposed to West German workers, thus including the circa two million foreigners working in West Germany in this concept) seemed intent on gaining more control over their lives via a thorough democratization of West German institutions in the course of the 1970s. To the workers, this mobilization "from below" also comprised a critique of the unions. This critique never questioned the fundamental value of the unions to the working class; as such, it was never antisystemic in the way many student radicals understood that term. It only demanded that the unions, in actual practice, live up to the spirit of their programmatic statements and expand their ambitions for reforms commensurate to their true capabilities. Thus, unlike much of the student movement, the workers' mobilization "from below" did not reject the reforms of the mobilization "from above" as being merely sugar-coated forms of co-optation. The workers simply wanted more of it and with the union leadership's enthusiastic support.

Despite being at odds over certain issues, the two mobilizations informing much of working-class politics throughout the late 1960s and early 1970s basically had very similar aims and hopes. Above all, they shared a sense of optimism perhaps unparalleled in the history of the FRG. This is all the more evident because it contrasted so sharply with the pessimistic mood that has engulfed much of the West German labor movement since the beginning of the crisis in 1973 and 1974. One thing can be said rather unequivocally: since the onset of the crisis, the SPD's participation in any forms of the mobilization "from above" has been severely curtailed, if not indeed completely eliminated. Following a rigid policy of cutbacks in public spending and relentlessly pursuing various other austerity measures, the SPD leadership has clearly opted to favor its hat of being the "party of government" over the other one, which it continues to claim, namely, that of being "the party of the workers." Indeed, to continue the analysis with the aid of our liberalism-collectivism dichotomy, the SPD's collectivism quickly vanished from the party's top policy-making bodies but reemerged among its middle-level and rank-and-file officials in the course of the latter half of the 1970s. The party's reaction seemed rather consistent with the legacy of its tradition and with social democracy's typical response under conditions of economic crisis: curtail all Marxist-collectivist aspects, propensities, and elements, as much as possible, in favor of the liberal dimensions of economic and political practice.

The unions, caught in a serious bind, responded rather predictably. Faced with the choice of an SPD-led government that fulfilled fewer and fewer of their needs and the prospects of a CDU/CSU return to power, the unions chose to go with the lesser of two evils, thereby replicating the famous "hostage-to-a-friendly-government" syndrome. This, of course, has left the unions in a precarious position. While, on the one hand, burdened with a staats-tragend obligation owing to the informal support of the SPD-led government, the unions have had to face an increasingly restive rank and file, but one that itself has undergone change. The rank and file has not been so much preoccupied with the far-reaching, optimistic reforms typical of the late 1960s and early 1970s, but with defensive issues aimed at the protection of its endangered jobs as a consequence of sluggish economic performance and heightened rationalization throughout much of West German industry.

Just like the SPD, the liberalism-collectivism dichotomy has experienced a shift in terms of intraorganizational emphasis among the unions. Not only have there been signs of a hierarchical cleavage in which collectivist dimensions seem to grow among the rank and file while the pursuit of liberal politics remains paramount for the leadership, but one can also perceive splits among the DGB's constituent unions into a group pejoratively known as the "chancellor's unions," denoting their strict allegiance to the SPD's government policy and an increasingly radical wing that wants to reemphasize the labor movement's "reliance on its own strength." The latter policy—definitely the more collectivist of the two—would clearly mean the abandoning of the SPD's almost exclusively liberal line in favor of a more active class politics based on the powers of the Einheits-gewerkschaft. It is important to understand, however, that precisely because of the all-encompassing form of the latter, this strategy merely calls to attention a genuinely felt disappointment in these unions for the austerity measures of the current SPD-led government. Yet, it in no way indicates a growth of radical syndicalism. Some unions' disillusionment with the SPD may in fact reinforce the unitary nature of their mandate thereby pushing them not only toward political independence, which they have claimed all along, but perhaps also toward political neutrality for the first time in the history of the Federal Republic of Germany.

CONCLUSION

Whatever the exact outcome of the unions' relations to social democracy, in general, and the SPD, in particular, will be, the zero-sum dimensions between their liberal and collectivist legacies continue to become accentuated with every additional day of crisis conditions in the West German economy. On the one hand, the unions' liberalism clearly wants the continued existence of the Bonn republic; it firmly believes in the legitimacy and overall necessity of an unimpeded success in terms of the implementation of a <u>Rechtstaat</u> on West German soil. In defense of this liberal democracy, the unions— true to their tradition— are determined to go very far. They are willing to make political sacrifices (most notably, of course, in terms of not pushing the SPD as hard as they could to obtain the reforms that they want), as well as bear economic burdens (mainly in the form of settling for rather modest wage and salary increases). On the other hand, it is precisely these <u>staatstragend</u> and moderate postures that have incurred the wrath of an increasingly insecure and restive rank and file threatened in an unprecedented way by the crisis befalling the West German economy.

Limited, perhaps even nonexistent, growth, coupled with intensified technological rationalization, poses a serious threat to the workers' standard of living. It is to the West German unions' credit that,
at least until the time of this writing, they have by and large succeeded in finding sufficient common ground between these two contradictory strains in their daily political existence. Part of this success
stems from the fact that the West German labor movement, unlike
some others in the capitalist world, has accumulated an impressive
history in terms of balancing its collectivist and liberal legacies for
nearly a century. Perhaps the best example in the hitherto successful reconciliation of these conflicting aims exacerbated by crisis conditions, stems from the unions' post-World War II organizational innovations, most notably the Einheits- and Industriegewerkschaft.
Centralization and their all-encompassing nature make the West German unions genuine class organizations without the necessity of radical rhetoric and undue militance. They are excellent defensive bodies,
quite true to one of their main mandates of being "protective organizations" (Schutzorganisationen).

Thus, it is not by chance that membership in West German
unions has consistently risen throughout the crisis. Repeated sur-
veys have confirmed that people join unions in West Germany in good
part because they feel more secure and better protected. So far, the
unions have, by and large, never disappointed their members. It is
important, however, to point out that the unions' past success coincided with a growing economy and other favorable conditions that have
become less certain in the West Germany of the 1980s. The balancing
act between the unions' liberal and collectivist legacies—so much
part of their daily politics throughout their existence—will become
increasingly difficult, perhaps even reaching the point of irreconcil-
ability. The continued compromise between these two traditions,
which has become the trademark of the West German unions' strategy
over the years and their major contribution to Model Germany, has
already shown signs of unusual and potentially damaging strain in
recent years. The crisis seems to push the unions toward an unen-
viable dilemma: either they increase their staatstragend, liberal
propensities (thereby, however, alienating a growing number of dissatisfied members), or they develop toward a more radical, Marxist-collectivist direction (thereby, however, risking an exclusion
from the mainstream of West German politics and the loss of their
carefully weaned access to institutional power). Both are less than
satisfactory choices, and the union leadership seems perfectly aware
of this dire fact. Further, in a more general way, both would severely
impair organized labor's effective participation in Model Germany,
thereby threatening the latter's very existence.

Characteristically, the solution that the West German unions
try to develop in countering this growing dilemma is once again based
on their major forte, compromise. Thus, for example, it is only
in this context that one can understand the unions' increasing militance
in nearly every recent bargaining round, as against the relatively
modest results attained. The first is intended as a response to the
growing restiveness of a mobilized base, whereas the second clearly
is an expression of the unions' concern for the overall welfare of the
West German economy. The novelty in this approach lies in the fact
that the margins of error have increased substantially as a consequence of the economic crisis. Thin lines will inform the West German unions' other paths as well. Thus, for example, it will become
increasingly difficult for the unions to maintain their antidestruction-
ist, anti-Luddite attitudes ("we are no machine wreckers") in light
of the adverse effects that the introduction of some new technologies
have had on their members.

Yet, it is rather unlikely that the growing radicalism on the
part of some unions will manifest itself in a wholesale negation of
technological advances, as has been the case in other advanced industrial countries. Rather, it seems much more probable that the
mobilization of the 1970s will demand concessions to the unions on
the issue of shop-floor control of these new technologies. In other
words, the unions will not obstruct the path of West German economic
development, provided they continue to receive substantial benefits
in return. The fact, however, that the unions will increasingly demand that these benefits be qualitative in nature, emphasizing the
unions' participation in the process of control, rather than mere
quantitative cushioning measures (monetarization) is certain to make
the compromise an even rockier endeavor than was hitherto the case.

But compromise there will be. This, perhaps more than any
other single attribute, has characterized the West German unions'
attitudes and behaviors over the years of their existence. It lies
very much at the heart of the liberal–democratic, as well as Marxist-collectivist, traditions. The first entails an interclass dimension
of compromise that the unions always saw as their important contribution to the stability and progress of a country with few other liberal
traditions and democratic structures. The second concerns an
equally important universalistic notion of intraclass solidarity, which
allowed the West German unions to be the true representatives of a
large and heterogeneous group of people rather than the narrow advocates of particularistic occupational interests. Both components
of compromise have helped the West German unions to reconcile their
seemingly disparate traditions of collectivism and liberalism, thereby,
in fact, creating yet a new level of compromise. They most certainly
contributed to the West German unions' reformism and gradualism

without, however, thus making them into "business unions" completely
accepting and uncritical of the overall political system. Both dimensions of compromise will continue to dominate the unions' existence
in the future. It is only in their respective weights vis-à-vis each
other and their particular manifestation in the West German political
economy as a whole that the future seems rather uncertain.

NOTES

1. I would like to express my gratitude to Thomas Ertman and
Gary Herrigel for their helpful comments on an earlier draft of this
chapter. I owe special thanks to John Herzfeld for his superb editing
efforts.

This chapter represents an interpretation of a rather complex
set of materials that I have had the pleasure of researching since the
summer of 1978. As such, it provides an analytic overview of some
detailed issues presented elsewhere in the course of this project.
Before listing the other writings in which I discussed various aspects
of the trade unions in the Federal Republic of Germany (FRG), I would
like to take this opportunity to thank three institutions whose help
proved indispensable in this lengthy endeavor. First, I owe special
thanks to the Ford Foundation, which financed a nine-month sojourn
in the FRG that formed the nucleus of my field work. Second, I
would have never been able to gain such superb access to countless
documents, research materials, and above all, people had it not
been for the wonderful support and hospitality I enjoyed throughout
my stay in the FRG at the Wirtschafts-und Sozialwissenschaftliches
Institut (WSI) of the Deutscher Gewerkschaftsbund (DGB). The institute's director, Heinz Markmann, and its associates proved not only
knowledgeable experts but also cooperative colleagues—indeed, good
friends. Last, I would like to express my gratitude to the International Institute for Comparative Social Research of the Science Center in Berlin and its directors, Karl W. Deutsch and Frieder Naschold, for providing me with the necessary funds and stimulating environment to spend an additional three months in West Germany as a
follow-up to the original nine supported by the Ford Foundation. The
following is a list of publications and conference papers in which specific topics concerning the politics of the trade unions in the FRG
have been discussed in some detail, accompanied by the appropriate
documentation. In the case of the unpublished conference papers,
interested readers are welcome to obtain copies from me.

"Neuorientierung deutscher Gewerkschaftspolitik durch die Wirt-
    schaftskrise der siebziger Jahre?," Journal für Sozialforschung
    21 (Spring 1981): 141-60.

This article discusses the West German unions' response to the economic crisis of the 1970s and contrasts their strategies to those pursued in the 1950s and 1960s.

"Trade Union Responses to the Contemporary Economic Problems in Western Europe: The Context of Current Debates and Politics in the Federal Republic of Germany," Economic and Industrial Democracy 2 (February 1981): 49-85, with Christopher S. Allen.

This article highlights the current strategies in terms of the unions' economic policies as a response to the crisis of the late 1970s. Particular attention is given to the so-called memorandum debate in the context of the politics of the unions' economic decisions.

"Power and Dissent: The Trade Unions in the Federal Republic of Germany Re-examined," West European Politics 3 (January 1980): 68-86, with Christopher S. Allen.

This article presents an overview of the West German unions' post-World War II development by mainly focusing on the different nature of their strategies.

"The Automobile Industry and the Metal Workers' Union in the Federal Republic of Germany: Changing Relationships in Crisis Conditions." Paper presented at the Second Conference of Europeanists, Washington, D.C., October 1980, with Christopher S. Allen.

This paper discusses the predicament of IG Metall in the ups and downs of West Germany's automobile industry, especially in regard to the technological changes affecting the nature of production.

"Class Power and Industrial Conflict in Advanced Capitalism: The Interaction of Business, Labor and the State in the Post-World War II German Steel Industry." Paper presented at the annual meeting of the American Political Science Association, Washington, D.C., August 1980, with Christopher S. Allen and Kenneth Gibbs.

This paper, also focusing on IG Metall, looks at the new difficulties faced by labor in an ailing industry. Specifically, it provides a detailed analysis of the country's steel strike in the winter of 1978 and 1979.

"Structural Change and Union Response in the Chemical Industry: The German Economy in Microcosm." Paper presented at the

New York State Political Science Association, Syracuse, New York, April 1980, with Christopher S. Allen.

The paper's major focus of analysis is the West German chemical union, IG Chemie-Papier-Keramik. In particular, we tried to assess the unions' politics in light of one of West Germany's most successful industrial sectors.

"Social Democracy, Communism and the West German Trade Unions: An Old Debate Re-opened." Paper presented at the annual meeting of the Northeastern Political Science Association, Newark, New Jersey, November 1979, with Christopher S. Allen.

This paper concentrates on perhaps the most controversial and contentious intraunion debates that emerged in the wake of the crisis of the 1970s. Focusing on the role of communism and Communists in today's union movement, the paper discusses the three major areas in which this issue has created the most heated intraunion arguments: economic policy (the memorandum debate), the interpretation of German labor history, especially in the latter Weimar period, and the political education of youth in the unions.

"The Experience of Labor in a Changing Market Economy: The Ambivalence of the West German Trade Unions." Paper presented at the Eleventh World Congress of the International Political Science Association, Moscow, August 1979, with Christopher S. Allen.

This paper tries to assess the potential new directions in collective bargaining that the unions have been developing in response to the economic crisis of the 1970s. By analyzing three major strikes in 1978 and 1979 in terms of their particular causes and aims, the unions' strategy of "relying on their own strength" is given empirical consideration.

"The West German Unions' Role in Democratization and Participation: Social Partnership or Class Conflict?" Paper presented at the Eleventh World Congress of the International Political Science Association, Moscow, August 1979, with Christopher S. Allen.

The aim of this paper is to analyze the unions' relationship to the state, political parties (notably the SPD), and capital in the 1970s.

Much of the above findings have also been reported in a lengthy chapter written with Christopher S. Allen. Entitled "The West German Case," it represents one of three parts of the social democratic case studies—the other two being the United Kingdom and Sweden—of the Ford Foundation Project. The chapter is to be published in Stephen Bornstein, Peter Gourevitch, Andrei S. Markovits, and Andrew Martin, eds., Trade Union Responses to the Economic Crisis in Western Europe—The Social Democratic Variant (London: George Allen & Unwin, 1982).

Last, a detailed volume discussing the politics of West German trade unions since World War II is in the process of being coauthored with Thomas C. Ertman. Entitled The West German Trade Unions: Structural Challenges and Strategic Responses, the book is to be published by OG&H, Cambridge, Mass., in early 1983.

2. In a broad way, one could see this collectivism deriving from two crucial traditions of German working-class history, both of which remain the pillars of today's unitary trade union movement (Einheitsgewerkschaft): Christian confessionalism and Marxism. Although both were important, it was mainly the latter in its various forms that informed the political ideology of the bulk of German unions at important junctures in their history. Thus, for the purposes of this chapter it will sometimes be helpful to use Marxism rather than collectivism or intraclass collectivism in describing the political character of the German unions.

3. Although the concept of "state fixation" (Staatsfixierung) has been widely used by West German scholars in their analysis of union politics, two articles mention this word specifically in an attempt to assess union strategy. For an analysis of state fixation in the context of the unions' ties to the SPD, see Bodo Zeuner, "Solidarität mit der SPD oder Solidarität der Klasse? Zur SPD-Bindung der DGB-Gewerkschaften," Prokla 26 (1977): 3-32; for the crucial issue of state fixation versus "relying on their own strength" as a union strategy, see Josef Esser, "Staatsfixierung oder 'Stärkung der eigenen Kraft'?", Gewerkschaftliche Monatshefte, June 1981, pp. 366-75.

4. Again, the concept of "juridification" (Verrechtlichung) frequently has been used by West German analysts of union politics. Among them, works by Thomas Blanke, Wolfgang Däubler, Michael Kittner, Ulrich Mückenberger, and Ulrich Zachert are of particular interest. Perhaps the most important monograph addressing precisely this particular question in West German industrial relations is Rainer Erd, Verrechtlichung industrieller Konflikte (Frankfurt: Campus, 1978).

5. This furnishes an excellent example of juridification as a consequence of state fixation.

6. In the following analysis, the concepts of organized labor and union movement will always refer to West Germany's DGB unions.

With 7.8 million members, the DGB federation represents far and away the most important labor organization in the FRG. It comprises about 85 percent of the 40 percent who are unionized workers in West Germany; furthermore, the DGB unions have consistently gained about 85 percent of the votes in the country's triannual works councils elections. On every other indicator, the discrepancy between the DGB and the four other federations in the FRG is equally substantial, if not more so. The other labor federations are the Deutsche Angestelltengewerkschaft (DAG)—an explicitly white-collar union; the Union Leitender Angestellten (ULA)—an organization for middle managers; the Deutscher Beamtenbund (DBB)—an exclusively civil servant organization; and the Christlicher Gewerkschaftsbund (CGB)—a barely existent, small confessional workers' association.

7. Originally, the DGB federation only had 16 constituent unions as its members. The Policemen's Union joined as the 17th member in April 1978. Although the bargaining of West German unions is rather centralized, it does not reach the levels attained by the Dutch, Austrian, and Swedish unions, for example, where the federations—the NVV, NKV (recently merged into the FNV), and the CNV; the ÖGB; and the LO, TCO, and SACO, respectively—conduct contract negotiations. In contrast the DGB has no such powers.

8. Protokoll—Gründungskongress des Deutschen Gewerkschaftsbundes, München, 12-14 Oktober 1949 (Cologne: Bund-Verlag, 1949), p. 318.

9. Ibid.

10. Not all DGB unions have this strict 75 percent rule. Thus, for example, the third largest union, IG Chemie-Papier-Keramik (about 675,000 members), provides some modifications as to this rule in its bylaws.

REFERENCES

The following is a selective list of works dealing all or in part with West German labor unions and/or their history. It in no way claims to be exhaustive.

English

Abraham, David. The Collapse of the Weimar Republic: Political Economy and Crisis. Princeton, N.J.: Princeton University Press, 1981.

Bergmann, Joachim, and Walther Müller-Jentsch. "The Federal Republic of Germany: Cooperative Unionism and Dual Bargain-

ing System Challenged," in Worker Militancy and Its Consequences, ed. Solomon Barkin, pp. 235-76. New York: Praeger,
1975.

von Beyme, Klaus. Challenge to Power: Trade Unions and Industrial
Relations in Capitalist Countries. Beverly Hills, Calif.: Sage,
1980.

Bundesministerium für Arbeit und Sozialordnung. Co-determination
in the Federal Republic of Germany. Geneva: International
Labor Organization, 1976.

Castles, Stephen, and Godula Kosack. "How the Trade Unions Try to
Control and Integrate Immigrant Workers in the Federal Republic of Germany," Race 11 (April 1974): 498-514.

Cullingford, E. C. M. Trade Unions in West Germany. Boulder,
Colo.: Westview Press, 1977.

Deppe, Rainer, Richard Herding, and Dietrich Hoss. "The Relationship between Trade Union Action and Political Parties," in
The Resurgence of Class Conflict in Western Europe since
1968, edited by Colin Crouch and Alessandro Pizzorno, vol. 2,
pp. 177-96. New York: Holmes and Meier, 1978.

Furlong, James. Labor in the Boardroom: The Peaceful Revolution.
Princeton, N.J.: Dow Jones Books, 1977.

Gerschenkron, Alexander. Bread and Democracy in Germany.
Berkeley and Los Angeles: University of California Press,
1943.

Jacobs, Eric. European Trade Unionism. London: Croom Helm,
1973.

Kassalow, Everett M. Trade Unions and Industrial Relations: An
International Comparison. New York: Random House, 1969.

Maier, Charles. Recasting Bourgeois Europe. Princeton, N.J.:
Princeton University Press, 1975.

Mann, Michael. Consciousness and Action among the Western Working Class. London: Macmillan, 1973.

Mueller-Jentsch, Walther, and Hans-Joachim Sperling. "Economic
Development, Labor Conflicts and the Industrial Relations Sys-

tem in West Germany." In The Resurgence of Class Conflict in
Western Europe since 1968, edited by Colin Crouch and Alessandro Pizzorno, pp. 257-306. New York: Holmes and Meier, 1978.

Spiro, Herbert J. The Politics of German Codetermination. Cambridge, Mass.: Harvard University Press, 1958.

Sturmthal, Adolf. The Tragedy of European Labor, 1918-1939.
New York: Columbia University Press, 1943.

Thimm, Alfred L. The False Promise of Co-determination. Lexington, Mass.: Lexington Books, 1980.

Willey, Richard J. Democracy in the West German Trade Unions:
A Reappraisal of the "Iron Law." Beverly Hills, Calif.: Sage,
1971.

German

Bergmann, Joachim, ed. Beitraege zur Soziologie der Gewerkschaften. Frankfurt am Main: Suhrkamp Verlag, 1979.

Bergmann, Joachim, Otto Jacobi, Walther Müller-Jentsch. Gewerkschaften in der Bundesrepublik. 2 vols. Frankfurt am
Main: Aspekte Verlag, 1976.

Borsdorf, Ulrich, Hans Otto Hemmer, Gerhard Leminsky, and
Heinz Markman. Gewerkschaftliche Politik: Reform aus
Solidaritaet. Cologne: Bund-Verlag, 1977.

Deppe, Frank. Autonomie und Integration: Materialen zur Gewerk-
schaftsanalyse . Marburg: Verlag Arbeiterbewegung und
Gesellschaftwissenschaft, 1979.

Deppe, Frank, Jutta von Freyberg, Christof Kierenheim, Regina
Meyer, and Frank Werkmeister. Kritik der Mitbestimmung:
Partnerschaft oder Klassenkampf? Frankfurt am Main: Suhr-
kamp Verlag, 1973.

Deppe, Frank, Georg Fülberth, and Juergen Harrer, eds. Geschichte
der deutschen Gewerkschaftsbewegung. Cologne: Pahl Rugen-
stein, 1977.

Grebing, Helga. Geschichte der deutschen Arbeiterbewegung. Munich: Deutscher Taschenbuch Verlag, 1979.

Jacobi, Otto, Walther Müller-Jentsch, and Eberhard Schmidt, eds. Gewerkschaften und Klassenkampf, Kritisches Jahrbuch. (Frankfurt am Main: Fischer Taschenbuch Verlag, 1972-75.

_____. Kritisches Gewerkschaftsjahrbuch. Berlin: Rotbuch Verlag, 1976 annually until 1981.

Klönne, Arno. Die deutsche Arbeiterbewegung: Geschichte-Ziele-Wirkungen. Cologne: Büchergilde Gutenberg, 1981.

Leminsky, Gerhard, and Bernd Otto. Politik und Programmatik des Deutschen Gewerkschaftsbundes. Cologne: Bund Verlag, 1974.

Schmidt, Eberhard. Ordnungsfaktor oder Gegenmacht: Die politische Rolle der Gewerkschaften. Frankfurt am Main: Suhrkamp Verlag, 1975.

Schuster, Dieter. Die Deutsche Gewerkschaftsbewegung: DGB. Bonn-Bad Godesberg: Vorwaerts-Druck, 1976.

Vetter, Heinz Oskar, ed. Vom Sozialistengesetz zur Mitbestimmung: Zum 100. Geburtstag von Hans Böckler. Cologne: Bund-Verlag, 1975.

8

BONN IST DOCH WEIMAR: INFORMAL REFLECTIONS ON THE HISTORICAL LEGACY OF THE FEDERAL REPUBLIC

CHARLES S. MAIER

Frequently during the last decade or even longer, we have been told "Bonn is not Weimar." The Federal Republic of Germany (FRG) happily was not vulnerable to the constitutional flaws, economic disaster, ideological polarization, aggrieved nationalism, or bitter class conflict that had brought down the first German republic. My title is <u>Nevertheless, Bonn is Weimar</u>. By this I do not mean to suggest that the FRG actually faces perils analogous to those of its predecessor, nor that ugly political extremism lurks beneath an apparently calm surface, nor that Germans never change. I think the Bonn regime has been a success story in terms of politics and economics; and while a greater degree of "mastering the past" (that is, really coming to terms with the historical burden of national socialism) might have been desirable, the workaday rationality with which West Germans reconstructed decent institutions has served them and Europe well. Nonetheless, every cliché should be critically tested, and even while we agree that the present regime is different overall from the Weimar Republic, it may be revealing to examine some ways in which it is not dissimilar. This chapter proposes, then, to argue, deliberately and admittedly perversely, the following theses:

1. That despite the radical discontinuities, the FRG shares essential characteristics of German statehood with its predecessor regimes;
2. That these characteristics involve not the strong state for which Germans are often criticized but a continuing German tradition of what might be termed insufficient statehood;
3. That the sources of statehood for the Germans must be sought outside the national or, in the case of the FRG, half-national framework; and that one finds where the state should be the forces of civil society instead.

Finally, we will be able to ask what is gained and what is lost without a state or without the idea of the state.

Before proceeding further, a word on what is meant by state is appropriate. Probably few other societies became so agitated as to whether they had a state or not. Not the French, because they could be certain that they did have one; it was and remains manifest in every subprefecture and prefecture in the land, at which every couple registers every child at birth and thereby gives him or her état civil ("civil status"). Nor have the British or Americans worried about their state; they never felt the notion was very relevant until recently; a state was not particularly perceived nor longed for. But for the Germans, obviously, state is an essential interpretive category. By and large both Left and Right thought they knew what a state should be, wanted one, and deplored that the regimes they lived under did not really make the grade. It is in light of their critiques that I should like to consider the Bonn Republic, but first let us review some of these criticisms.

Remember that for Hegel the state by definition had to partake of a high degree of rationality: not every political structure was a state, and certainly the associative level of human transactions—markets, corporations, guilds—did not possess statehood because they could not generalize the needs of citizens. Germans have been pretty demanding about the governments they lived under in terms of awarding them state status or not, and indeed, many of the regimes that one might ordinarily think passed muster have been contemptuously dismissed. Even Bismarck's Second Reich fell short of real statehood for many conservative critics who yearned for an integral and mystical authority far more transcendent than the flummery of William II or the jostling interests of the new rich, the professors, and grasping rye farmers seemed to allow. Indeed, for these critics from the turn of the century on, the German regime appeared less a state than just what Hegel would have termed civil society with a lot of military trappings: the naked struggle among social forces and "interests"; a menacing social democracy that wanted to level all cultural and material distinctions on the one side, a bunch of arrogant parvenu businessmen and drunken university Burschen on the other.

Of course, the critiques of the Second Empire were mild compared with those leveled against the Weimar Republic. On the one side were the right wing critics—Carl Schmitt being perhaps the most sophisticated—who argued that as a parliamentary regime Weimar did not attain the character of a state. Functionally, its party fragmentation did not permit the concentration of power that a state had to represent, and during the last stages of its existence, conservative forces offered schemes for constitutional reform that would have erected a strong upper house, made voting favor old adult males, and sought to

give the Reich's executive the authority he was largely to claim under
Article 48. What Article 48 provided as an emergency procedure,
the Right wanted as the normal construction of the regime. Underlying Schmitt's calls for authority was the counterposing of pluralism
(a set of multiple roles for individuals and groups with no decisive
political fulcrum or priority for the political) and the state—"the decisive case, the authoritative entity."[1] The political entity decided
what was political; what was political was ultimately the distinction
between us and them, friends and foes, foes abroad (enemies in war)
and foes presumably at home. In this sense liberalism represented
not politics but the critique and negation of politics. Despite the en-
shrining of liberal hypocrisies in the Versailles Treaty, despite the
making of a regime out of pluralism, Schmitt affirmed, state and
politics could not be exterminated. "Us" and "them" remained the
primal distinction; internal or foreign war the final or underlying
relationship; the state, the final "decider."

Given these criteria the Weimar Republic could hardly represent a state. It incorporated a flabby and feeble pluralism, paralyzed
by its inability to transcend group interests (especially the interests
of labor) and, of course, discredited by its inability to invoke full
sovereignty internationally. This critique is familiar to us all.
Schmitt gradually worked his way toward praising a presidential
regime as Guardian of the Constitution, then went on to praise the
will of the Führer as incorporating the decisionist entity.

These conservative critiques, which became the common currency of fashionable rightist circles, are certainly well known. Still,
it is worth stressing the points of tangency with the criticisms of the
Left. Consider Otto Kirchheimer's analysis of the Weimar constitution as one that gave the Left political guarantees (that is, assured a
formal democracy) but denied them social guarantees (that is, precluded a socialist outcome) and, hence, remained a constitution without decision.[2] Or recall Franz Neumann's classic analysis of the
Weimar constitution in the introduction to <u>Behemoth</u>, where the republic was analyzed as resting upon several fundamental compacts
among social forces: that between the army and the Social Democratic
party (SPD) (the famous Groener-Ebert telephone conversation) and
between the unions and industry (the Stinnes-Legien agreement).[3]
For the SPD critics Weimar, too, was a halfway house to political
rationality and decision, hence more of a set of social compacts than
a state per se. Left and Right together were convinced that the republic was an unfortunate and feckless structure.

Now the regime that followed certainly remedied some of the
flaws that the Right especially felt. But resources of coercion were
not enough. Friend and foe together also bridled at allowing the Third
Reich to claim statehood. Sympathizers and Nazis did not really wish

to be a state; the notion of "movement" and of leader gave them a
more direct expression of political community that supposedly recon-
ciled popular with absolute power. "State" was a rather fusty concept
suitable for the halfway authoritarianism of von Papen but not really
"decisive" enough to unite absolute sovereignty and perfect representation. Nor did the Left wish to give the Third Reich the honor of being a state. What can be called the Morningside Heights analysis
of Nazism (referring to Columbia University's hospitality to the
"Frankfurt School" refugees) applied to the Third Reich the same criteria it had imposed upon Weimar and found that the Third Reich, too,
was merely a set of social compacts, or the upshot of raw social
forces that never achieved the rationality of a state. Herbert Marcuse in Reason and Revolution (1941) sought bravely to acquit Hegel
of any intellectual paternity of the Third Reich by arguing that the
system of power Hitler had instituted was the opposite of a Hegelian
state: it was irrationality in power, not rationality; it was a raw expression of Volksgemeinschaft, hardly elevated and mediated. [4] Likewise for Neumann, the regime represented the result of old and new
authoritarian forces: monopoly capital, bureaucracy, the Junker
landowners, and the army. Once again a German regime lacked real
statehood. As Kirchheimer also noted in 1941, it was useful to think
of three stages of political compromise: liberalism meant agreement
among parliamentary representatives or between them and a government; mass democracy à la Weimar meant compromises between voluntary associations; and fascism corresponded to "the treaties with
which the elites of the estatist orders, organized by constraint, divided power and booty." [5] In sum, no more than the Weimar Republic could the Third Reich count as a state. Faced with these critiques
we are left with the question, Where and when has the state existed
among the Germans?

    In this perspective of insufficient statehood, the Bonn Republic
follows historical tradition. In formal constitutional terms this was
clear to the delegates of the 1948-49 Parliamentary Council. Their
Basic Law was provisional, to be displaced automatically (Section
146) when a constitution decided by the German people came
into force. It was limited, ceded by the occupying powers or at least
three of them, and with the spheres of foreign relations, economic
determination over the Ruhr and military action, sharply curtailed.
    As telling as the formal limitations, however, was the histori-
cal formation of the regime as a political and social collectivity. The
Bonn Republic was Bizonia with juridical functions fleshed out on
its originally economic ones. If you will recall the prehistory of the
Bonn Republic (a prehistory that can be followed in the "Z" series of
documents at the Federal Archives in Koblenz) its major point of con-

ception was the U.K.-U.S. decision to join their zones of occupation at the end of 1946. The economic administrative agencies that were established at the outset of 1947 served as embryonic state agencies: more than the Länderräte of the U.K. and U.S. zones, the Wirtschaftsrat für das vereinigte Wirtschaftsgebiet (Economic Council for the United Economic Region) became the parliamentary analogue, and the Verwaltungsrat für Wirtschaft, the protoexecutive. It was there that Christian Democrats, Liberal Democrats, and Social Democrats discussed the restricted area of public policy that was open to them, namely, organization of the economy.

Perhaps all the decisions were foreclosed. Once the United Kingdom was persuaded to join with the U.S. occupying powers in Bizonia, the forces of the moderate Left among the West Germans lost their natural stronghold in industrial North-Rhine Westfalia. The consequences for the Christian Democratic Union (CDU)—the eclipse of the collectivist Karl Arnold tendency and the Ahlen Program to the benefit of Adenauer and Erhard's revised capitalism—would become evident only later. The immediate consequence was the Social Democratic reversion to the opposition when the party failed to secure direction of the Wirtschaftsamt in the new Bizone. Thereafter, Social Democrats attacked Erhard's economic policies, defending planning and considerations of social equity against his frank and ultimately successful wager on growth.

These debates between 1947 and 1949 were more than merely technical economic controversies. In fact, they provided the framework of political, as well as political economy, alternatives during a period in which the West Germans had not yet achieved even limited political decision-making power. Planning, currency reform, the Lastenausgleich ("compensatory levies") for those left propertyless by the war were technical subjects; however, as Erhard told the Wirtschaftsrat, "economics threatened once again to become Germany's fate."[6] By the time the formal Constitutional Council convened in late 1948 the major parameters for West German institutions had already been set implicitly: the geographic division of the country, of course, had been imposed from the outset; the federalism rested upon a convergence of CDU interests and U.S. convictions; the strongly capitalist commitment to the economy was ratified when the Socialists decided on an oppositional role, if not earlier. This is not to say that an SPD that retained control of the Bizonal institutions could really have imposed planning, preserved controls, and constructed a more centrally managed economy. Nonetheless, SPD opposition and Erhard's dominance did sanction a go-for-broke unleashing of private energies. A year later, at the talks in Königstein among socialist, Christian Democratic, and economic leaders, it became evident that the future West German emphasis on intense export and value-added strategies at the expense of more social consumption at home was already emerging. [7] The postponement of a tax to compensate those whose assets had been lost with defeat, the Lastenausgleich, and the stress on accumulation and on producing competitive exports entailed a whole political, as well as economic, orientation.

In this economic determination of a political order, the Bonn Republic followed squarely in the German historical tradition. Even Bismarck's state had been foreshadowed first by the Zollverein, a Prussian-dominated customs union, and then by the Zollparlament, which brought together delegates from the southern German states and the new North German Confederation between 1867 and 1870. Indeed, it was the adverse elections in the Zollparlament that revealed the strength of anti-Prussian forces and persuaded Bismarck as minister president of Prussia he had best force national unification by means of exploiting foreign crisis and war. The Economic Council of Bizonia served, in a sense, as the Zollparlament for the Bonn Republic; foreign policy decisions, however, lay beyond its competence.

For the Weimar Republic—as Neumann suggested—the truly constitutive moments considered are the Arbeitsgemeinschaft of November 15, 1918, the Ebert-Groener arrangement, and we can add, the acceptance of the Versailles Treaty by the Reichstag. The Arbeitsgemeinschaft meant a fundamental social compact between leading industrialists and labor chiefs and established the political centrality of the eight-hour day. Industry's acceptance of the eight-hour day, under the duress of the revolution; then its suspension at the end of 1923, with the consequent withdrawal of the Social Democratic party into four years of opposition; and what amounted to renewed breakdown of the underlying labor-industry social compact with the Ruhr lockout of 1928 and the failure of the Great Coalition over social insurance in 1930 were crucial issues—not merely for politics but for the constitutional order of the Weimar Republic. These junctures established and then disestablished the fundamental social compromises that were the basis of the Weimar regime. In its intimate connection with these social compromises, Weimar's statehood did not extend beyond the forces of civil society.

The other major "contracts" that Neumann described were also constitutive. The Versailles Treaty limited the sovereignty of the German Republic, and more important, it established a clear issue of foreign policy—acceptance or revision—as a crucial domestic issue as well. The Republican forces were those that accepted the European order imposed by Versailles, or at least those who were willing to wait for its peaceful erosion and amendment. Finally, the military-civilian pact served to allow a civilian regime legitimacy for an initial decade, but then increasingly eroded its independence. The Groener-Ebert Pact, so to speak, established the critical and ambiguous position of the instruments of force that the Reich had at its disposal; it both leashed the army and precluded its effective reform. It ensured its perpetuation as the price for its limited intervention in politics. By 1930 and with increasing intensity during the crisis of 1932-33, as the focus of power switched to the presidential rather than parliamentary and party offices, the limitation on the army meant less and less.

If any characteristic marked the Weimar political order, it was precisely the rawness of these political and social forces: their direct intrusion into the realms of power and the allocation of authority, without a real state to mediate them. In this sense Bonn has recapitulated much of Weimar: not in the balance among the constitutive social forces, but in the immediacy of their decisional role. As Ernst Nolte has pointed out in what is otherwise a somewhat eccentric book, Deutschland und der Kalte Krieg, the truly constitutive moments in the history of the FRG were not those of the noted Herrenchiemsee discussions of 1949, but subsequent formative debates; namely, the rearmament controversy of 1950-51 and the adoption of Ostpolitik at the end of the 1960s. These major reconsiderations of what the Bonn polity represented in terms of its domestic social forces and international role were the truly formative political foundations. [8]

I think Nolte's insight is correct, although I would nominate other crisis points alongside those that he emphasizes: for domestic policy, the SPD decision to go into the opposition in 1947, and then its repeal of that decision, in effect, at the Bad Godesberg party conference 12 years later; perhaps the Spiegel Affäre of 1963 in providing some specificity to the guarantees of dissent (though here the Radikalenerlass might have to be coupled with the dismissal of Strauss as setting an outer periphery); and finally the participation of the SPD (and especially its economics minister, Karl Schiller) in the Great Coalition of 1966-69. [9] For the Schiller experience in effect meant that the Bonn government would add to its capacities the commitment for active macroeconomic intervention (that is, would become, like the other European nations, a Keynesian polity) in exchange for which the Social Democrats would accept not merely the renunciation of collectivism that they had already buried at Bad Godesberg, but the implicitly monetarist and explicitly export-oriented economic strategy that had prevailed since 1949, when they were in the opposition. The year 1966, like 1959, made social democracy safe for capitalism in general and for West Germany's capitalist strategy in particular; in return it sanctioned a more buoyant and expansionist emphasis in this strategy, allowed some shifting of national income to labor after 15 years of renunciation and capital accumulation that had followed the currency reform, and provided the social presupposition of Ostpolitik.

Today, 15 years after this West German "opening at the Left," we see evidence that the FRG will shift gears once again. With measurable unemployment; pressure from a major ally to increase its defense spending; increased pressure from within the SPD Left; the disappearance of the chancellor's major friend abroad (Giscard d'Estaing); and the bellwether reversion of, so far at least, one important Free Democratic group to a CDU alliance, the handwriting on the wall is apparent. What the present moment suggests is that the moments of turning in economic policy or political economy represent significant political shifts as well. In this sense, the recent debates and moods in West Germany are reminiscent of those late 1920s when the forces of capital complained they could not afford the social programs of the Great Coalition, felt that their domestic and foreign markets were near saturation, and worried that the level of German real wages had become prohibitively high. Then, too, the financial managers of the Weimar Republic had to be concerned about the vulnerability of their international economic situation as U.S. funds began to falter, reparations remained a problem, and domestic interest rates had to remain high. Today, it is Arab oil and high U.S. interest rates that impose the constraints upon West German financial management; but many of the conjunctural stresses that Bonn must undergo in the twilight of Keynesianism are those that Weimar underwent before its dawn. This is not to say that the upshot will be the same. Bonn ist doch Weimar— but Weimar without Junkers, without an inflation-expropriated middle and professional class, without an ulcerating national issue, and so far still without mass unemployment (and, of course, without half of its territory). But like Weimar, its most basic political alignments and policy commitments rest upon the interplay of working-class and capitalist interests; like Weimar, it is a regime that rests upon the transactions of highly organized social forces; like Weimar (as Weimar was diagnosed by both Left and Right), it remains as much civil society as state.

When I proposed this interpretation to a friend I was asked, How come there are so many policemen? Who hires the police? It befits us to ask where the state lies in West Germany, if not in Bonn. To which might be added the question, Does any modern regime really represent a state in the stringent Hegelian or Morningside Heights sense? Do we need a state? C. B. Macpherson has recently asked, "Do we need a Theory of the State?"[10] He decided that Marxists certainly did, and quasi-Marxists or social democrats would benefit as well. I guess that all the spiritual children of the Suhrkampkultur (by which is meant the readership of those little volumes whose covers range over the rainbow and whose contents run from pink to red) do need a theory of the state. I am not so sure that we really need a state, however. But to know what we are missing, we should at least be able to talk about what it might be like if it were there. For Macpherson, as for other Marxists, the modern state is characterized by a certain symbiotic relationship with capital; the state fragments capital by dealing with particular segments of organized industry and the economy (including unions) but can exist only insofar as it advances the accumulation of capital in general. Whether this particular theory of the state gets us beyond the tautological, I find it hard to say. Indeed, I think most arguments about the state attribute to its existence the way the ontological argument attributes existence to God. Capitalists deal with ministerial officials and legislatures; the process by which they become the state for professors is often very mysterious.

The question remains, Who hires the policemen? For West Germany the answer is clear, and illuminating. The federal states, or Länder, hire the majority of policemen, excepting the Grenzschutz; and everyone would agree that insofar as there is a Grenze, there must be some degree of statehood. Even under Germany's most powerful regime the police began as a Land function, and then became less a nation-state one then a party one (that is, the Gestapo started as Prussia's secret police, and the SS was the party's). When critics complained of Weimar's insufficient statehood or even of Bismarck's, they did have a model of a sufficient state before them. It was Prussia. Nobody ever questioned whether Prussia was an adequate state. They asked only whether it was an adequate nation. The greatest of Prussia's kings defined his role as first servant of the state. It is no surprise that a certain nostalgia for Prussia exists today in both Germanies. After all, not even the Weimar constitutional drafters could bring themselves to split up Prussia, although it was likely to claim all the historical legitimacy there was to go around. The East German regime, which has no doubt that it represents or should represent a state, feels quite comfortable annexing the Prussian tradition: the great equestrian statue of Frederick has now been moved back from Potsdam, where I viewed it 15 years ago, to Unter den Linden. (There is an equally fine equestrian sculpture of the Great Elector by Schlüter in front of the Charlottenburg palace, but it has hardly the same resonance.) In West Germany nostalgia for a state should become all the more acute when the pluralist nature of the Bonn compromises are particularly exposed. Given the fact that economic changes are intimately bound up with, indeed codetermine, quasi-constitutional discussions in West Germany, the vulnerability of the present moment should naturally awaken some longing for the German state that did exist.

In theory there were other contenders for sufficient statehood: Austria and Bavaria. But Austria proved an impossible state frame for Germans (which is what the history of the nineteenth century regimes is about), and Bavaria can claim no attractive power of its own. Although it remains the only historical state intact within the West German polity, it cannot serve as paradigm: the last national election just confirmed that Modell Bayern is hardly for export north of the Main.

All this suggests that the Bonn Republic is condemned not to have a state. As I stated at the outset, this establishes the regime squarely in the tradition of German national structures, each of which was lamented as unvollendet, incomplete territorially, of course, and somehow incomplete spiritually, or as a state entity.

By now, however, the West Germans should understand that this situation brings more opportunities than liabilities. Despite the current nostalgia for Prussia, it is useful to be reminded, as Hans Ulrich Wehler has recently done, that the Prussian liabilities were often devastating. If living as a Bavarian is hardly to be taken seriously, living as a Prussian was hardly to be taken as fun. Conversely, as historians, we can transcend the nineteenth century perspective that criticized the Holy Roman Empire as just a shambles of sovereignties and an impediment to rational progress. In retrospect, its intricate curiae, states, circles, estates, towns, and the like sanctioned rich if fragmented communities. I hardly wish to substitute a nostalgia for the institutions of the Holy Roman Empire in the place of a longing for Prussia, but only to suggest that in the conditions of a wartorn Central Europe—confessionally divided, as was no other area in the world—the empire's version of "incomplete statehood" at least supported other civic aspirations.

To return to the Bonn Republic, being liberated of a state means that Germans in the West finally do have a chance—and have exercised the chance—to be modern. The real German revolution took place only in 1945: part of that revolution was the work, in effect, of 1789, eliminating finally the role of a landed upper class. But part of that revolution involved eliminating statehood (for a while eliminating even incomplete statehood). Indeed, all of us—not merely Germans—could learn a useful lesson by learning how to live without a state. This was Dahrendorf's plea in Society and Democracy in Germany about 15 years ago. The difficulty is how do we live without a public interest or a common good. By being openly an insufficient state, a pluralist bargain, the Bonn polity has served all of us a paradigm of corporatist modernity. It has embodied the burdens of our future as well as of our past. But neither in Bonn nor elsewhere in the West—where the state in the Morningside Heights sense is in disarray—do we have an answer as to how something more comes out of a corporatist pluralism than the interests of the stronger. For some of the hardy neoconservatives of the American Enterprise Institute, of Commentary and The Public Interest, even for a liberal such as Dahrendorf, this result is healthy. They in a sense have taken Carl Schmitt and validated him at the subnational level, celebrating the struggle between friend and foe as a healthy one, provided precisely that it does not take place at the level of the state (that is, provided that it eliminate the political). For those of us who have some nostalgia for the exiles of Morningside Heights, this answer seems insufficient. How to provide a better one cannot be the task of this brief study. My purpose has been to show that in some elemental ways Bonn faced anew, and still faces, the task that Weimar faced, albeit unsuccessfully: constructing a democratic order on the basis of limited statehood and restricted sovereignty. Filling this task is an opportunity for all of us in the West who must outgrow, indeed are being compelled to outgrow, the nineteenth century state, but who have yet to think through what concept of res publica or commonwealth to put in its place.

NOTES

1. Carl Schmitt, The Concept of the Political, trans. George Schwab (Brunswick, N.J.: Rutgers University Press, 1976), p. 44.

2. Otto Kirchheimer, "Weimar—und was dann? Analyse einer Verfassung," in Politik und Verfassung (Frankfurt am Main: Suhrkamp, 1964), p. 15.

3. Franz Neumann, Behemoth: The Structure and Practice of National Socialism (New York: Harper Torchbook, 1966), pp. 11-13.

4. Herbert Marcuse, Reason and Revolution: Hegel and the Rise of Social Theory (Boston: Beacon, 1960), pp. 409-19.

5. Otto Kirchheimer, "Strukturwandel des politischen Kompromisses," in Von der Weimarer Republik zum Faschismus: Die Auflösung der demokratischen Rechtsordnung (Frankfurt am Main: Suhrkamp, 1976), p. 213.

6. Records of Vollversammlung des Wirtschaftsrates, 21-22, April 1948, Aktenbestand Z 3, vol. 20, Bundesarchiv [Federal Archive], Koblenz.

7. From the 1949 Königstein discussions, Aktenbestand Z 13, vol. 63, Bundesarchiv [Federal Archive], Koblenz.

8. Ernst Nolte, Deutschland und der Kalte Krieg (Munich and Zurich: Piper Verlag, 1974), pp. 248-55, 329, 579-85.

9. For Schiller's role, see George H. Küster, "Germany," in Big Business and the State: Changing Relations in Western Europe, ed. Raymond Vernon (Cambridge, Mass.: Harvard University Press, 1974), pp. 64-86.

10. C. B. Macpherson, "Do We Need a Theory of the State?" Archives Européennes Sociologiques, 18 (1977): 223-44.

9
WEST GERMANY AS NUMBER TWO: REFLECTIONS ON THE GERMAN MODEL

PETER J. KATZENSTEIN

For the last thirty years political analyses of German history have centered upon two sets of questions, Why World War I and World War II? Why Hitler and Auschwitz? These questions have invited what by now are familiar answers. Delayed political unification and late but rapid industrialization in the second half of the nine-teenth century led to a combination of extreme military aggressive-ness abroad with extreme political illiberalism at home. Such has been the conventional depiction of the "German problem."

The preoccupation with the German problem is gradually fad-ing in the scholarly analyses of the Federal Republic of Germany (FRG). Fears are receding of a revival of German militarism and authoritarianism feeding on the sore of national reunification and re-inforced by a downturn in the economic fortunes of the Bonn Republic. In the eyes of many, West Germany has succeeded in combining Anglo-Saxon liberalism with continental statism in a modern social welfare state. A successful capitalism and a stable democracy have emerged, which provide other advanced industrial states with a "German Model" of what their own future might look like. This chap-ter describes the institutional characteristics of the German Model,

This chapter summarizes some of the arguments made at greater length in a book on public policy in West Germany and inte-grates them with parts of an essay, "Problem or Model? West Germany in the 1980's," World Politics 32 (July 1980): 577-98. I would like to thank the editors of World Politics for granting me the permission to reprint portions of that article—copyright © 1980 by Princeton University Press— and the German Marshall Fund for supporting generously the research project of which this is one part.

analyzes how they fit together politically, and speculates about their possible changes in the 1980s.[1]

INSTITUTIONAL STRUCTURES IN THE
PUBLIC AND THE PRIVATE SECTORS

West Germany's social forces were influenced greatly by fascism, Germany's defeat in World War II, and the Allied occupation. As a result of these cataclysmic changes, two of the most important traditional actors, the landed gentry east of the river Elbe and the military, were eliminated as serious contenders in the political arena. The procapitalist and anticommunist imperatives of the U.S. occupation sought to recreate West Germany in the image of the United States. For the first time in modern German history the Bonn Republic permitted a convergence of political conservatism with economic liberalism typical of the Anglo-Saxon countries.[2] Discontinuity was most pronounced in the political realm. Allied insistence on the dispersion of state power converted West Germany into a little United States with its own brand of the separation of power but, significantly, with the bureaucracy largely unchanged. Under U.S. tutelage the postwar party elite designed a system of popular participation that transformed national conservatism and prohibited the emergence of extremist political movements of the Right or Left.

In the private sector, change and continuity were more evenly balanced. The elimination of the Junkers and the army enhanced the political importance of a centralized business community and a centralized labor movement. Gladly accepted by an overwhelming majority of West Germans at the time, the U.S. occupation thus imposed what Charles Maier has aptly characterized as a U.S. vision of the "politics of productivity."[3] As a result, throughout the history of the Bonn Republic economic issues have remained central to virtually all questions of public policy. The changes brought by the Allied occupation, in what the Germans call Hour Zero (Stunde Null) in 1945, were much greater in the decentralized structure of the West German government than in the organizational centralization of social and economic institutions.

The decentralization of the power of the West German state is reflected everywhere. West Germany's courts are powerful and active. They combine the U.S. system of judicial review with the continental system of administrative justice; in addition they have well-defined jurisdictions in a number of areas, such as labor or social issues. Like the United States and unlike France, West Germany has a strong federal system, which gives the 11 states (Länder) constitutional prerogatives in areas such as education. In the 1970s in particular the Federal Council (Bundesrat), which represents these states in the policy-making process at the federal level, has become increasingly important. Finally, the federal bureaucracy in Bonn lacks the kind of social cohesion and ésprit de corps characteristic of the French civil service.

The decentralization of the West German state combines U.S. political precepts (a strong federalism, judicial review, and an independent Federal Reserve) with the emerging political properties of the FRG (the perpetuation of coalition governments, the growing importance of the Federal Council, and increasing judicial activism in policy making). Countervailing tendencies, to be sure, did exist. Bonn's "chancellor democracy" offers great power to the man at the top who has the instinct and talent to exploit fully the advantages of his office; a complex system of interbureaucratic relations provides a substantial measure of effective policy coordination. But these countervailing tendencies notwithstanding, numerous recent studies have illustrated that the decentralization of the state has created a reactive rather than an active West German public policy in both domestic and foreign affairs.[4]

In sharp contrast to the decentralization of power in the public sector, West Germany's private sector organizations are thoroughly centralized and very encompassing. The business community, for example, founded its first peak association in the 1870s, some 90 years before a similar institution finally emerged in the United Kingdom. After 1945 West Germany's unions decided on a united, industrywide form of organization, which stands in striking contrast to the decentralization of the United Kingdom's industrial unions, France's syndicalist labor movement, and Japan's company unions. West Germany's integrated financial structures give the large private banks as well as the regional banks of the Federal Reserve, rather than the federal government, control of the commanding heights of the economy. The United Kingdom, by way of contrast, still lacks West Germany's large-scale and effective investment banks; and, unlike the Federal Republic, in France large public-sector investment banks are effective instruments in the hands of the state bureaucracy. Furthermore, West Germany's powerful churches and social professions illustrate that the centralization of power in the private sector is not confined solely to economic institutions but characterizes West German politics more generally.[5]

This high degree of centralization in the private sector is very significant for the process of policy making. "Interest associations are more inclusive, more tightly organized, and occupy a more privileged position in the public policy processes than their American counterparts . . . traditional patterns of functional representation that bypass political parties have been complemented by the marked

increase in collaborative interelite relations."[6] The political foundations of the business community and of the Bonn Republic are inextricably merged. Like the military in Latin America or the state bureaucracy in Japan, the credit that business (rather than the government or fortuitous circumstances) has been given for the "economic
miracle" of the 1950s has provided it with a pervasive legitimizing
myth. As a result, it still enjoys today a preeminent place in West
Germany's political life.

A unified labor movement emerged in West Germany only in
response to fascism. Although the centralization of labor is less
strong than that of business, what matters is the political acceptance
of the unions as a legitimate spokesman for the interests of organized
and unorganized workers alike. Centralized and powerful interest
groups are represented directly in the political parties, their "study
groups" (Arbeitskreise), and in parliamentary committees dealing
with matters of special concern to them. Habit, as well as the law,
assure these groups of privileged access to the state bureaucracy.
Elaborate institutions typically delegate political authority and limit
political participation. These arrangements have two consequences.
"First they encourage behind-the-scenes interelite bargaining and
accommodation among pressure group spokesman and key public officials. . . . Second these procedures induce the rank-and-file members of interest associations to depend on their formal representatives
to obtain satisfaction for their policy demands and compel the constituent organizations of federal peak associations to rely on top interest
group elites who have direct access to national policy makers."[7]

PARAPUBLIC INSTITUTIONS AND
POLITICAL PARTIES

The decentralized system of government and centralized interest
groups merge in a variety of powerful, parapublic institutions, such
as the Federal Reserve, the Labor Office, or the Social Welfare
Funds.[8] These institutions provide the key to a relatively quiet and
harmonious process of debating and implementing policy away from
the controversies of partisan politics. Some of these institutions,
like the self-administered social welfare funds, have a long history
dating back to the nineteenth century. Others, like the Federal Reserve, are the creation of Allied policies after 1945. Still others are
West Germany's political imitation of foreign practices (the Concerted
Action influenced by French policies in the early 1960s) or of indig-
enous institutions (the German Research Council in the mid-1960s).
Some of these institutions are active in only one problem area, while
others are concerned with a whole range of policy problems. During

the past three decades these institutions have worked relatively smoothly, especially in the management of economic and social welfare issues because of the peace that has prevailed between the social forces of the Left and the Right since 1945.

The parapublic institutions are in intimate contact with a variety of political institutions, most importantly with the political parties that provide a second institutional arena where a decentralized state and a centralized private sector link up. On depoliticized issues political parties, like the parapublic institutions, further elite collaboration. But when issues become politicized, they are the most important institutional vehicle for mass political participation. From the outset of the Bonn Republic, political parties in the new "party state" (Parteienstaat) enjoyed a paraconstitutional position; later they came to benefit from substantial state subsidies.[9] In linking a decentralized public and a centralized private sector on politicized questions, political parties draw together around one table all of the important contestants for power in West Germany's electoral arena. But owing to the gradual institutional implantation of West Germany's party system during the last three decades, in the 1970s electoral pressure group politics was much less important than in the early days of the Bonn Republic. Instead, the transformation in the 1970s of the West German party system to a bloc system has made intra-bloc politics (within the Social Democratic party-Free Democratic party [SPD-FDP] government and Christian Democratic Union-Christian Social Union [CDU-CSU] opposition) more important to the process of policy initiation than interparty competition (between SPD-FDP and CDU-CSU). With the passing of time, elite collaboration in the West German party system has become an important supplement to the parapublic institutions.

Fifteen years ago Ralf Dahrendorf discerned in his celebrated book, Society and Democracy in Germany, an elite cartel founded on anxiety;[10] its political manifestation was the official Grand Coalition of 1966-69. In a recent textbook Lewis Edinger describes, instead, elite collaboration based on self-confidence; its political reflection has been the secret Grand Coalition since 1976.[11] In trying to master West Germany's two postwar recessions, unlike the United Kingdom both coalitions elevated the search for consensus above confrontation. The fusion of Germany's statist tradition with the West German party state has made all of the major parties into instruments of responsible governance, as well as democratic participation. There is less to the partisan conflict between West Germany's administered people parties than meets the eye. SPD Chancellor Helmut Schmidt, as the West German synthesis of both "Reds" and "Experts," is the best CDU chancellor the FRG ever had.

With the exceptions of the elections of 1969 and 1972, during the last two decades the major parties have been in astonishing agreement on most matters of political substance. The undeniable ideological intensification of the debate between the SPD-FDP government and the CDU-CSU opposition in the last decade stems in part from the necessity to emphasize differences in political style in the interest of electoral mobilization. To some it betrays an increase in the irresponsibility of partisan politics in the FRG; to others it is growing irrelevance. The diffusion of conflict and demobilization of the electorate, which derives from West Germany's state parties, creates its own political opposition. Serious political opposition derives from the existence of political movements questioning the basic consensus among party leaders and offering to a party able to accommodate them the prospect of electoral enlargement.

In the 1950s rearmament and nuclear weapons became the focus of a movement that was still related in part to the, then, oppositional SPD. In the 1960s emergency legislation and the Grand Coalition created its own extraparliamentary opposition and boosted the strength of the student movement. In the 1970s, the number of people who at one time or another had participated in civic initiative groups (Bürgerinitiativen) was probably larger than the combined membership of all the established political parties. The "green parties" of the ecology movement, though small, are of sufficient attraction to some segments of the voting public to have an important effect on the delicately balanced relations in West Germany's party system, especially at state and local levels of government. The antinuclear movement is challenging the leadership of all the major parties on an issue of vital importance to West Germany's future. At the outset of the 1980s different social movements that find themselves out of step with the country's established political elites are pressing for change on issues as disparate as defense and housing policy.

But opposition movements questioning West Germany's basic consensus are not likely to become a major political force, shaping West German policies in their own rights, in the foreseeable future. West Germany's dilemma of democratic participation in policy making is thus revealed in the tension between the pressures of electoral competition and the politicization of state institutions during the past 15 years of Social Democratic ascendance on the one hand and the smooth functioning of parapublic institutions as key guarantors of West Germany's substantial policy achievements on the other. These institutions have afforded West Germany's new, self-confident political class of professional powerbrokers the opportunity to shield policy making in the 1970s from a declining social and political consensus. When this opportunity was found to be too costly politically or otherwise unavailable, political leaders have preferred the legalization of politics through recourse to an activist Constitutional Court rather than a prolongation of intensive partisan debate and conflict. Focusing political attention on a strong CDU Chancellor Konrad Adenauer in the 1950s and a reform-minded SPD coalition government headed by Chancellor Willy Brandt in the early 1970s captures only the visible parts of West German politics. Its invisible features are the quiet collaborations of party leaders that are facilitated by the parapublic institutions that the dominant coalition (the CDU-CSU until 1966 and the SPD-FDP since 1969) has found, for a variety of reasons, difficult to conquer. The key to an understanding of the German Model lies in a rough symmetry between the power of the Left and the Right and in the multiple, invisible links between public and private centers of power.

The political logic of West Germany intersects in plausible ways with the political logic of the problems the country has faced during the last three decades. In the two areas that have been West Germany's proudest achievements, a highly successful management of the economy and the growth of a mature welfare state, the public and private sectors have been linked by parapublic institutions. [12] On the other hand, in the two areas where the West Germans have been conspicuously unsuccessful in implementing reform, administrative and educational reform, no such institutional link between the public and private sectors has existed. [13] Indeed, the absence of parapublic institutions was a great impediment to the unsuccessful attempts of overhauling the administrative apparatus of the federal bureaucracy or of providing advanced, high-quality education to a growing number of citizens. In the cases of policy success, political compromises were struck among elites in the insulated confines of highly centralized peak associations dealing with economic issues and in a social welfare bureaucracy that is largely independent of the state. By contrast, in the cases of policy failure the lack of any central coordinating forum encouraged political confrontation; hence, policy reform could not overcome the resistance of autonomous ministries, as in the case of administrative reform, or it was vulnerable to the disruptive pressures of partisan politics, as with university reform. The success of the German Model illustrates its democratic dilemma. Where the public and private sectors are linked by parapublic institutions, West Germany's political parties are part of the policy solution whose effectiveness in not necessarily matched by the norms of democratic accountability. Where these parapublic institutions are absent, political parties often reinforce the policy problem despite and sometimes because of fulfilling their mandate of democratic participation.

West Germany's way of organizing power creates distinctive capacities and incapacities for public policy. To many, West Germany

is a model because in the last two decades our attention has focused
so much on questions of economic policy and social welfare broadly
defined. In an era of volatile and expensive energy supply, high inflation, growing unemployment and low economic growth our attention
to and our assessment of West Germany are unlikely to change in the
1980s. But it is important to recognize that the success and effectiveness of any political model has its limits. This is the lesson to be
drawn from West Germany's experience with administrative and university reform policies.

Thus, political interpretations characterizing the FRG as a
party state that, for the first time in the last century, has secured
a liberal democracy in Central Europe contain only a partial truth.
Equally important is the way parapublic institutions and political
parties intersect in creating a political model marked by a distinctive
preference for political stability. The tension between democracy
and stability is of course not unique to West Germany. But against
the backdrop of modern German history, that tension acquires a
richer and more ominous meaning. It requires a more probing political analysis than can be found in the often unqualified admiration
that "Europe's New Giant"[14] is now receiving, especially in North
America.

THE PROBLEM OF CHANGE: WEST
GERMANY IN THE 1980s

Historical continuities in the evolution of West Germany's political institutions and practices must be balanced against questions of
change. Perhaps the most important political lesson West German
politics in the 1970s can teach us is the pervasive influence durable
institutions had in shaping the objectives and absorbing the policies
of an SPD government, which, at least in the early 1970s, was committed to the issue of social reform. Why were the accomplishments
of SPD reformers, measured against their own aspirations, so modest? The answer proffered by the preceding analysis is the durability
and resilience of the distinctive institutions of the FRG. Yet, no system of governance is immutable, and none is ever protected from
the possibility of fundamental change. But how does one think about
political change in West Germany, since change can be measured
neither by right-wing radicalism discredited by the Nazi past nor by
left-wing radicalism discredited by the East German neighbor?

Regime change could effect either mass participation or elite
collaboration as the two defining characteristics of the FRG. From
the vantage point of the late 1970s, it appears unlikely that a coalition
of the antidemocratic forces of prewar Germany could once again

attract widespread popular support for the cause of fascism. The first economic recession of the FRG led to sharp gains in the electoral strength of the neo-Nazi National Democratic party (NDP) in the years 1966-68. In sharp contrast, West Germany's Right has failed utterly in exploiting the more prolonged and serious economic crisis after 1973. Similarly, parties to the left of the SPD have been conspicuous electoral failures throughout the 1960s and 1970s. In response to growing challenges to the party's commitment to détente abroad and social reform at home, debates within the SPD will surely intensify, thus possibly precipitating a change in government. But the institutional form of mass political participation in West Germany is unlikely to be challenged in the 1980s. More likely are realignments and possibly transformations in West Germany's system of elite collaboration. Elite collaboration is likely to continue functioning across partisan lines. In the 1950s and 1960s the unions and CDU-led governments cooperated effectively in part because of the incomplete implantation of the unions on the party's left wing. In the 1970s the business community had few problems cooperating with an SPD-government whose Eastern policy opened new export markets and whose domestic economic policies since 1973 were favorable to business.

A more probable source of friction affecting elite collaboration in the 1980s lies in the gradual erosion rather than rapid transformation of the relations between the SPD and the unions.[15] The success of the stabilization policies of the SPD depends in large measure on the active cooperation of union leaders with firm control over their followers. In the medium term the political compensations for union "responsibility" must exceed the mere prospects of an SPD government staying in power. If they do not, a growth of militancy at the base may eventually offset not only the political bargains struck at the summit but also alter the institutional centralization of the entire system of elite collaboration. This does not mean that the German Model is likely to contract the British disease. The legal constraints imposed on West Germany's labor movement, the self-perceptions of union leaders, and the nature of union-party ties all militate against it. But the complaint that the Employers Association brought in 1977 before the Federal Constitutional Court against the Codetermination Law of 1976, the subsequent official withdrawal of the unions from participation in West Germany's income policy via the so-called Concerted Action in 1977, and the costly steel strike in 1978-79 indicate that West Germany's social partnership is not immune to gradual erosion. At the point at which such incremental changes were to transform the role of the unions from a stabilizing factor (Ordnungsfaktor) to an oppositional movement (Gegenmacht), West Germany's entire system of elite collaboration would undergo a qualitative transformation.

Reflections about the possible causes and consequences of instability in West Germany are based on the political experience of the 1930s. Far-reaching political change is a possibility only if West Germany's social forces are fundamentally affected by external developments, be it in the form of Soviet tanks or a grave crisis in the world economy. But short of truly catastrophic economic conditions transforming the political regimes throughout the advanced industrial world, the dangers confronting the substance, if not the form, of West German democracy in the 1980s derive not from the lack of stability but from its excesses. The institutional features of the German Model faithfully reflect the very low tolerance the West German population exhibits for all forms of political disorder. The ramifications of West Germany's monetary policy and the all-out attack on terrorism illustrate the potentially enormous political costs, both at home and abroad, accompanying the West German yearning for a degree of stability and security that will probably be unobtainable in the 1980s.

Hailed by many as the most important step on the long road to European unification in the past decade, the enlargement of the deutsche mark snake to a European currency bloc (European Monetary System [EMS]) in 1979 is a West German attempt to create greater stability throughout Europe at the price of marginally higher inflation at home. The establishment of the EMS was feasible in West Germany's domestic politics because it met long-standing demands of the dissatisfied unions for monetary expansion, curbed the power of the central bank, and, with the prospect of a small devaluation of the deutsche mark against the dollar in European markets, promised to slow down the general upward drift of the deutsche mark, which had become a major problem for West Germany's export industry. Internationally the EMS is an attempt to insulate the FRG at least in part from the deleterious consequences of a lack of U.S. leadership by constructing a West European complement to the Eastern policy. The stabilization strategy underlying West Germany's mercantilism of the 1950s and 1960s was narrow. The policy of undervaluation of the deutsche mark and of fiscal restraint collapsed, together with the Bretton Woods system of fixed-exchange rates.[16] The stabilization strategy informing West Germany's internationalism in the 1980s is likely to be based on the quiet assumption of political responsibilities on a global scale. West Germany will not play the role of the strong locomotive pulling others out of their economic troubles; more likely it will attempt to become the engine switching trains in the yard and heading them in the direction of stability. Rather than the historical memory of two inflations, the force propelling this stabilization strategy is the German Model. The political contradiction it faces in the 1980s derives from the necessity of

having to invest in the economic and political stability of Europe in
the full knowledge that the success and the uniqueness of the German
Model rests to some extent on the conditions perpetuating weak regimes in Western Europe.

West Germany's policy of internal security complements its
efforts of economic stabilization. Bismarck's reformist social legislation in the 1880s rounded out his repressive anti-Socialist policy.
In the 1970s the SPD's policy of domestic security (Politik der Inneren
Sicherheit) complemented its policy of domestic reforms (Politik der
Inneren Reformen).[17] Forty years after the Nazis cleared the state
bureaucracy and the profession of what they regarded as subversive
elements, an SPD government dedicated to the extension of democracy
joined hands with the CDU-CSU opposition in imposing its own version
of the Berufsverbot. The erosion of civil liberties in West Germany
in the 1970s began as a defense against the alleged long march of
left-wing radicals and reformers through the educational institutions
of West Germany. That erosion accelerated as the terrorist pressure of the Baader-Meinhof group and subsequent generations of Red
Army cells encouraged the illegal activities of West Germany's
modernized internal security forces and spawned the most advanced
computerized method of citizen surveillance anywhere in Europe and
perhaps in the advanced industrial world. Yet, the FRG is still a
Rechtstaat. At the height of the terrorist wave, for example, the
debate about preventive detention was brief, conducted in low voices,
and restricted to conservative circles. Moreover, a recent debate
within the SPD about the Berufsverbot may move policy back to a
more liberal course, at least on this one issue.

But the 1970s are noteworthy not for the courageous defense of
liberal norms of privacy but for the speed with which traditional civil
liberties were sacrificed in the interest of internal security. This
encroachment on West German democracy was inaugurated and supervised neither by authoritarian Junkers, nor aggressive generals,
nor anti-Semitic Nazis. Well-intentioned Social Democratic reformers legitimized political practices that, under conservative auspices,
would have elicited much sharper political protests at home and
abroad. West German democracy would be taxed to its limits, and
perhaps beyond, to survive the magnitude of civil strife of the United
Kingdom's or Italy's daily life. The question of internal security
thus illustrates, like the issue of economic stability, the distinctiveness of the FRG in the 1980s: compared with the other large advanced industrial states, West Germany is likely to have a lower domestic tolerance of change.

Before World War II the danger in the "German problem" was
that it combined too much change within Germany with too little
change without. The danger in the German Model may be that it

blends too little change within West Germany with too much change without. If West Germany in the 1980s should become an inverted mirror of its past, the German Model will again become the German problem.

CONCLUSION

A cursory glance at other large, advanced industrial states reveals the distinctiveness of the German Model.[18] Unlike France and Japan, West Germany lacks a radical labor movement and an assertive state bureaucracy. Organized labor in West Germany is very much part of the dominant coalition, and the gradual politicization of the top civil service has secured further the position of party leaders. Unlike the United States and the United Kingdom, West Germany's social market economy lacks the sharp distinction between state and society and features an intimate fusion between industry and finance. Unlike Italy, West Germany shows no trace of the political exploitation of the economy and the state bureaucracy by a conservative, broadly based coalition intent on defending its power against a Communist party of growing strength. The small rather than the large advanced industrial states approximate more closely the German Model. Like Sweden, West Germany has succeeded in combining political adaptability with economic prosperity; like Sweden, West Germany has affected important institutional modifications of a capitalist economy; and like Sweden, West Germany has encouraged extensive elite collaboration without negating the effect of electoral competition. Unlike Sweden, reform policies in the FRG have been less energetic for two reasons. West Germany's Social Democratic party has a weaker political base than Sweden's; and, critically for this argument, West Germany's institutional features tend to inhibit government activism in the pursuit of social reform.

The distinctiveness of the German Model among the advanced industrial states has both international and domestic roots. The reduction in Germany's size after 1945, rather than Social Democratic hegemony in the 1970s, induced a relatively decentralized form of neocorporatism distinctive also of some other small European states, such as Switzerland or the Netherlands since the late 1960s. Elite collaboration in a system of statist political parties and of social partnership between the business community and the labor unions is the West German contribution to a long-standing tradition of Central European political culture.[19] Despite its distinctiveness, the German Model may well be critical in offering a common reference point for a political interpretation of other large advanced industrial states. Political change in statist or liberal forms of capitalism is rendered

more intelligible by measuring it against the institutional structures
of the FRG rather than against one another. In their different political
traditions, all large advanced industrial states are experimenting with
institutional modifications of industrial capitalism. With the possible
exception of Japan, the relative size of these countries in the international economy is shrinking not only in objective terms but also in
the perception of their political elites. This is not true of West Germany. In the 1980s we shall not be able to overlook the effect of
West Germany on others, be it as a model or as a problem.

U.S. attitudes toward West Germany have changed since 1945.
Anxiety has been replaced by indifference, and indifference has given
way to admiration. From a distance West Germany's democracy looks
stable, its economy prosperous, its politics bland. The specter of
a revival of authoritarian nationalism had receded and communism
has chosen to contain its appeals through concrete walls and barbed
wires. Other countries make for better copy. What are the politics
of declining empires in modern times? What are the prospects of
communism in democratic capitalism? Will state bureaucracies defend national autonomy in an international economy? Can social
democracy combine equality with prosperity? These are the questions that excite the political imagination of those thinking and writing
about the United States and the United Kingdom, Italy and France,
France and Japan, and the United Kingdom and Sweden. The literature on contemporary West German politics lacks a central problem.
True to its subject matter, it is both competent and dull. To restore
that literature to the brilliance and political relevance of the generation of emigré scholars who left so few U.S. disciples requires rethinking the ways in which West Germany is a model and in which it
is a problem. In that enterprise of intellectual reorientation con-
verting the central premise of analysis into the central question may
be as good a beginning as any. Will the cunning of West Germany's
future point to the same lesson as the tragedy of Germany's past?
Can democracy and peace be endangered by too much stability, as
well as too little?

In the 1980s our attitudes toward the FRG will be a mixture of
pride and prejudice. West Germany is likely to become both a
model and a problem. After a long vacation, the advanced industrial
world will return to political normalcy in the coming decade. The
ungovernability of democracy and the crisis of capitalism have, after
all, been with us since the middle of the nineteenth century. West
Germany is likely to stand as a model for how to reap the benefits
of the politics of productivity at home and abroad. It is likely to become a problem in West Germany's manner of imposing the costs
of its policies on marginal or dissenting sectors of West German society and on other countries endowed with less industrial prowess

and more social conflict. Like all advanced industrial states, West
Germany will confront the universal task of adjusting domestically
to changes imposed from abroad. But its predicament will be unique,
bringing in harmony an unusually large international demand for
change with an unusually small national tolerance for change. In the
1970s West German policemen in search of political terrorists and
West German bankers in search of fiscal restraint became a common sight far beyond West German borders. Stability made in West
Germany has become a distinctive trademark. This reminds us
that the new Germany, like the old, is projecting abroad its distinctive (in)capacity for domestic adjustment. Ironically, the transformation of Germany from problem to model reaffirms an old
maxim: when the Germans agree, others worry.

NOTES

1. Growing fascination with the West German Model explains
perhaps why recent years have witnessed the publication of a growing
number of English language textbooks and bibliographies, including
Walter S. G. Kohn, Governments and Politics of the German-Speak-
ing Countries (Chicago: Nelson-Hall, 1980); David P. Conradt, The
German Polity (New York: Longman, 1978); Lewis Edinger, Politics
in West Germany, 2d ed. (Boston: Little, Brown, 1977); Gunther
Kloss, West Germany: An Introduction (London: Macmillan, 1976);
Arnold J. Heidenheimer and Donald P. Kommers, The Government
of Germany, 4th ed. (New York: Crowell, 1975); Guido Goldman,
The German Political System (New York: Random House, 1974); Kurt
Sontheimer, The Government and Politics of West Germany (New
York: Praeger, 1972); and Alfred Grosser, Germany in Our Time:
A Political History of the Postwar Years (New York: Praeger, 1971).
The most important English-language bibliographies include the first
four volumes of German Political Studies (Beverly Hills, Calif.:
Sage, 1974-80), each of which includes an extensive bibliographical
essay or bibliography; Douglas E. Ashford, Peter J. Katzenstein,
and T. J. Pempel, Comparative Public Policy: A Cross-National
Bibliography (Beverly Hills, Calif.: Sage, 1978), which contains a
selected, annotated bibliography of West German material in eight
public policy cases; Anna J. Merritt and Richard L. Merritt, Politics,
Economics, and Society in the Two Germanies, 1945-1975: A Bibliography of English-Language Works (Urbana: University of Illinois
Press, 1978); Arnold H. Price, The Federal Republic of Germany:
A Selected Bibliography of English-Language Publications, 2d ed.,
rev. (Washington, D.C.: Library of Congress, 1978); David P. Conradt, ed., Research Directory 1976 (n.p.: Conference Group on

German Politics, 1976); and Gisela Hersch, A Bibliography of German Studies 1945-1971 (Bloomington: Indiana University Press, 1972).

2. Hans-Jürgen Puhle, "Conservatism in Modern German History," Journal of Contemporary History 13 (October 1978): 697, 713.

3. Charles S. Maier, "The Politics of Productivity: Foundations of American International Economic Policy after World War II," in Between Power and Plenty: Foreign Economic Policies of Advanced Industrial States, ed. Peter J. Katzenstein (Madison: University of Wisconsin Press, 1978).

4. Renate Mayntz and Fritz W. Scharpf, Policy-Making in the German Federal Bureaucracy (Amsterdam: Elsevier, 1975); Helga Haftendorn, Wolf-Dieter Karl, Joachim Krause, and Lothar Wilker, eds., Verwaltete Aussenpolitik: Sicherheits- und entspannungspolitische Entscheidungsprozesse in Bonn (Cologne: Verlag Wissenschaft und Politik, 1978).

5. Clause Offe, "The Attribution of Public Status to Interest Groups: Observations on the West German Case," in Organizing Interests in Western Europe: Pluralism, Corporatism and the Transformation of Politics, ed. Suzanne D. Berger (Cambridge: At the University Press, 1981), pp. 123-58; Heinz Josef Varain, ed., Interessenverbände in Deutschland (Cologne: Kiepenheuer, 1973); Gerard Braunthal, The Federation of German Industry in Politics (Ithaca, N.Y.: Cornell University Press, 1965); Walter Simon, Macht und Herrschaft der Unternehmerverbände BDI, BDA und DIHT (Cologne: Pahl-Rugenstein, 1976); and Joachim Bergmann, Otto Jacobi, Walther Müller-Jentsch, Gerwerkschaften in der Bundesrepublik: Gewerkschaftliche Lohnpolitik zwischen Mitgliederinteressen und ökonomischen Systemzwängen (Frankfurt: Europäische Verlagsanstalt, 1975).

6. Edinger, Politics in West Germany, pp. 211, 219.

7. Ibid., p. 216; see also pp. 248-49.

8. The category "parapublic institutions" is broad. It figures prominently in the legal and professional literature on particular policy problems.

9. Gordon Smith, Democracy in Western Germany: Parties and Politics in the Federal Republic (New York: Holmes and Meier, 1979); Kenneth H. F. Dyson, Party, State, and Bureaucracy in Western Germany (Beverly Hills, Calif.: Sage, 1977); Wolf-Dieter Narr, ed., Auf dem Weg zum Einparteienstaat (Opladen: Westdeutscher Verlag, 1977); and Jürgen Dittberger and Rolf Ebbighausen, eds., Parteiensystem in der Legitimationskrise: Studien und Materialien zur Soziologie der Parteien in der Bundesrepublik Deutschland (Opladen: Westdeutscher Verlag, 1973).

10. Ralf Dahrendorf, Society and Democracy in Germany (Garden City, N.Y.: Doubleday, 1969), pp. 252-65.

11. The "secret" coalition between 1976 and 1980 was due to the dominance of the CDU-CSU in the Federal Council (Bundesrat) and its control over the arbitration committee, which resolved conflicts with parliament (Bundestag).

12. See, for example, several chapters in Peter Flora and Arnold J. Heidenheimer, eds., The Development of Welfare States in Europe and America (New Brunswick, N.J.: Transaction Books, 1981); Ray C. Rist, Guestworkers in Germany: The Prospects for Pluralism (New York: Praeger, 1978); Graham Hallett, The Social Economy of West Germany (London: Macmillan, 1973); and references cited in Ashford, Katzenstein, and Pempel, Comparative Public Policy.

13. Fritz Scharpf and Renate Mayntz, eds., Planungsorganisation: Die Diskussion um die Reform von Regierung und Verwaltung des Bundes (Munich: Piper, 1973); Joachim Hirsch and Stephan Leibfried, Materialien zur Wissenschafts- und Bildungspolitik (Frankfurt: Suhrkamp, 1973); and references cited in Ashford, Katzenstein, and Pempel, Comparative Public Policy.

14. Hugh Patrick and Henry Rosovsky, eds., Asia's New Giant (Washington, D.C.: Brookings Institution, 1976).

15. This topic is explored fully in a research project undertaken by Andrei S. Markovits and Christopher S. Allen. See, for example, their article "Power and Dissent: The Trade Unions in the Federal Republic of Germany Re-examined," West European Politics 3 (January 1980): 68-86; Wolfgang Streeck, "Organizational Consequences of Corporatist Cooperation in West German Labor Unions: A Case Study" (Paper presented at the Ninth World Congress of Sociology, Panel on Interest Intermediation, Uppsala, Sweden, August 14-18, 1978).

16. Michael Kreile, "West Germany: The Dynamics of Expansion," Between Power and Plenty: Foreign Economic Politics of Advanced Industrial States, ed. Peter J. Katzenstein (Madison: University of Wisconsin Press, 1978), pp. 191-224. Susan Strange, "Germany and the World Monetary System," in West Germany: A European and a Global Power, ed. Wilfrid L. Kohl and Giorgio Basevi (Lexington, Mass.: D. C. Heath, 1980), pp. 45-62; Wilhelm Hankel, "West Germany," in Economic Foreign Policies of Industrial States, ed. Wilfrid L. Kohl (Lexington, Mass.: D. C. Heath, 1977), pp. 105-24.

17. Manfred G. Schmidt, "Die Politik der SPD- und CDU-Regierungen: Eine vergleichende Analyse der Politik der Länderregierungen in der BRD 1952-1977" (Paper presented to the DVPW-Arbeitskreis "Parteien, Wahlen, Parlamente," Neuss, February 1979); Jane Kramer, "A Reporter in Europe," New Yorker, March 20, 1978, pp. 44-87; Edinger, Politics in West Germany, pp. 360-62; Günter Minnerup, "West Germany since the War," New Left Re-

view 99 (October 1976): 40-43; Terrorism and Politics in West Germany (Cambridge, England: CAPG, n.d.); Wolfgang Krieger, "Worrying about West German Democracy," Political Quarterly 50 (April-June 1979): 192-204; Sebastian Cobler, Law, Order and Politics in West Germany (Harmondsworth: Penguin, 1978); 'Radikale' im öffentlichen Dienst: Eine Dokumentation (Frankfurt: Fischer, 1973); Wolf-Dieter Narr, ed., Wir Bürger als Sicherheitsrisiko (Reinbek bei Hamburg: Rowholt, 1977); and Manfred G. Schmidt, "The Politics of Domestic Reform in the Federal Republic of Germany," Politics and Society 8 (1978): 165-200.

18. Berger, Organizing Interests in Western Europe; Philippe C. Schmitter and Gerhard Lehmbruch, eds., Trends toward Corporatist Intermediation (Beverly Hills, Calif.: Sage, 1979); Katzenstein, Between Power and Plenty; and Heinrich August Winkler, ed., Organisierter Kapitalismus: Voraussetzungen und Anfänge (Göttingen: Vandenhoeck, 1974).

19. Gerhard Lehmbruch, "Consociational Democracy, Class Conflict and the New Corporatism" and "Liberal Corporatism and Party Government," in Trends toward Corporatist Intermediation, ed. Phillipe C. Schmitter and Gerhard Lehmbruch (Beverly Hills, Calif.: Sage, 1979), pp. 53-62, 147-84; Gerhard Lehmbruch, "Das politischeSystem Östereichs in vergleichender Perspektive," Österreichische Zeitschrift für öffentliches Recht 22 (1971): 35-56; and Gerhard Lehmbruch, Proporzdemokratie: Politisches System und politische Kultur in der Schweiz und in Österreich (Tübingen: Mohr, 1967).

10

CONCLUSION: THE FEDERAL REPUBLIC OF GERMANY AND THE UNITED STATES—AN UNEASY PARTNERSHIP

ANDREI S. MARKOVITS

It would be a mistake to view this collection of essays as an attempt—no matter how indirect— to present "Model Germany" as a model in a normative sense (that is, as a construct that should be imitated). More specifically, this book does not purport to provide answers even in their most tentative form. It certainly avoids pointing the finger at other countries and showing them how to improve their own fate. Briefly put, this volume does not extol the Federal Republic of Germany (FRG) as a panacea. Rather, it represents a collection of critical essays the shared purpose of which is to help highlight some of the intricacies of the West German puzzle. This task, already quite formidable, will most likely increase in the future in direct proportion to the world's growing complexity. Aspects of this complexity have also affected West German-U. S. relations since the latter part of the 1970s. While the bonds between these two countries are still unusually strong and will most likely remain so for the foreseeable future, certain strains and tensions have recently appeared that signal the necessity for reflection and evaluation concerning this important partnership. In the following few pages I would like to present a set of ideas that bear some relevance to this topic. They also relate to the implicit theme of this volume, which is that an understanding of the way West Germany functions will be crucially important to the United States in the coming decade.

In the course of the last few years, one could observe a definite increase in incidents where West Germany's and the United States' aims were clearly at odds in the areas of economic and foreign policy. Paradoxically, the roots of this conflict lay precisely in the success of Model Germany, which the United States actively helped get started in the reconstruction era of the 1950s. Indeed, to many Americans, the FRG's stellar performance provided a concrete vindication of their belief in the moral and instrumental superiority of liberal democracy as a political system. Yet, suddenly the United States found itself challenged on various fronts by a country that until very recently was loath to participate in the international political community on a level commensurate with its economic prowess (the famous "economic-giant-political-dwarf" syndrome). It was hard to cover up the fact that by the late 1970s the objective interests of the United States and the FRG had begun to diverge. This growing disparity of interests was both economic and political. As to the former, West Germany's export orientation made the FRG one of the United States' most threatening competitors in the world market. By 1980 West Germany had become the world's largest exporter in absolute terms. It not only dominated the markets of Western Europe, but it also was far and away the most important capitalist trading partner with the USSR and Eastern Europe. Moreover, West German exports to the United States itself increased steadily over the last half of the 1970s. In short, the United States and the FRG clashed with increasing frequency in the ever-growing competition of global capitalism. Adding insult to injury, West Germany seemed to prevail in many of the head-on confrontations.

Sooner or later, this acute economic rivalry was bound to have political repercussions. Exacerbated by a U.S. return to an increasingly "hard line" vis-à-vis the USSR in the wake of the latter's invasion of Afghanistan, the foreign policies of the FRG and the United States began to drift apart, especially in relation to the USSR and Eastern Europe. The West German government openly defied both the Carter and Reagan administrations in their quest to curb the FRG's economic ties with the USSR. This has led to considerable tension between Washington and Bonn. Indeed, it was the difference in the way these two countries viewed their respective economic positions in the world market that induced yet another growing disagreement in the realm of foreign policy. West Germany's desire to continue the course of détente and Ostpolitik—a phenomenon that has received wide coverage in the U.S. media almost exclusively under the concept of "neutralism"—can only be interpreted in the context of the FRG's redefinition of its "national interest" in light of its economic engagements. Since this approach clashes with Washington's view of the world, which in turn, is influenced by a different set of economic criteria, it seems only natural that a growing chasm determines the interaction between these two most important allies/rivals of the capitalist world at the beginning of the 1980s.

These objective conflicts between the FRG and the United States are further compounded by important subjective dimensions, such as the interpretation and presentation of events. It has always amazed this writer that despite the jet age, television, and other forms of rapid communication, deep-seated prejudices and stereotypes continue to inform each country's image of the other. The lack of under-standing of "what makes the other guy tick" is rather pervasive in all social strata on both sides of the Atlantic. Indeed, so-called elites, which include policy and opinion makers, can hardly be exempt from letting superficial half-truths determine their consequential thoughts and actions. Since the task of this volume is to provide a better un-derstanding to a predominantly U.S. audience of "what makes the FRG tick," I will refrain from discussing the numerous sources of mis-understanding and misinformation that continue to exist in West Germany concerning the United States. Rather, I would like to point briefly to three areas that have been among the sources of U.S. mis-interpretation of today's Federal Republic of Germany.

The first consists of an intellectual underrepresentation of contemporary West German politics in our university curricula, pub-lished works of scholarship and journalism, and in the media. Per-haps for understandable reasons, Americans still are much more preoccupied with Nazi Germany, Weimar, and even earlier periods of German history than with events in the FRG. There are thousands of books on all aspects of the Third Reich, but barely a handful on West Germany in the English language. Peculiar as it may sound, the numerous Hollywood films about World War II that played in our cinemas in the 1950s and 1960s and have now been relegated to the status of an occasional late-night television rerun, influenced our view of Germans more than we care to admit.

In addition to being outdistanced in academia by its earlier pre-decessors, the FRG also suffers relative neglect at the hands of other European countries, which have consistently benefited from more prominent exposure in social science courses at U.S. universities. In the case of the United Kingdom, the reasons are rather evident. Blessed with more or less the same language and a similar culture, the United Kingdom could be studied by researchers with much less effort in terms of setup costs than just about any other European society. Also, being the European country that is "most like us," a common cultural bond developed in the course of three centuries that clearly translates into active interest in current affairs as well.

Sweden, in turn, seems to have assumed a primus-inter-pares position as far as the study of social democracy and the welfare state is concerned. It is largely owing to these two characteristics that this country has received so much attention in the areas of compara-tive politics and public policy in U.S. academe. None of the other comparable "small democracies"—be they Austria, Switzerland, Hol-land, Belgium, or Sweden's Scandinavian neighbors—have attained a similar level of exposure as Sweden. Indeed, it has been my experi-ence that, on the whole, the functioning of Sweden's political and eco-nomic system is better known, even among the small group of "Euro-peanists" in the social sciences, than is the FRG's.

France, Spain, and Italy command considerable attention as a consequence of their militant labor movements, numerous strikes, and—in the case of the latter two—by being the main representatives of "Eurocommunism." Something seems to be "happening" there all the time; they are different in the sense of being "exotic," "mysterious," ungovernable," even "sexy." The FRG, in notable contrast, appears boring. It lacks the excitement of the Latin-Mediterranian political systems, the cultural closeness of the English-speaking world, and the readily apparent uniqueness of Sweden or Japan. Moreover, the temporal proximity of national socialism—without a doubt among the most shameful experiences in human history—still maintains a sufficient level of fascination to "crowd out" interest in contemporary West German politics. It is also in this context that a disproportionate amount of attention has been given to manifestations of both rightist and leftist radicalism in the FRG. Somehow, West Germany's undemocratic dimensions still elicit greater interest with U.S. audiences than its democratic ones.

The second area that has been a source of U.S. misinterpretation of today's FRG is closely tied to the first. It basically pertains to the ambivalent emotions on the part of the United States vis-à-vis West Germany and the still-pervasive U.S. doubts as to the durability of the FRG's democratic structures and outlook. Only in this context can one explain the oscillations that characterize much of the reporting on West Germany in the U.S. media. Thus, for example, as amply discussed in the introduction to this volume, in 1979 and 1980 the celebration of Model Germany's successes reached nearly adulatory levels in some of the United States' most prestigious publications. There was a genuine feeling of happiness and vicarious pride in the FRG's achievements, which assumed almost self-congratulatory dimensions. Somehow one could not help but perceive a definite sense of vindication in these laudatory reports. A country we helped create and wean was not only our most reliable ally but also a bastion of liberal democracy and economic stability. But was it really?

Certainly one could hardly reach the same conclusion barely one year later. At the time of this writing in the fall of 1981, one report after another mentioned various problems in the FRG, often resorting to an alarmist tone. Thus, for example, Helmut Schmidt, "superchancellor" 12 months ago, had become Europe's most embattled leader. One had the distinct impression that he was engaged in a daily life-or-death fight to keep his job. The economy was suddenly portrayed to be in shambles. Zero growth for 1981 and the highest unemployment figures in 29 years were described in language that hinted at more than an economic crisis. Something systemic, structural, and fundamental seemed to have gone awry in the FRG.

In an almost caricature-like fashion symbolizing this sudden reassessment by the U.S. media of West Germany, John Vinocur, who barely a year before had extolled Helmut Schmidt and the FRG as the new leaders of the Western world, published yet another cover story in the New York Times Magazine (November 15, 1981), this time with the telling title "The German Malaise." This general "malaise" received added corroboration by certain concrete political developments, all of which had anti-U.S. overtones. Over 100,000 demonstrators opposed Secretary of State Alexander Haig's presence in West Berlin; hardly a week passed without an overt act of violence perpetrated by left-wing radicals against U.S. forces in West Germany; and an increasing percentage of the FRG's population was against U.S. attempts to deploy neutron bombs and Pershing missiles on West German soil. Finally, when Helmut Schmidt, Willy Brandt, and other major public figures in West Germany, supported by both labor and capital, urged caution and prudence in the West's response to the repressive measures of the military dictatorship in Poland, many Americans felt openly betrayed by their model ally. Visions of neutralism regarding West Germany's position in world politics began to appear with serious frequency in the U.S. media's interpretation of events in the FRG. Worst of all, much of this political "neutralism" seemed to gain legitimacy among the public and in respectable political circles by assuming certain nationalist overtones.

In short order, the glowing accounts of Model Germany as an economic success story and a reliable political ally had changed. Instead, the media portrayed a picture of an economically struggling country that was also politically unstable. Furthermore, this instability endangered the North Atlantic Alliance and thus posed a direct threat to U.S. security. West Germany, in the view of some U.S. commentators, had not only developed into a full-fledged economic rival, but was on its way toward becoming an unreliable political ally. This was seen by some in this country as selfish and thankless, especially in light of what the United States had done for West Germany. Some of the tone could be likened to a disappointed father's lamenting the independent actions of a wayward son. The U.S. ambivalent emotion vis-à-vis West Germany had gone from euphoria in 1979 and 1980 to dejection in 1981.

The third area of U.S. misinterpretation concerning the FRG derives from the truly complex nature of the latter's institutional arrangements. On the one hand, they seem deceptively similar to certain parallels in the United States, only to surprise the unknowing researcher by fulfilling very different tasks. Moreover, the language of West German politics is profoundly different from its U.S. counterpart. This adds yet another level of difficulty to the proper deciphering of concrete political behavior in the FRG. Roughly speaking, one can discern a clear case of what could be called "crisis posturing" on the part of most political actors in West Germany. To the untrained eye, this "posturing" reveals a gravity of conflict far beyond its actual content, which, however, is perfectly understood by the participants. As an illustration, here is a typical example from the area of industrial relations: nearly every bargaining round is accompanied by a barrage of the gloomiest predictions from both sides. Labor regularly resorts to "crisis posturing" by painting the most dire picture in terms of mass unemployment, technological de-qualification, deterioration of work conditions, and other calamities as inevitable consequences if it does not obtain its demands. Capital, in turn, always argues that it cannot yield even an inch this time, since it is faced with increased global competition; moreover, it barely escaped total disaster as a consequence of the previous bargaining round. Following this display of mutual antagonism and distrust, it indeed is truly surprising that in the vast majority of cases a compromise is found that seems to satisfy both parties, at least to a tolerable degree. This is not to say that serious conflicts, hostilities, and disagreements are absent in the FRG. It is only to convey the fact that a "crisis language" understood by all the players may lead outsiders to take its form at face value, thereby distorting its content by inflating its true meaning. Indeed, one could make the generalization that this "crisis posturing" is a necessary prerequisite for Model Germany's compromise politics.

Again, this in no way tries to negate the serious economic predicament that the FRG will have to confront in the course of this decade. The West German economy is in a crisis at the time of this writing. Moreover, the social effects of this crisis are unevenly distributed. Nevertheless, it would simply be wrong and unrealistic to view the West German crisis either as comparable to difficulties in other countries—say the United Kingdom, Italy, Belgium, Holland, or even the United States—or as threatening the democratic fabric of the FRG. Given a longitudinal analysis of the FRG's economic performance during the post-World War II period, the present figures certainly look somewhat troublesome. If, however, the basis of comparison is the current performance of other countries belonging to the Organization for Economic Cooperation and Development, for example, then the FRG's overall position assumes a much brighter outlook. Indeed, what is rather surprising and perhaps also telling of the Model's tenacity and adaptability is how little the turbulence in the world economy has actually effected the FRG. Indeed, as leftist critics of the Model have correctly pointed out, its main participants (that is, organized labor and export-oriented capital) have hardly felt any adverse effects in the wake of the crisis. It was precisely the "marginal" elements of West German society (that is, those excluded by the Model, such as women, foreign workers, the handicapped, youth, and small businesses) who have become the main victims of the crisis. Up to now, the Model's welfare functions have by and large succeeded to "cushion" the fall for these people. The degree to which the welfare state will be able to be maintained will, however, depend on West Germany's relative success in the world market.

Herein lies the ultimate danger for the Model but also its high predictability, dependability, and staying power. The danger is clear: a serious breakdown in economic demand, especially in the advanced industrialized world, would spell disaster for the FRG. Short of this scenario, however, it seems fairly evident that all West German governments, regardless of the particular party or parties in power, will continue to pursue a policy designed to buttress the country's export orientation. Moreover, this course of action will be pursued with the support of both social partners, labor and capital. Compromises will be harder to come by and will most likely be accompanied by more vociferous "crisis posturing" on the part of both parties, but they will be made. Labor will not jeopardize the necessity of West Germany's export performance by insisting on excessively high wages and/or by pursuing a Luddite-like policy against technological innovation; capital, on the other hand, will hardly dare dismantle the welfare state and will reluctantly, but surely, continue to share some of the "spoils" with labor, including a certain degree of control over the introduction of new technologies.

Briefly put, short of an exogenous collapse in the world economy, there are few endogenous indications that the fundamental economic and social arrangements of Model Germany will undergo substantial changes in the near future. Their maintenance will become increasingly difficult and will require utmost caution, delicate diplomacy, and a readiness to compromise. All these qualities, however, have been honed to an exceptional degree by all the participants in the Model over the last three decades.

Yet, the Model is not beyond serious threats. However, these seem to emanate primarily from the area of foreign policy and its domestic ramifications. The cleavages, which at the time of this writing are disrupting the FRG's political landscape, center on issues such as the neutron bomb, the deployment of additional nuclear warheads in West Germany, the FRG's role in the North Atlantic Treaty Organization, and ultimately West Germany's relationship vis-à-vis the United States. It is these cleavages that have severely shaken the Social Democratic party—after all, one of the major facilitators, if not originators, of the Model—and which, in fact, may well catapult this party and its chancellor out of power by the time this volume is published. There are many indications that the fundamental disagreements currently debated will not abate, thereby po-

tentially causing major disruptions to the political arrangements of
Model Germany.

As already stated, the essays in this volume do not provide answers. They do, however, offer some insights as to the functioning
of the FRG's political economy in an increasingly complex world.
As such, they highlight the precarious nature but also tremendous
achievement of a particular system of conflict management in a
liberal democracy here referred to as Model Germany. The United
States had a role in creating it. It continues to hold a responsibility
in maintaining it. Following the sketchy thoughts delineated above,
this means turning away from the unsympathetic attitude toward the
FRG shared by both the Carter and Reagan administrations. Our
policy makers have to realize that bullying the FRG into following the
dictates of our immediate strategic interests may succeed in the
short run—albeit with tremendous costs—but will most certainly prove
disastrous in the long run, both for West Germany and the United
States. For West Germany's economy to be successful, its foreign
policy has to enjoy a great degree of independence and autonomy.
This in no way implies a lessening of the alliance between these two
countries; if anything, it means just the opposite. For only full political autonomy will prove an ultimate guarantor of democracy in the
FRG. We assisted in the construction of the first successful and
lasting democracy in German history. It is incumbent upon us to see
to it that it not be jeopardized by anybody, including ourselves.

SELECTED BIBLIOGRAPHY ON
MODELL DEUTSCHLAND

BOOKS

Brandes, Volkhard, Jens Huhn, and Joachim Hirsch, eds. Wie
  Phönix aus der Asche? Energiekrise und "Modell Deutschland."
  Offenbach: Verlag 2000, 1982.

Hauff, Volker, and Fritz W. Scharpf. Modernisierung der Volkswirtschaft: Technologiepolitik als Strukturpolitik. Frankfurt
  am Main: Europäische Verlagsanstalt, 1975.

Hirsch, Joachim. Der Sicherheitsstaat: Das "Modell Deutschland,"
  seine Krise und die neuen sozialen Bewegungen. Frankfurt am
  Main: Europäische Verlagsanstalt, 1980.

Kohl, Wilfrid, and Giorgio Basevi. West Germany: A European and
  Global Power. Lexington, Mass.: D. C. Health, 1980.

SPECIAL JOURNAL ISSUES DEVOTED
TO MODELL DEUTSCHLAND

Leviathan, vol. 1 (1979)

   Deubner, Christian. "Internationalisierung als Problem
     alternativer Wirtschaftspolitik." Pp. 97-124.

   Esser, Josef, Wolfgang Fach, Gerd Gierszewski, and Werner
     Väth. "Krisenregulierung—Mechanismen und Vorausset-
     zungen." Pp. 79-96.

   Junne, Gerd. "Internationalisierung und Arbeitslosigkeit:
     Interne Kosten des 'Modell Deutschland.'" Pp. 57-78.

   Leviathan editorial board. "Das 'Modell Deutschland' und
     seine Konstruktionsschwächen." Pp. 1-11.

   Schlupp, Frieder. "Internationalisierung und Krise—das
     'Modell Deutschland' im metropolitanen Kapitalismus." Pp.
     12-35.

Simonis, Georg. "Die Bundesrepublik und die neue internationale Arbeitsteilung." Pp. 36-56.

Prokla, vol. 40, no. 3 (1980).

Esser, Josef, Wolfgang Fach, and Georg Simonis. "Grenzprobleme des 'Modell Deutschland.'" Pp. 40-63.

Hirsch, Joachim, and Roland Roth. "'Modell Deutschland' und neue soziale Bewegungen." Pp. 14-39.

Prokla editorial board. "'Modell Deutschland'—Anatomie und Alternativen." Pp. 1-13.

Sozialistische Studiengruppe. "Eine linke Alternative zum gescheiterten 'Modell Deutschland'?" Pp. 64-90.

Taeger, Jürgen. "Die 'süsse Gewalt' des Rechtsstaates. . . Rück- und Ausblicke auf eine Politik der Inneren Sicherheit." Pp. 93-112.

Prokla, vol. 41, no. 4 (1980).

Adler, Alexandre. "Der 'historische Block' des 'Modell Deutschland.'" Pp. 93-104.

Hübner, Kurt, and Michael Stanger. "Schwierigkeiten der Begründung alternativer Wirtschaftspolitik." Pp. 107-29.

Jäger, Michael. "Sozialliberaler Korporatismus: die Zukunft des 'Model Deutschland.'" Pp. 131-43.

Markovits, Andrei S., and Thomas Ertman. "Das 'Modell Deutschland': Eine Herausforderung für die U.S.A." Pp. 6-31.

Prokla editorial board. "'Modell Deutschland' in der Diskussion." Pp. 1-5.

Weill, Claudie, and Friedrich-Karl Frettchen. "Ein 'Modell Deutschland' in den Farben Frankreichs?" Pp. 77-90.

West German Politics, vol. 4 (May 1981).

    Issue entitled "The West German Model: Perspectives on a Stable State."

OTHER ARTICLES

Altvater, Elmar. "Deutschland—eine Modellskizze." In Die Linke, edited by Hermann L. Gremliza and Heinrich Hannover, pp. 39-56. Hamburg: VSA-Verlag, 1980.

Deubner, Christian, Udo Rehfeldt, and Frieder Schlupp. "Deutsch-französische Wirtschaftsbeziehungen im Rahmen der weltwirtschaftlichen Arbeitsteilung: Interdependenz, Divergenz oder strukturelle Dominanz." In Deutschland—Frankreich—Europa, edited by Robert Picht, pp. 91-136. Munich: Piper Verlag, 1978.

Esser, Josef, and Wolfgang Fach. "Gewerkschaften als Säule im 'Modell Deutschland'?" In Moderne Zeiten—Alte Rezepte: Kritisches Gewerkschaftsjahrbuch 1980/81, edited by Otto Jacobi, Walther Müller-Jentsch, and Eberhard Schmidt, pp. 51-62. Berlin: Rotbuch Verlag, 1980.

Esser, Josef, Wolfgang Fach, and Werner Väth. "Die sozialen Konsequenzen einer modernisierten Volkswirtschaft: Arbeitslosigkeit und gesellschaftliche Disintegration." PSV Sonderheft 9 (1978): 140-68.

Kreile, Michael. "West Germany: The Dynamics of Expansion." In Between Power and Plenty: Foreign Economic Policies of Advanced Industrial States, edited by Peter Katzenstein, pp. 191-224. Madison: University of Wisconsin Press, 1978.

_____. "Die Bundesrepublik Deutschland—eine 'Economie Dominante' in Westeuropa?" PSV Sonderheft 9 (1978): 236-56.

Narr, Wolf-Dieter, and Claus Offe. "Was heisst hier Strukturpolitik? Neokorporativismus als Rettung aus der Krise?" Technologie und Politik Aktuell-Magazin 6 (December 1976): 5-26.

Schenk, Thomas. "'Modell Deutschland': Bedingungen gewerkschaftlicher Politik in den 80er Jahren." Express 20 (January 1982): 8-9.

Schlupp, Frieder. " 'Modell Deutschland' and the International Division of Labor: The Federal Republic of Germany in the World Political Economy." In The Foreign Policy of West Germany, edited by Ekkehardt Krippendorff and Volker Rittberger, pp. 33-100. Beverly Hills, Calif.: Sage, 1980.

_____. "Die Bundesrepublik in Westeuropa—heimliche Grossmacht oder un-heimliche Dominanzmacht?" Gewerkschaftliche Monatschefte 30 (September 1979): 563-75.

Schmidt, Manfred G. "The Politics of Domestic Reform in the Federal Republic of Germany." Politics & Society 8 (1978): 165-200.

Wiseman, Carter S. "Germany: The Model?" Newsweek (European edition), September 27, 1976, pp. 7-12.

INDEX

Accumulation strategy, 92-93, 106

Added-value manufacturing system, 17

AEG-Telefunken Company, 20

Afghanistan, 217

Africa, 98, 105, 106

Agenor, 103

Aggregate demand, 79

Algeria, 17

American Enterprise Institute, 197

American Motors Bayer, 20

Anti-communism, 162-63, 164, 171

Antiinflationary coalition, 69

Arbeitsgemeinschaft, 193

Argentina, 20

Austria, 1, 118, 196, 218

Automation, 131

Bad Godesberg Conference (1959), 194

Bad Godesberg reforms, 171

Balance of payments, 17, 92, 98, 99

Bank(s), private, 63-64 (see also Bundesbank)

Bank deutscher Lander, 60

Bank für Gemeinwirtschaft, 19, 65

Banking and industry, close fusion between, 19-21

Bankruptcy, 20

Bargaining autonomy (Tarif-autonomie), 165

Barre Plan, 112

Bavaria, as state, 196-97

Behemoth, 190

Belgium, 218, 221

Berlin Wall, 13

Bizonia, 191, 192

Bonn Republic, 119; as insufficient state, 191, 197; and Weimar, similarities of, 10, 188-98

Borrowing powers, of government, 62

Brazil, 20

Breslau Congress (1925), 126

Bretton Woods exchange rate system, 61, 91, 94, 96, 208

Budgetary Structure Law, 86

Bundesbank, 5, 8, 15, 57, 58, 60-62, 69, 70, 77, 78, 79, 80; and European Community, 95-96, 99, 101; exports and, 64-65; and private sector, 62-70

Bundesrepublik, 148, 151

Canada, 34

Capital: internationalization of, 40; output per unit of, 26, 27

Capital accumulation, 29, 30-31, 32, 56

Capital formation (1950-77), 30

Capitalism: v. economic democracy, 125, 130; Mitbestimmung and, 161-62; modifications of industrial, 211; monopoly, 129; organized monopoly, and planned production, 127; restoration of West German, 58-59; social democracy and, 194

Capital labor/ratio, 32

Capital markets, 16

ABOUT THE EDITOR AND CONTRIBUTORS

ANDREI S. MARKOVITS is currently Assistant Professor of Government in the Department of Government at Wesleyan University and Research Associate at the Center for European Studies at Harvard University. He received all his university degrees from Columbia University (B.A., 1969; M.B.A., 1971; M.A., 1973; M.Phil., 1974; Ph.D., 1976). Dr. Markovits's main teaching and research interests lie in the areas of comparative politics, political sociology, and comparative industrial relations. He is the coeditor of three books and author of numerous articles and reviews in journals, such as Comparative Politics, West European Politics, Economic and Industrial Democracy, New German Critique, European Studies Newsletter, Social Science Information, Journal für Sozialforschung, Prokla, and Gewerkschaftliche Monatshefte. Dr. Markovits's current projects include the completion of a major study of the West German trade unions since World War II, coauthored with Thomas C. Ertman and entitled The West German Trade Unions: Structural Challenges and Strategic Responses (Cambridge, Mass.: OG&H Publishers, forthcoming).

DAVID ABRAHAM is currently Assistant Professor of Modern European history at Princeton University. He received all his university degrees at the University of Chicago (B.A., 1968; M.A., 1971; Ph.D., 1977). Dr. Abraham's main teaching and research interests lie in the areas of modern German history, class conflicts and the state, social democracy, and political economy. He is the author of The Collapse of the Weimar Republic: Political Economy and Crisis (Princeton, N.J.: Princeton University Press, 1981) and of numerous articles and reviews, which have appeared in journals such as Politics and Society, Political Power and Social Theory, Past and Present, and Journal of Modern History. He also contributed an article to Business and Politics in Modern Germany, edited by Theodor Hamerow (New York: Holmes & Meier, 1982). Dr. Abraham is in the process of embarking on a long-term project to explore the transformative potential and limits of northern and central European social democracy since 1914.

GUIDO G. GOLDMAN is currently Senior Lecturer on Government in the Department of Government at Harvard University and Executive Director of the Center for European Studies at Harvard University. He received his postsecondary education at Harvard

(B.A., 1959; M.A., 1964; Ph.D., 1969). Dr. Goldman's main teaching and research interests lie in the areas of modern German politics, German foreign policy, and German-American relations. He has authored The German Political System (New York: Random House, 1974) and coauthored, with Samuel Beer, Adam Ulam, and Suzanne Berger, Patterns of Government (New York: Random House, 1972).

PETER J. KATZENSTEIN is currently Professor of Government in the Department of Government at Cornell University. He received his B.A. (1967) from Swarthmore College, his M.Sc. (1968) from the London School of Economics and Political Science, and his Ph.D. (1973) from Harvard University. Dr. Katzenstein's main research and teaching interests lie in the areas of international relations, comparative politics, political economy, and public policy. He has written numerous articles, reviews, and books dealing with these topics. Among them are A Semisovereign State: Policy and Politics in West Germany (Philadelphia: Temple University Press, forthcoming) and "Problem or Model?: West Germany in the 1980s" (World Politics 32 [July 1980]: 577-98). He has also edited Between Power and Plenty (Madison: University of Wisconsin Press, 1978). Dr. Katzenstein's current research focuses on the small European states in the context of the international economy.

CARL F. LANKOWSKI is currently Assistant Professor of Economics in the Department of Economics at Hobart and William Smith Colleges. He received his B.S.F.S. (1971) from the School of Foreign Service at Georgetown University, his M.S. (1973) from Southern Connecticut State College, his M.Phil. (1975) from Columbia University, and his Ph.D. (1980) also from Columbia University. Dr. Lankowski's main teaching and research interests include the political economy of Western Europe, comparative politics, and the political economy of international organization. He has published an article with Donald Puchala in the Journal of Common Market Studies. Dr. Lankowski's current projects include an analysis of social democracy in a comparative context and the preparation of his dissertation Germany and the European Community: Anatomy of a Hegemonial Relation for publication.

CHARLES S. MAIER is currently Professor of History in the Department of History at Harvard University and Research Associate at the Center for European Studies at Harvard University. He received his B.A. (1960) from Harvard, studied at St. Antony's College at Oxford University in 1960/61 and was awarded the Ph.D. by Harvard University in 1967. Dr. Maier's main research and teaching interests fall in the areas of twentieth-century European history, issues in political economy in a historical and contemporary perspective, and the politics of economic reconstruction. Among Dr. Maier's numerous publications are Recasting Bourgeois Europe: Stabilization in France, Germany and Italy in the Decade after World War I (Princeton, N.J.: Princeton University Press, 1975) and his edited book The Origins of the Cold War and Contemporary Europe (New York: Franklin Watt, 1978). Dr. Maier is currently engaged in three research projects: a Brookings Institution project with Leon Lindberg on the politics of world inflation, a book on inflation to be published by Basic Books, and another on U.S. and European reconstruction after World War II.

JEREMIAH M. RIEMER currently teaches in the Department of Government at Oberlin College. He received his B.A. (1974) from Harvard University and his M.A. (1977) and Ph.D. (1982) from Cornell University. Dr. Riemer's main teaching and research interests lie in the areas of comparative politics, with a special focus on Western Europe, comparative labor movements, political economy and economic policy, as well as modern political and social thought. Dr. Riemer is currently engaged in completing a study on West German crisis management in the recession of 1966/67 and the stabilization crisis after 1973.

WILLI SEMMLER is currently Assistant Professor of Economics in the Department of Economics at the New School of Social Research. He studied political science, philosophy, and economics in Hamburg, Munich, and Berlin and received his Diplom (1972), Dr. rer. pol (1976), and Habilitation (1980) from the Free University in Berlin. Dr. Semmler's main teaching and research interests include the areas of Marxist economics, public finance and theories of the state, mathematical economics, theories of value, industrial organization, and post-World War II growth in Western countries. Dr. Semmler's numerous publications include Zur Theorie der Reproduktion und Akkumulation (Berlin: Olle und Wolter, 1977), and he has coauthored with Elmar Altvater and Jürgen Hoffmann, Vom Wirtschaftswunder zur Wirtschaftskrise: Ökonomie und Politik in der Bundesrepublik (Berlin: Olle und Wolter, 1979). Dr. Semmler has also coedited two volumes, Handbuch Staat (Frankfurt am Main: Europäische Verlagsanstalt, 1977) and Monopol kontrovers (Berlin: Olle und Wolter, 1980). Dr. Semmler's current projects include the completion of a volume on competition and monopoly and another one on theories and empirical evidence.